Praise For *Be The Revolution*

"Be The Revolution *offers important insights into some of the most significant developments in modern America, based on intimate knowledge and direct participation.*"

~Noam Chomsky

"*Jay Ponti is a legendary long distance revolutionary thinker and activist whose vision, analysis and courage are a beacon of hope in our bleak times! Don't miss this jewel of a book!*"

~Dr. Cornel West

"*We should thank Jay for his life's work. As an organizer, he is a wonder to watch in action. This accounting of events of the last ten years is a profound and seismic piece of American political, and cultural history that has gone all but unnoticed in the mainstream.*

Be The Revolution *is not about a battle of right or left, but the battle for humanity and the natural world. The timing of this book couldn't be more right, nor the message more on point.*"

Ken Burns should do a doc on this!"

~Mark Ruffalo

"Be The Revolution *is a love letter to our movements, an honest and searching testimonial from the heart of the grassroots.*

Jay Ponti is a ride or die revolutionary who has given us a glimpse into some of the most important moments of political struggle in the last decade.

This is the book the establishment doesn't want you to read."

~Nina Turner
Former State Senator

Be The Revolution *is an important first-hand account of the efforts led by Occupy Wall Street and Bernie Sanders' inspired activists to resist the forces of neoliberalism and mobilize for an equitable future. This history is crucial to understand if the human race is going to save itself from the climate emergency and rise of neofascism.*

~Thom Hartmann

"*Stories are vitally important when it comes to the thing called politics. Jay Ponti has done everyone on the left a remarkable service by telling stories that could so easily be lost.*"

~Timothy Morton
Author, Philosopher and Professor

"*The prevailing narrative of American politics is not the real story. It obliterates the deeper reality of who we are as people and the overarching meaning of struggles for justice.*

Beneath the corporate-created hype and the games of our political establishment lie the activism and sacrifices of real people doing the gut-wrenching work of trying to further and save our democracy. Be The Revolution *tells the story of those people.*"

~Marianne Williamson
Author and Political Activist

Praise For *Be The Revolution*

Wopila (Thank you) for writing the blow by blow actions of the War we faced at the Oceti Sakowin Camp (Standing Rock). Jay Ponti had great influence on the two Declarations written at Oceti Sakowin , particularly the Divestment Treaty among Nations. The First Declaration defies the Doctrine of Discovery and illegal actions used by it.

The second called for Divestment by countries from fossil fuels, especially by DAPL, and all other oil corporations. Thank you for your written words.

~Phyllis Young
American Indian Rights Activist

"This book is a great history of progressive action from the Occupy moment to the present—clear, invigorating, and encouraging of future efforts. We owe Jay Ponti a big thank you for his tireless efforts to change the American political landscape, and thus to help save Earth's biosphere from a catastrophic mass extinction event. It's crucial work he describes here, and joining the effort can give anyone a project that includes meaning and hope."

~Kim Stanley Robinson
Author of Ministry for the Future

BE THE
REVOLUTION

HOW OCCUPY WALL STREET AND THE BERNIE SANDERS
MOVEMENT RESHAPED AMERICAN POLITICS

JAY PONTI

Be the Revolution: How Occupy Wall Street and the
Bernie Sanders Movement Reshaped American Politics

Copyright © 2023 by Jay Ponti

All rights reserved.

Soft Cover - ISBN: 979-8-9892668-4-5
Hard Cover - ISBN: 979-8-9892668-6-9
E-book - ISBN: 979-8-9892668-5-2

Fire Drill Press, 2023.

Very Special Thanks

Rev. Bill McDonald, Mom & Dad (Mike & Diane Ponti), my editor Alex Zaitchik, my copy editor Tarryn Thomas, Julian Xeer, Adam Junod for the cover design, my agent Bill Gladstone, Michelle and Joe Radomski for beautifully formatting this book, Charles Lenchner, Joye Braun, Mark Ruffalo, Susan Sarandon, Alex Ebert, Thom Hartmann, Zack Exley, Claire Sandberg, Bill McKibben, RL Miller, Mondale Robinson, Alex Lawson, Troy Miller, Jocelyn Keatts, Harry Waisbren and everyone at Act.tv, Noam Chomsky, Jake DeGroot, Russell Greene, Mimi Kennedy, Conor Boylan, PDA, Kat Brezler, Daniel Moss and Michelle Garrison, Kerri Evelyn Harris, Jodie Evans, Nomiki Konst, Brett Banditelli, Patricia Brooks, Bertram Mark Seabrooks, Nathan Kempe, Paul Eichorn, David Braun, Dr. LaNada War Jack, Lisa Fithian, Sioux Z Desbah, Justine Medina, Tatiana Seryan, Jason Lowenthal, Cory Archibald, Julian Xeer, John Bito, Ilana Orea, Gina Kim, Jason Ackerman, Ann Szalkowski, Cliff Tasner, Betty Faye Doumas, Sue-ling Braun, and Sam Mickens.

This book is dedicated to political revolutionaries everywhere.

To everyone who stands shoulder to shoulder for Occupy, Black Lives Matter, Climate Justice, Medicare for All, a Free Palestine, and an end to immoral wars.

To Heather Heyer, who paid the highest price in Charlottesville. And to Erica Garner who devoted her life to justice.

To Uncle Noam Chomsky, Dr. Cornel West, Maya Angelou, James Baldwin, David Graeber and Hunter S. for your inspiration.

Sioux Z Dezbah and Sophia Wilansky who sacrificed their bodies at Standing Rock. To Rattler, Red Fawn and all other water protector political prisoners.

To Myron Dewey and Joye Braun, who were two of the real ones.

To the future generations who I pray are born into a sustainable and just world.

To all of my mentors and teachers who made me the man that I am.

To everyone who contributed to the creation of this book.

To my loving wife Perla—I would never have finished this book without your support and encouragement.

And this book is dedicated to you, reader. You are the leader you've been waiting for.

Always remember…

ALL THINGS ARE POSSIBLE!

TABLE OF CONTENTS

It takes courage to tell the truth about oneself, about one's own defeat. Many of the persecuted lose their capacity for seeing their own mistakes. It seems to them that the persecution itself is the greatest injustice. The persecutors are wicked simply because they persecute; the persecuted suffer because of their goodness. But this goodness has been beaten, defeated, suppressed; it was therefore a weak goodness, a bad, indefensible, unreliable goodness. For it will not do to grant that goodness must be weak as rain must be wet. It takes courage to say that the good were defeated not because they were good, but because they were weak.

~ Bertolt Brecht, *Writing the Truth: Five Difficulties*

QR codes appear throughout *Be The Revolution* that connect to videos and links related to the material. Here are some instructions on how to scan QR Codes:

iPhone users:
1. Open the camera app
2. Focus the camera on the QR code and gently tap the link that appears

Android users:
1. Open the Google app
2. Click on the Google Lens icon

3. Focus the camera on the QR code and gently tap the link that appears

Preface

Most of us are fighting a war we don't even know is happening.

We may have some vague notion that the super rich run the world, and that this is unnatural, unjust, and dangerous. But we are too consumed with daily survival to give this overwhelming fact much thought. It remains a hovering abstraction, one that will always be there, perhaps, because it is one we believe we can do little to change.

There have always been the rulers and the ruled, we may think. Pretending otherwise won't help us to pay the rent, put food on the table for our families, and survive the police state, the rise of neofascism or the climate apocalypse.

And yet throughout history there have always been two paths, two ways things could go. There is the path of resignation and stasis, and a path trodden by people who believed that they could write a new history—and did.

Be the Revolution is a collection of stories about the second group—the people who cleared away, widened, and walked the path of change. I wrote these stories not only to record episodes and movements in which I played a role, but also because they hold lessons about tactics, strategy, and how to approach and construct something like a general theory of political change.

The first draft of this book, written over the course of five years, was more explicitly theoretical, and took the form of a 700-page word document titled *The Political Revolutionary's Handbook*. I got some sage advice from a comrade publisher who told me "Jay, no one is going to want to read a seven hundred-page book about organizing."

I had to concede that this was a fair point.

So I rewrote and restructured it. The new version consists of stories that illustrate this theory of change, grounded in my experience as an activist and organizer at the forefront of several earth-moving political movements during the second decade of the twenty-first century.

The Political Revolutionary's Handbook will subsequently offer a more in depth instructional guide to tactics and theory.

Though each of these political movements is often viewed as a separate occurrence, this book will show how each one of them is in many ways a continuation of the same uprising.

These stories challenge narratives that have taken root across the political spectrum, especially in progressive and leftist circles. Perhaps you've heard the one about Occupy Wall Street ending in failure, or the one about Bernie Sanders emerging from nowhere in 2015, only to flame out after making a bunch of unrealistic promises to naive millennials?

This book will show that Occupy organizers were the principal force behind Bernie Sanders's decision to run in 2016, and will detail how Occupy's national grassroots network was the key factor in the campaign's record-breaking fundraising and volunteer efforts. It will excavate the roots of Occupy in the early aughts, long before there was anything like a national progressive movement, and show how that lineage endures into the present.

Preface

We will go behind the scenes at pivotal events during the 2016 and 2020 Democratic primaries and national conventions. We'll meet the secret group of Sanders organizers and influencers known as Bernie's Avengers that challenged the Democratic establishment at the 2016 convention, then traveled west to join the historic pipeline fight at Standing Rock. Along the way, we'll explore the factors that led to Donald Trump's election and the rise of neofascist conspiracy culture on the right.

It is important for me to be clear that none of this was part of the plan for my lifepath. I had no intention of joining a class war or the fight against fossil fuels and toxic banks, the fight for the future of humanity. If not for a few pivotal experiences that changed my worldview and trajectory forever, I would have been teaching meditation, playing music and producing film and television content.

The following pages are not a blanket endorsement or condemnation of anyone. There may be events concerning various individuals that I mention herein that give more context or illustrate harm. I apologize in advance if anyone mentioned has caused harm that the author is unaware of. My goal is to record these events as I saw them and offer my lessons learned and a general theory of change.

I do not speak for these movements. I only speak for myself. This work by no means represents everyone who played a pivotal role in the shaping of the outcome. In some ways it was the collective actions of everyone who participated, just as the ocean that forms a tidal wave is but the sum total of small individual drops of water.

I wrote this book because I believe it is impossible to see the present clearly, or to confront the future, without understanding the decade of historic uprisings that began in 2011. Those uprisings changed the world forever, and yet many of our political organizing tactics remain stuck in the 1970s. The ways we communicate with each other and the world continue to alienate many of those outside of our (increasingly social media-filtered) ingroup silos.

You will not hear this version of history from the corporate media. If it were up to the stakeholders of the corporate state, these events and those who shaped them would fade into the dust of time, without a ripple in the narrative of the dominant culture.

This book demonstrates the power of individuals and small groups of committed citizens determined to break out of these silos and alter the course of history. If humanity is to save itself from the impending climate apocalypse, we must understand the events of the past ten years and the opposition we face, and thus operate out of a theory of change that will fundamentally transform our culture and political systems.

I wrote this book because we don't have time as a species not to learn lessons from the movements of the last ten years. The next generations don't have the luxury of learning how to mobilize, only to be crushed by the corporate state and then beginning again as we did.

According to the latest IPCC (Intergovernmental Panel on Climate Change) report, the human race as of 2023 has less than seven years to reduce carbon emissions by 50%, or else there will be little that we can do to salvage a habitable earth. The report was generated by 234 scientists from sixty-six countries who analyzed more than fourteen thousand peer-reviewed studies, and there is no more debate about this. Unless the governments of the world act to end fossil fuel consumption, deforestation, and factory farming, we will face extinction-level events.

It is obvious that our elected officials lack the political will and survival instinct for the preservation of our species, because they are enabling the expansion of these practices for the benefit of their corporate donors. As Frederick Douglass once said, "power concedes nothing without a demand,"—therefore it is evident that it is up to us, the 99 Percent, to stand together. It is up to us to lift our voices, it is up to us to use our bodies to stop the gears of the political machines of the corporate state, which are fueling all the crises we face.

I hope this book will give you the confidence to believe that you too can make an impact—because you can—as well as the inspiration to think boldly about solving the planetary crisis we face—because we must.

Jay Ponti
Los Angeles
January 2023

PART ONE

Chapter 1

OCCUPY

There was an eerie calm just before the riot police descended on us.

It was a cool midnight on November 26, 2011. I was standing with my comrades on the steps of Los Angeles City Hall, surveying a scene of thousands of Occupiers who were prepared for an assault that was widely believed to be imminent. Without warning, hundreds of police in full riot gear burst from the double glass doors behind us. They fell on us with fury, like a swarm of angry black wasps or the locusts from *The Mummy*.

It was the second time that week that approximately fifteen hundred police had been mobilized to clear the Occupy Los Angeles encampment. This time they would finish the job.

Since September, more than a thousand Angelenos had been encamped around the perimeter of City Hall, occupying every available square foot of lawn. The social experiment was a punk rock circus of civil disobedience—part siege, part festival, part modern-day agora. It was a magnificent island of broken toys, and it was all about to come to a dramatic end.

Occupy began with a clarion call to action by the radical anti-consumerism Canadian magazine *Adbusters*, who had invited tens of thousands to take over Wall Street. They'd distributed an image of a ballerina balancing atop a bull on one toe—an artistic way of taunting America to stand up to the big banks that had ruined their lives.

The tactic of taking over public spaces was present in the air that year, as the Arab Spring uprisings had recently swept governments from power across the Middle East. It was also part of a long and proud tradition of national protest dating back to the nineteenth century. United Auto Workers union members had engaged in sit-down strikes at General Motors factories over brutal working conditions in Flint, Michigan in 1936–37. In 1968, Dr. Martin Luther King Jr., Rev. Jesse Jackson and other black leaders occupied the National Mall in Washington for several months as part of a Poor People's Campaign. Indigenous activists occupied and held the island of Alcatraz for almost two years starting in 1969 when plans were announced to sell "The Rock" to a billionaire.

Indeed, occupation is as American as apple pie.

When people answered the call to congregate on Wall Street, however, it marked the first time in post-9/11 America that the people had stood up to the corporate state. Their commitment would prove the state's hegemony was more fragile than anyone had realized.

At first only a few hundred people showed up at Zuccotti Park in downtown Manhattan, near some of the most powerful financial institutions in the world. The earliest iteration of the occupation was called Bloombergville, to put the billionaire mayor on blast for being the poster man-child of the country's Wall Street-owned government. (Bloomberg was also hated as the progenitor of the unconscionable stop-and-frisk policy that terrorized black people in New York City.)

I first became directly involved with Occupy on the other side of the country, after I received a call from local organizers with Occupy LA. They were putting together a concert and rally at City Hall. I had been referred to them as someone who could help with the production and planning. At the time I was busy organizing other shows, but the offer to put on a major Occupy event in my hometown was too good to pass up. One of my favorite local acts, Ozomatli, who were also old friends, was scheduled to perform. The speakers list included liberal economist Robert Reich.

When I was eighteen, Reich's *The Work of Nations* had opened my eyes to the realities of globalization and the "race to the bottom." Reich's politics had veered to the left since his years as Labor Secretary in the Clinton administration, and now Occupy was spurring my own radicalization. I felt the camps across the country represented the real possibility of people waking up and taking on structural inequality and systemic corruption. I was thrilled at the prospect of being involved in helping it to grow. I happily accepted the offer to help manage the City Hall event.

Even after I had become an OLA regular myself, and even as I watched the LAPD riot police coming at us like black-clad storm troopers, I had no idea that the camps and the people in them would alter the course both of my life and national politics as profoundly as they have.

My road to Occupy started the same as most people's: with shock and anger over the lack of accountability for the 2008 financial crisis. There was no mystery about what had happened. Wall Street had built fortunes playing games with the financial system and the housing market. At the bottom of the pyramid scheme was an industry based on fraudulent and predatory subprime loans.

When it all came crashing down, millions of Americans were homeless, broke, or faced with the real threat of becoming one or the other. Those responsible, meanwhile, were not only bailed out by the government, but they were allowed to keep hundreds of millions in profit and bonuses.

Some of them even got Cabinet positions in Obama's administration.

Soon sales of luxury items were rising sharply, even as 50 million Americans in the immediate post-crash years were living below the poverty line. If you want to understand how this could happen, I highly recommend watching Adam McKay's Academy Award-winning film, *The Big Short*, which deftly illuminates this travesty of late-stage crony capitalism.

The impunity granted those responsible was a political choice by the Obama administration. In Iceland, three dozen bankers judged to have committed fraud were sent to jail in response to these events, which had triggered a global financial crisis. The country also allowed three major banks to fail, accepting short-term pain as the cost of longer-term health and sanity in the national economy. Many former financiers went back into the industry of their ancestors: fishing. A decade later, Iceland has made a full recovery with employment reaching an all-time high.

In Washington, DC, there was no talk of justice. If the people wanted justice, they would have to occupy something, anything— everything. In mid-September 2011, the first of the occupations took place in buildings throughout New York's financial district. Then, on September 17, an encampment at Zuccotti Park was established. The first week of the camp received little media coverage.

The break came on October 1, when seven hundred occupiers were arrested during a protest that shut down the Brooklyn Bridge. The police action was covered widely by professional and citizen journalists, and the message of the protest went far and wide. Within days, occupations by a national movement of people calling themselves the 99 Percent popped up across the nation, from Boston to my home city of Los Angeles.

David Graeber is generally credited with coining the phrase, "We are the 99 Percent!" Graeber was an activist and academic, one of the nation's foremost anthropologists, and an avowed anarchist. His slogan was incredibly important, because it so simply and elegantly communicated the concept of a plutocracy, or a society controlled by a tiny number of wealthy people

The first time I remember hearing a reference to the 99 Percent was in Michael Moore's 2009 documentary, *Capitalism: A Love Story*. The filmmaker's voiceover uses the phrase to reference a leaked 2005 Citigroup document to its superwealthy shareholders, celebrating the death of democracy and the birth of plutonomy, or "a society controlled exclusively by and for the benefit of the top 1 percent of the population." The letter then goes on to reference the greatest danger to the hegemony of the new aristocracy: that the 99 Percent control 99 percent of the vote! Moore's documentary may have been the first time many Americans were first introduced to Senator Bernie Sanders talking about democratic socialism.

This concept of wealth inequality was all but unmentionable in the public discourse prior to Occupy, but it quickly became an identity and a rallying cry for working people—to bring them together to join a phenomenon that was quickly outgrowing its origins as an isolated protest.

Before they were forcibly ended later that winter, camps would appear in 951 US cities. But the outrage and determination embodied by the camps was not limited to the United States. Within a month, protesters in over eighty countries around the world would participate in a day of Occupy solidarity actions. Something had snapped; a global movement was in the process of being born.

As the Occupy encampments spread, they grew into increasingly complex, tech-savvy communities. Participants were forced to build infrastructure quickly as their numbers grew. They organized concerts and speaking events, provided security, established rules, and built mess halls and media operations, with tents focused on press, social media, building secure websites, and using search engine optimization strategies. This helped raise hundreds of thousands of dollars for camps nationwide, which allowed for the renting of porta-potties and the distribution of food, legal aid, and tents for the hundreds of young people arriving every day. In Los Angeles, more than a thousand people occupied the lawn surrounding City Hall for almost two months.

Strategy discussions and collective decision-making took place at nightly general assembly meetings. In these experiments in direct democracy, people broadcast their thoughts using a method known as the "people's mic." First deployed during the anti-nuclear movement of the 1980s—shortly after the time it also appeared in Monty Python's *Life of Brian*—the method is simple and ingenious for large protests without a speaker system: a speaker shouts a sentence and then waits for the crowd to repeat it, amplifying it for everyone to hear.

This became a necessary tactical response to the ban on megaphones enacted by Mayor Bloomberg's administration.

Occupy

Public discussions began with someone shouting, *"MIC CHECK!"* The crowd would then echo it back: *"MIC CHECK!"* This simple exchange could be powerful—it allowed everyone to experience not only being heard, but having their voices lifted up. It was tremendously empowering, and forged an immense feeling of connection and solidarity.

Occupy encampments were armies of the doomed—people whose lives had been upended or forestalled by the crashed economy and crushing student debt burdens—but the mic check system gave everyone a sense of having agency over some aspect of their lives and, if not over society at large, then at least the miniature, temporary societies of the encampments.

Within the mic check system, a series of hand gestures people could utilize to communicate concepts including approval (a jazz hands-inspired wiggling of all ten fingers), disapproval, requests for clarification, and so on were widely adopted.

Sometimes daily business would be conducted directly within the general assemblies. Other times, representatives from working groups would delegate or organize various functions of the encampments.

There was this palpable sense that we knew we were on the precipice of changing the world, even if no one could quite define it. It was like a great tsunami that had swept across the globe—and the butterfly wings that had begun the gale were a few handfuls of radicals in Zuccotti Park. These grassroots cantonments attracted leftist intellectuals and activists who could have deep conversations with normies about class consciousness and theory.

I spent most of my time in the communications tent. It was there that I met Lisa Clapier, who in time would become a key figure in one of the most devastating online psyops in history. Lisa and I both gravitated toward meditation, the peace communities, and Eastern spirituality. But she was much more into the New Age than I was, and for a while she tried to get people at the encampment to call her The Dalai Mama.

Lisa had seven children, but was determined to help the camp deploy new, independent media platforms to elevate the movement. I was pulled in by her because in many ways we both shared a vision of a world that didn't exist—a world where humans had awoken to a shared reality that transcended our petty differences of politics and ideology, and a world where humans had connected with the Oneness of a Spirit that binds us all.

I was convinced that there was a monolithic untapped power in the yoga and New Age world that could be mobilized to support the 99 Percent agenda, which we talked about for hours. This was one of the reasons I would collaborate with Rep. Tim Ryan, who later emerged as an unlikely leader of the mindfulness movement in Washington. If I had known Lisa would eventually (allegedly) put this idea into practice by helping to weaponize an online, live action role-playing game called QAnon in 2017, I would have kept my mouth shut. But we're getting ahead of ourselves.

The encampments were not without their challenges. In many ways we were trying to build an airplane while flying it. In some cities, tensions flared between the day-trippers and "tourists" who showed up in support and left after one cold night, and those who had really dug in to make the camps their temporary homes. The local unhoused population could also present unique challenges to security and optics, sometimes making the movement vulnerable to criticism by the corporate media. Our capitalistic society and local government had failed this population, which had grown considerably since the financial crisis.

Because the concept of the 99 Percent was so inclusive, it sometimes brought together groups that wouldn't normally organize together. This could result in clashes of worldviews and prejudices that complicated the process of onboarding and orienting new supporters. Cliques emerged, sometimes driven by ideological differences. There weren't sufficient training sessions to help people unpack what was unfolding, or help them heal traumas caused by racism, misogyny, classism, and poverty.

This had implications for strategy. The culture within the movement often gave way to *prefiguratism*, a concept defined by the academic Carl Boggs as a decentralized, anti-hierarchical movement that practices the participatory democracy it wants to bring to the dominant society. Prefiguratism starts with a vision, but when it skips over the strategy and tactics required to realize that vision, it can greatly complicate getting anything meaningful accomplished.

Conceptually, having a leaderless movement might prevent the corporate state from dismantling that movement by eliminating central figureheads, but it also can result in what civil rights and women's liberation activist Jo Freeman calls the "tyranny of structurelessness."

In her eponymous essay, Freeman argues that attempts to achieve pure democracy can become "a smokescreen for the strong or the lucky to establish unquestioned hegemony over others ... because the idea of 'structurelessness' does not prevent the formation of informal structures, but only formal ones." Many are the masks of power.

The problems mounted as winter neared and intra-camp violence—some of it caused by police agents—became more common. But overall the camps continued to draw wide support and notice into November. The Los Angeles and New York encampments were the most high-profile of the camps and the most star-studded. Among the celebrities to visit and address the camps were Noam Chomsky, Susan Sarandon, Mark Ruffalo, Rage Against the Machine's Tom Morello, Tim Robbins, Danny Glover, and Michael Moore, as well as entertainers like Bill Maher, Jeff Ross, Patton Oswalt, Kanye West, Russell Simmons, and Russell Brand, whose platforms brought media attention to the movement.

It would not be the last time some of these influencers would stand together for justice with the 99 Percent. Indeed, several would play important roles in the Bernie Sanders and Standing Rock movements. One musician and radical leftist Occupy Oakland organizer named Boots Riley would go on to make the dystopian, futurist cult movie *Sorry to Bother You*, which dealt subversively with themes of class and race.

My own favorite memory of Occupy Los Angeles doesn't involve a celebrity—it concerns a meal. Specifically, the Thanksgiving dinner I shared with a thousand comrades in front of LA City Hall, just a few nights before it all came crashing down.

★ ★ ★ ★ ★

It was a holiday with a complicated legacy, especially in a space as charged with politics as the camps. But on this night, we put aside the contested nature of Thanksgiving and let ourselves be happy—well fed, thankful, and awash in tryptophan and a spirit of love and common struggle. And yet there was an ominous undercurrent we couldn't quite escape. We knew this was the calm before the storm. A week before, the NYPD had evicted our comrades in Zuccotti Park, arresting more than two hundred people in the process.

We'd watched the whole thing on livestream. We knew it was just a matter of time before they came for us on the other side of the country.

By then I had spent more than a month at camp, leading classes about Gandhian non-violent civil disobedience and teaching Himalayan breathing techniques to help people manage their stress, both on the daily and during any escalations. I had spent the previous four years studying in India with Himalayan meditation masters and was an acharya (teacher) of my lineage. I did my best to make people understand that what had happened in Zuccotti was a window into our future. More than likely, the very near future.

I had recently met with then LA City Council Member Bill Rosendahl, the city's first openly gay city council member. Bill was outrageous and flamboyant and principled, but he was also a seasoned politico. He'd witnessed Rev. Dr. Martin Luther King Jr. deliver his "I Have A Dream" speech, and had been with Robert Kennedy at the Ambassador Hotel in Los Angeles in 1968 the night he was assassinated. He'd worked on RFK's historic primary campaign as well as those of Eugene McCarthy and George McGovern.

Though he'd invited me to a meeting with his chief of staff because he sympathized with our efforts, he couldn't say so publicly for political reasons: he knew any comments would be seized on by the Tea Party, the right-wing populist movement that had claimed eighty-seven GOP congressional seats in the midterm election of 2010. Of course they were largely an astroturf movement—a fake grassroots army supported by dark money flowing out of Koch Brothers-funded think tanks like Americans for Prosperity. But no elected official wanted to be on the receiving end of this well-financed operation with a deep bench of media allies.

I wasn't sure how to approach my meeting with Bill. He'd asked to see me because of my role in the concert mentioned above, but I was not anything like a major organizer, and I didn't speak for anybody. To be honest, deep down I believed it was too late for a lone Democratic city politician to make a difference, and I wasn't even sure what my ask was.

I had organized a few fundraisers for Green Party candidates in my hometown over the years, but I didn't know the first thing about back-channel politics. I just knew how to organize a good party. I'd cut my teeth organizing punk rock shows and had produced events at Queer Lounge at the Sundance film festival. (Incidentally, straightguy@queerlounge.org was my all time favorite email address.)

If nothing else, the meeting gave me a chance to summarize my thoughts about the movement, and see it through the eyes of the political establishment. I told him that in my opinion, one of the biggest missed opportunities of the Occupy encampments was their failure to make clear policy demands on local, state and federal officials, and then leverage collective power to push those demands through in the form of legislation.

Bill agreed, and he would become my mentor in politics, helping me work through the lessons of Occupy as grassroots political activism took over my life. (I would say I was a "full time" activist and organizer, except for the fact that I did not make any money doing it. There were times I would have gone hungry if not for my government-issued EBT card and local soup kitchens. If there's anything I hope people take away from this book, it's that one person can make a difference even if they are poor and lack resources.)

The concept of developing organizing strategies inside electoral politics was an important take-away for many Occupy activists, who learned the hard way that standing outside of buildings with bull-horns and shutting down streets is not enough.

You need to occupy the structures of power.

Like most populist movements, Occupy was a very big tent, and it attracted a vast spectrum of ideologies. Many of the core organizers were anarchists, like Graeber, who fiercely rejected any strategy that involved electoral politics.

Soon enough, we would come to see the place where ideology meets the reality of a policeman's boots and baton. *Praxis* is a term to describe a theory of change that holds water in the real world. Fred Hampton said, "Theory is cool, but without praxis, theory ain't shit."

So many armchair leftists read books and comment from the safety and comfort of their homes about theory. They viciously attack anyone whose ideas or actions do not conform to their very specific notion of leftism. But political revolution is not a theory; at some point you've got to get out from behind the keyboard and organize real humans in the real world. That is not to say that a sound theory of change is not critical. We must have both a sound theoretical framework and committed action.

I wish we could pass out copies of Jonathan Smucker's triumphant work, *Hegemony How-To*, to leftists the way they used to pass out laundry detergent samples in the mail. Smucker, a veteran Occupy organizer, deftly elucidates how prefiguratism sabotages meaningful leftist efforts.

Unfortunately this book hadn't yet been written. In November 2011, we were all about to learn these lessons the hard way.

The Whole World is Watching

A week before that first and only Occupy Thanksgiving, a campus policeman at UC Davis had brazenly pepper-sprayed nonviolent Occupy protesters sitting quietly on campus. The officer at the center of the assault, Lt. John Pike, would soon regret his actions: the digital dexterity of Occupy and its network of supporters kicked in and quickly made Pike a meme legend. There were memes of his face inserted into iconic images, rendering him casually spraying mace at the Beatles walking on Abbey Road, at Jack and Rose on the Titanic, and at God Himself in Michaelangelo's famous ceiling mural at the Sistine Chapel.

This social media campaign was the biggest, but not the first or only such campaign to target instances of state repression and violence.

Three weeks earlier, without provocation, police fired a tear-gas canister point blank at the head of an Iraq War veteran and Occupy Oakland activist, Scott Olsen, fracturing his skull. When others rushed to assist the fallen Veterans for Peace demonstrator, police threw a concussion grenade into the middle of the group. It was captured on video. In another instance, a uniformed officer was caught on video punching a young woman in the face without provocation. The advent of citizen journalism was clearly an issue for the police state, so anyone with a camera—journalists covering the OWS events included—was also targeted and arrested.

Soon Occupy was loud with a chant not heard in many years: "The whole world is watching!" Whenever police confronted occupiers with batons, chemicals, and threats, we let them know that their actions were being recorded and would be projected on the national stage.

This explains why the detention of journalists, and the use of tear gas and other suppression tactics against them, emerged as a major storyline of Occupy. It eventually got so bad that some cops spoke out. The most vocal was retired NYPD Captain Ray Lewis, who joined the occupiers in Zuccotti and was arrested in full uniform. He told reporters that police are also members of the 99 Percent, and that "corporate America must be stopped."

However, cops like Lewis were in the minority. The dominant view was expressed during the violent clearing of Zuccotti on November 15, when Mayor Bloomberg ordered the forceful eviction of the Occupy encampment.

We would later learn that the sweep had been in the works for a long time. According to FOIA documents obtained by the Partnership for Civil Justice Fund (PCJF), the FBI's New York branch was preparing for Occupy as early as August 19, before the encampment even took proper shape. The documents include a report by the Domestic Security Alliance Council (DSAC), which is described by the federal government as "a strategic partnership between the FBI, the Department of Homeland Security, and the private sector."

In other words, the FBI was conspiring with the criminals on Wall Street from the start, to protect their interests from the people they had robbed and subvert the first seedlings of protest by those demanding justice. It was always a safe bet that a similar alliance was at work within the power structures of California and the city of Los Angeles.

This was the corporate state in full effect: multiple agencies of the federal government, working in concert with corporations to plan the demise of a populist movement whose members were only exercising their constitutional right to protest the corruption of this unholy alliance. They knew this whirlwind was a threat to the hegemony of the corporate state and were intent on suppressing it.

Night of the Locust

After the Zuccotti Park camp was cleared on November 15, protesters in New York turned to the direct occupation of financial crime sites: banks, corporate headquarters, board meetings, foreclosed homes, and college and university campuses.

Meanwhile, the Los Angeles occupation remained in the sprawling green around City Hall.

During the last week in November, the LAPD made two appearances to warn us to leave. On the first night, thousands had shown up in solidarity, following a mayoral announcement that the police would forcibly take down the camp, as was happening at Occupy protests across the country.

On Sunday, November 26, a ten-block perimeter was created around City Hall to cut off the possibility of thousands more supporters entering the area. I had been away from the camp when they set it up, but was able to find a weak spot and make it through. The mood was tense for several hours, as fourteen hundred black-uniformed shock troops stood shoulder to shoulder under the ominous orange incandescence of the streetlights overhead.

To help people manage their anxiety, I organized a large meditation circle of about fifty people on the south steps of City Hall. I distributed some candles I had left over from the 11.11.11 Peace Concert and led an Earth Peace Meditation that I'd learned at the feet of the Himalayan master I'd been studying with since 2008. We set the following intention: that the night would end in peace.

Two hours later, at around 3 a.m., a voice came over a megaphone. The police were withdrawing from the area. Though we knew it was only a temporary victory, it felt like a victory nonetheless. Those of us who'd participated in the meditation felt a special peace amidst the chaotic scene. It was a beautiful moment, and we allowed ourselves to wonder if our collective intentions perhaps had had some influence on the outcome.

Two days later, the scene would not end so peacefully.

On Monday morning, November 28, at 12:01 a.m., Los Angeles Mayor Antonio Villaraigosa gave an ultimatum to the occupiers to disperse. "It is time to close the park and repair the grounds so that we can restore public access to the park," he declared.

Were we not the public? Did we deny anyone access to the park? No.

We knew this was part of a coordinated statewide effort, because the Mayor of Oakland had told the BBC that mayors from eighteen cities had recently participated in a call organized by the US Conference of Mayors. It was a strategy call about how to dismantle the Occupy encampments in their respective cities.

This time, instead of approaching the camp directly and setting up a perimeter, fourteen hundred police burst through the double doors of the south lawn of City Hall in full riot gear— there were so many it looked like an army division—and it sent us instinctively scattering. They quickly formed ranks, a spectacle of force meant to intimidate us. There were tense stand-offs as some groups refused to be pushed off the grounds by approaching flanks. Some occupiers shouted and taunted the police; a few, possibly instigators, clearly wanted to incite violence. Unfortunately, the police were more than eager to oblige.

Together with my best friend and fellow activist Steven Weinglass, I attempted to reduce tensions by using de-escalation techniques. Steven was more practiced at handling such situations than I was. His brother was the renowned civil rights attorney Leonard Weinglass—whose clients had included the Chicago 7, the American Indian Movement activists prosecuted for the standoff at Wounded Knee, and Mumia Abu-Jamal—and he had been around resistance movements and direct action protests his whole life. He'd told me stories of his teenage memories spending time with Abbie Hoffman, Tom Hayden and other icons of that era. Steve had been in Chicago during the 1968 Democratic Convention, when the cops had busted the skulls of anyone with long hair they'd found in Lincoln Park after 11 p.m.

Steven and I were attempting to de-escalate confrontations between occupiers and law enforcement when I was knocked down by a sudden sharp pain in my back. A member of the LAPD had thrust the butt end of his baton into the back of my ribs.

Everything changed for me at that moment. I understood for the first time, in every fiber of my being, that the class war is real.

This was a pivotal moment in my life and politics. What I had previously known only in theory, I now understood in my gut: the state and its police force are not neutral referees in a society of contending interests. They are on the side of the rich and powerful. It was the final event in my transition from liberal to radical.

Incidentally, the word *radical* is derived from the Latin word "radix," meaning "root," and implies the root giving life to the "extremities" (think radish = root vegetable). So, in truth, being radical just means getting to the root of the issues. I think we need to reclaim and destigmatize this word that has become a term of abuse to de-legitimize activists challenging the status quo.

Altogether, the clearing-out lasted several hours. As the lawn was forcibly emptied, police began to take down the tents. Meanwhile, the confrontations and stand-offs spilled out into the streets. One hero remained in a tree on the south lawn, refusing to leave. The police crowded around below, looking like angry firemen trying to figure out how to get a defiant cat down from its high perch.

Two hundred and ninety-two people were arrested that night. They were loaded onto buses as teams moved in to remove the tents and other structures. Throughout it all, the police marched in tight ranks, breaking up groups of protesters with force and intimidation. A perimeter was created around City Hall, and people trying to get through were arrested, often without being read their Miranda Rights. Police separated protesters whose arms were interlinked. They stomped on people's feet and twisted their legs until they let go. The media complied with orders not to broadcast the images of violence. This was perhaps the perfect living metaphor for the corporate state versus populist movements.

Looking at the former encampment suddenly without people, I realized something. The next morning, the city and the media would justify the eviction on public safety and public use grounds: the lawn outside City Hall, they would say, needed to be repaired and cleaned up. I suspected this narrative would focus on unsanitary conditions surrounding the camp and the hazards to public health. And the visuals didn't lie: like a fairground after a festival concert, the park was filthy.

A little after 3 a.m., I found a box of two hundred trash bags and began to approach the people now wandering aimlessly under the ghostly orange streetlights. They looked as if they had just awoken from a dream to find themselves in a waking nightmare.

Did they want to help me to clean up the lawn and monkey-wrench the coming media narrative? They all dismissed me in a blank daze. Nobody was ready to care about anything again just yet.

After all, what was the point?

When I noticed a small circle of people sitting on the lawn that included some of the more active organizers, I made one last try.

If what you are doing isn't working, then pivot and change your tactics. Hopefully before you reach this point, you have thoroughly flushed your vision for what success looks like. The most successful campaigns are clear about this. They know what their mission is, what their goals and objectives are, what the strategies, tactics and theory of change that will bring victory are, and they are prepared to adapt when the landscape changes.

At this point we were long past all of that.

"*MIC CHECK!*" I screamed, addressing the cohort huddled together with their arms interlocked preparing to make their final stand.

"*MIC CHECK!*" they responded.

It had worked. I'd cut through the despair of the moment.

My heart was pounding and my hands were trembling as we volleyed the following sentences back and forth:

> *TOMORROW MORNING, THE NEWS IS GOING TO REPORT THAT THEY HAD TO TAKE DOWN OUR CAMP BECAUSE OF THE TRASH.*

> *WE HAVE THE OPPORTUNITY RIGHT NOW TO SHOW THEM WE ARE BETTER THAN HOW THEY HAVE TRIED TO PORTRAY US.*

> *WE CAN TAKE CONTROL OF THE NARRATIVE. I HIGHLY SUGGEST WE TAKE THESE TRASH BAGS AND CLEAN UP. RIGHT NOW!*

I held the roll above my head.

One by one, everyone came and took a trash bag. Some asked for several. They spread out. More people drifted over, joined us. Eventually, I gave the roll to someone else who took over distribution. It seemed like a hundred people were walking around picking up trash from the lawn and surrounding area.

The cops had full riot gear, helmets, paddy wagons, buses for those who'd been arrested, mace, and other weapons. We were armed with nothing but rolls of garbage bags, the truth, and each other. If you saw this scene in a movie, you might think it was corny and contrived. But it was among the most powerful and inspiring moments of my life. We were going to throw away their lies with the remains of Occupy LA.

I eventually went home as dawn broke in time to catch the morning news. Sure enough, the local reporter on-scene delivered the city's statement claiming the encampment was ordered down due to health risks caused by garbage. But there wasn't any garbage left on the lawn. The camera guy had to do a zoom-in of a solitary McDonald's bag on the grass.

The lesson I learned that day was to seek out those who had the most influence to make a big call to action. Think of it like starting a fire—you need the most flammable kindling first before you build up to the bigger logs (the bigger logs in this case are a metaphor for the broader public). I also took away from this experience that it is always important to anticipate how the media will seek to undermine your efforts, and to devise optics to act as countermeasures to those false narratives.

What did it all mean?

The significance and legacy of OWS are not easily summarized. But few would deny that the place to begin any summary is the broad shift it caused in our political language and thinking. Before OWS, there was almost no popular or mainstream recognition or even consciousness around the root causes of society's ills, and the profound and growing inequality that increasingly defined that society. Nobody talked about the man (or the math) behind the curtain. If you worked hard but slipped through the cracks, it was your fault. Few understood how completely the game had been rigged. This was then proved by French economist Thomas Piketty in 2013, with seven hundred pages of cold hard data in his landmark work, *Capital in the Twenty-First Century.*

Occupy gave permission to millions of people to acknowledge, name, and resist the corporate state. The concepts of the 99 and the 1 Percent not only provided a handle for grasping the enormity of the problem, it illustrated how skewed the numbers on each side really were. For the first time since the anti-war demonstrations and liberation movements of the sixties and seventies, the self-satisfied establishment and the status quo it upheld were shaken. Nothing would be the same.

The corporate state tried to bury us. But what it did not understand—what nobody really understood in 2011—was that the Occupy encampments were not trees that had been uprooted, but seeds that had been scattered.

The encampments were vibrant centers of public discourse, art, ideas, and connectivity. They got people out of their houses and into the streets. Atomization, or the fragmenting of meaningful human communities into individuals, is a function of end stage capitalism. This is the reason Amazon is the most profitable company in the world—its business model preys on lonely people filling the void in our desperate lives by buying things we don't need without having to leave our caves.

Occupy camps were places for those displaced by the housing crash, to go and feel like they were part of the solution. For every day the camps stood, more Americans were connected to the power and possibility that is created when people come together and make a stand. It was a place to discover and experience real solidarity in the face of state oppression, which gave us the opportunity to feel courageous.

OWS also served an important role in building an intergenerational tissue among activist networks. It attracted seasoned organizers, who brought their experience and knowledge into the camps. The decentralized, internet- and tech-savvy rabble rousers were the first to use livestreaming to allow the public to follow events on the ground, leading many to see firsthand how the corporate media lied, undercovered or manipulated the truth.

These relationships added heft to a decentralized network that would emerge from the ashes of OWS, to move the chains on multiple fronts. This network was flush with the realization that all you needed to make a serious impact was a couple hundred people. You didn't even need a permit—just the guts to stand up to the corporate state.

By the early months of 2012, it was clear the movement's energy had been harnessed and co-opted by labor unions and community activists across the country. As history has shown time and again, the ruling class will brutally suppress leftist movements, then co-opt the innovations that arise from those movements to maintain power. Obama, after supporting the corporate state's efforts to dismantle our movement, adopted the Occupy narrative to defeat Mitt Romney. OWS enabled the Obama campaign to frame Romney as the living avatar of the 1%.

Also in 2012, Occupy Sandy mobilized a mutual aid volunteer network to rapidly respond when the eponymous hurricane devastated New York City. Occupy Sandy, working with InterOccupy and the OWS Tech Ops group, leveraged the power of the internet to source desperately needed aid to the victims of the climate catastrophe. As extreme weather calamities continue to escalate due to the climate apocalypse, this model may one day be what keeps our society from collapsing.

You could find Occupy DNA in city, state and national minimum wage movements, anti-foreclosure campaigns, and the revitalized campaign for racial justice that would eventually influence the creation of Black Lives Matter. (This DNA reached across the globe, and the Occupy movement was credited with inspiring the Umbrella Movement in Hong Kong, the Pirate Party in Iceland, and Podemos in Spain.)

There was another branch of the Occupy legacy. While some veterans of the camps continued to focus on the streets, others turned their attention to the ballot box. A number of people who had participated in or were deeply affected by OWS decided to run for public office. Those who saw a need to build electoral power as well as grassroots power began to plan for local, state and national races. One of the first Occupy candidates was Kshama Sawant, who in 2013 ran for Seattle City Council on a "$15 Now" platform as a "voice for the 99 Percent."

She defeated an opponent bankrolled by CEOs and landlords. Movements for divestment, debt forgiveness, public banking and fighting foreclosures were led by Occupy organizers. Members of the OWS tech ops group like Harry Waisbren, Brad Gans, Kelli Daley, and Julianna Forlano would go on to create Act.tv, one of the left's most effective media platforms for uplifting grassroots political organizing and direct actions. Jerry Ashton, who had come to OWS as a debt collector, emerged to start the organization RIP Medical Debt, which was responsible for billions of dollars in debt relief and was even featured on the John Oliver show.

Then there was the group of former occupiers who had a more ambitious goal: a presidential candidate that represented the 99 Percent. They believed the time had come to occupy the Democratic Party and—just maybe—the White House.

Chapter 2

THE PEOPLE FOR BERNIE SANDERS

If there is no struggle there is no progress—
power concedes nothing without a demand.
-Frederick Douglass

In 2014 Tim Carpenter, the founder of the Progressive Democrats of America, while lying in bed dying of cancer, asked a group of colleagues a question: "What if we could get Bernie Sanders to run for president?"

A rotund redhead with an easy smile and a relentless passion for organizing, Tim had founded the Progressive Democrats of America to oppose the militaristic corporate agenda of the modern Democratic Party. He often wore a "Healthcare not Warfare" T-shirt under his blazer and sweated profusely. His colleagues had enormous respect for him, but not for this latest idea.

"He's an Independent, he's not even a Democrat!" huffed the PDA's political director, a bearded Irishman named Conor Boylan. Others chimed in with their own objections.

Tim was unmoved; his vision and intentions were clear. He saw something that his team could not, as Barack Obama entered the home stretch of his second term: a *future we could all believe in.*

"Slow down," said Tim. "Hear me out."

He asked the group to remember why they'd gotten involved in politics. "Think about all you've had to deal with," he said. "All of the campaigns, all of the issues we've fought for. Bernie ticks every box. We are going to be out in front of this. We are going to get him to run, and run as a Democrat. It's going to be fun."

Years later, Conor recounted this deathbed conversation with his old friend, boss, and mentor. He said something had seemed to click inside of Tim, who'd beamed with energy as he spoke about the prospect of Bernie Sanders 2016.

"None of us could see it at the time, or thought he would win," said Conor. "Tim had a way of seeing around corners that we couldn't see."

Tim died in April of 2014, too soon to see his dream of a Bernie Sanders candidacy realized. John Nichols, a writer and co-conspirator, would later recall in *The Nation*, "Not many hours before I learned that he had passed, Tim had been on the phone with me, running through the latest numbers from a national petition drive he and the PDA had organized to urge Vermont Senator Bernie Sanders to seek the presidency. There were over ten and a half thousand. A few hours after the call, he emailed me, with more numbers. There were over eleven thousand. That was typical Tim. His enthusiasm for politics was immeasurable and infectious."

Carpenter founded the Progressive Democrats of America during the 2004 Democratic National Convention, together with former staffers and supporters of the failed Dennis Kucinich campaign. That year, the Kucinich campaign had been the chosen vehicle for delegates and activists concerned about the centrist and rightward trends in the party.

Kucinich, US Rep. Barbara Lee, the Reverend Jesse Jackson, Tom Hayden, Marianne Williamson, and Code Pink's Medea Benjamin had helped to launch the organization, the idea for which had been brewing throughout the campaign. Kucinich's campaign manager Dot Maver and her then-assistant Charles Lenchner had led the brainstorming about how to capitalize on the energy and enthusiasm around the campaign, to continue mobilizing the grassroots after the election.

The small group had no idea at that moment that they were planting the seeds for what would become the Bernie Sanders movement. Until now, the established narrative has excised the role Charles Lenchner played in launching this initiative; a void I hope to rectify in these pages. Political revolution is messy work, and it is natural for facts to be distorted by biases and the rivalries that happen in the rough and tumble of organizing.

At the time, Tim Carpenter had joined the Kucinich campaign as a field organizer. When the Democratic Convention finally arrived, it was he who ran with the idea. Tim and a few others managed to get their hands on the email addresses of every Kucinich delegate, which they used to launch the PDA early the following year. It's a moral gray area, but sometimes political revolutionaries need to color outside of the lines. Just think of the world we would be living in if Tim Carpenter hadn't commandeered the campaign email list. Kucinich never really operationalized it for grassroots activism and without those contacts, PDA might never have gotten off the ground, and subsequently would never have encouraged Bernie to run. Sanders had no ambition to seek the Oval Office

He needed a big push from the people.

Following the Kucinich campaign, the group put the entire mainstream of the party in its sights. The Clinton Administration had cemented a political realignment that had shifted the party so far to the right that they were basically like the Republicans of the 1970s. After seeing the party repeatedly get their asses kicked by Reagan, Clinton's Third Way Democrats were happy to finally have corporate America behind them.

These "new Democrats" despised Tim and the PDA. The group's first supporters in Washington were few, largely limited to Maxine Waters, Barbara Lee, and Lynn Woolsey (known as the "triad," they were akin to an original "squad"). After the 1994 election cycle, the new Republican Speaker of the House Newt Gingrich shifted the entire strategy of the GOP to focus on fundraising.

Democrats soon followed his lead and thus Congress began its descent into the bowels of the corporate money swamp.

Later, in 2002, Nancy Pelosi (one of the wealthiest women to hold elected office would become House Minority Whip, then rise to House Minority Leader in 2003. According to PDA members active at the time, Pelosi despised the triad, and did her level best to bring them to heel.

Back then there was no such thing as a "progressive movement." People identified as "liberal," but that had become a squishy term. People hadn't identified as "progressive" since Teddy Roosevelt, who had been a Republican. Tim's genius was to rebrand the movement to the left of the party as forward-looking and distinct from Clinton, Pelosi and other "new" Democrats.

After Tim died, PDA was left without a leader. But the team was motivated by a desire to fulfill Tim's dying wish of a Sanders presidential campaign. They organized PDA events for Bernie in

Iowa and elsewhere, even as Sanders himself remained wary of the idea. The senator from Vermont didn't know if he could raise enough money, and had apprehensions about subjecting his family to the scrutiny and spotlight of a national campaign.

But there were too many impassioned supporters of the idea to just let it dissipate. One of them was RoseAnn DeMoro, a member of Tim's kitchen cabinet and an organizer with National Nurses United. The nurses' union was the PDA's top funder and worked to make free universal healthcare the center of the Democratic platform. At the time, single-payer healthcare was considered a fringe idea, but DeMoro believed Sanders could move the issue toward the center of the party platform. "History does not reward timidity in bringing about social justice to the healthcare arena," she once said in a 2007 interview with Physicians for a National Health Program.

The PDA was not the first group to try and entice Sanders into running for president. In 2014, the Green Party courted Sanders to run on its presidential ticket. That same year, a schism developed within the Democratic Socialists of America over whether or not to support a Sanders campaign. Tim, a long-standing member of the DSA, had been a close friend of its founder, Michael Harrington, whom he believed would have supported Sanders as part of an *inside-outside strategy*, or the leveraging of grassroots power to win elections and eventually control institutions.

In 2014, the DSA had only five thousand members nationally. Its debate over whether to work within the Democratic Party or to break from it echoed earlier debates among socialists over whether or not to oppose FDR's New Deal and military alliance with Stalin and Churchill. Within the DSA, a caucus known as Bread and Roses vehemently opposed the party's support for a Sanders presidential run.

Meanwhile, the PDA was not waiting for anyone else to settle their debates. It began laying the groundwork to elect Bernie with hundreds of "We Want Bernie" house parties and fundraisers. Wherever Sanders went, he was stalked by sign-carrying PDA members chanting, "RUN BERNIE RUN!"

Occupy the White House

On April 30, 2015, Bernie Sanders convened a small press conference in Burlington, Vermont, to announce that he would seek the Democratic nomination for president. The Washington establishment and corporate media shrugged it off. To them, it was a foregone conclusion that Hillary Clinton would be the nominee after winning a primary campaign with no legitimate challenger.

Two former Occupy Wall Street organizers named Charles Lenchner and Winnie Wong did not share this certainty. They not only believed Sanders could be a strong candidate, they thought the candidacy could reignite the movement. Unlike many of his cohorts, Charles was committed to building electoral power—the "inside" of the inside-outside theory of radical change—and carrying forth the lessons learned in his experiences with the Dennis Kucinich campaign.

Like many members of OWS, Charles and Winnie had experienced first-hand the power of the corporate state to systematically dismantle populist uprisings. Charles especially was no stranger to state oppression. He had previously been jailed as a soldier in Israel for refusing to serve, in protest of the government's treatment of Palestinians.

Although she is Asian-American, Winnie has always reminded me of Emma Goldman in appearance and spirit. It is unclear who coined it, but Winnie was an early adopter and promoter of the hashtag that would come to define the movement—*#FeelTheBern*.

Before Bernie Sanders made his intentions known, Charles created a group, "Ready for Warren," to push the Senator from Massachusetts to challenge Clinton, the anointed candidate of the oligarchs. When asked what they would do should Elizabeth Warren refuse to run, Lenchner responded, "We'll pivot to Bernie Sanders." He had seen how well Sanders memes performed on social media, and he believed he and Warren were natural allies. Both had taken strong and consistent positions against the big banks and the billionaire class. When Warren finally told Charles's affinity group to leave her alone, the group was quickly rebranded as The People for Bernie Sanders.

Charles and Winnie were both DSA members, and they brought a small cohort from the DSA into the new group. All of the new group's members had to face vocal opposition from factions within both OWS and the DSA who believed that nothing good could come from contact with Bernie.

Their arguments have not aged well.

To many observers, Bernie's candidacy simply went viral. Because his brand so perfectly fit the zeitgeist of the moment, it was destined to happen. While there is some truth to this, it ignores months of advance planning by Occupy veterans who pushed Sanders to run while also pursuing the "outside" strategy of mobilizing national networks forged during OWS. Meanwhile, the PDA had prepared a volunteer army for immediate deployment as soon as the announcement was made.

This was profoundly important.

Consumerism is so deeply entrenched in our mindset that we unconsciously view politicians as products—supporting the political brand that most aligns with our worldview. From this perspective, we choose candidates the same way we might choose our favorite organic kombucha. Personally, I hate kombucha.

We have internalized an expectation that society will deliver to us whatever we want or need, whether it's a pizza or a presidential candidate. The baseline assumption here is that it is the job of someone else to "do democracy" for us. This has been the brand that the Democrats have been selling since the Third Way neoliberals abandoned unions and working people for the narrative that the meritocracy of college educated professionals would do a good job of governing, leaving liberals to go about their lives as consumers.

Despite the narrative that "the smart Ivy-Leaguers were taking care of everything," Occupy organizers had learned the truth too well the truth—if poor working people wanted justice and equality, it was up to us to fight for it.

It is crucial to understand that Bernie did not simply "go viral" or emerge from the free market, driven by his appeal to unrealistic young Millennials. Bernie was a tactic of the PDA and Occupy activists.

The People for Bernie group was able to engage with and grow online audiences with their Facebook page, which soon swelled to 2 million followers. It was a digital megaphone that helped guide the tone and message of the movement.

When Bernie Sanders made his campaign announcement, his name recognition nationally was only 1 percent. Hillary Clinton, meanwhile, was one of the most well-known and powerful people on planet Earth.

The People for Bernie group helped to gather more than a hundred thousand people together, by hosting house parties and grassroots events across the country after the campaign launched.

The Occupy movement not only didn't fail—it had never ended.

Many may assume that Bernie emerged from nowhere and became an "instant phenomenon," but that was not the case. For Bernie organizers, the campaign was a tactic. Without the *Feelthe-Bern* hashtag going viral, the activation of the decentralized tech savvy OWS network of organizers, and the massive digital reach nationwide, it's unlikely the Sanders campaign would have generated as much momentum as it did.

The People for Bernie Sanders social media platform went on to gather over a million followers. Without their organizing efforts, and the efforts of the PDA, history would have played out very differently. In fact, the success of the Sanders campaign was largely driven not by the hired professional consultants, but by the collective efforts of Sanders supporters. This is a key distinction. It marked the first time in the American experience that a grassroots movement of ordinary citizens legitimately challenged the corporate state's political machine. The People for Bernie then went on to ignite organizing efforts nationwide.

Only by understanding the landscape of progressive leftist movements prior to 2016 can we fully appreciate the impact that a small group of committed people had, by igniting a movement that reshaped American politics.

"Real change," Bernie liked to say in his stump speech, "always takes place from the bottom up, when people at the grass-roots level stand up and fight back."

Despite its lack of institutional support, the People for Bernie organization became an effective platform for people standing up, but it did not appear out of thin air. Its foundation was built up by a core team of Occupy veterans that formed days after Bernie's announcement. Joining Charles and Winnie in early May were Kat Brezler, Brett Banditelli, and Moumita Ahmed (founder of Millennials for Bernie), a crew with decades of combined experience in electoral politics, labor and grassroots organizing—up to and through the recent encampments.

They activated the national email list of Occupiers, sending out a big call to action and an open letter with influential OWS organizers urging Occupiers to support Bernie as the candidate of the 99 Percent.

When asked about the connection between the 2016 Bernie campaign and OWS four years earlier, Charles described the lessons offered by its successes and failures: "Occupy was very successful in attracting the attention of the world and in the messaging around inequality and corporate greed," he said. "But after organizing and mobilizing large numbers of people, it was sort of a shock to discover it was not going to last forever. One of the greatest things that came out of the Occupy movement is that the organizers met each other and learned to build. They built power that culminated in one of the most significant presidential campaigns in history."

One of the OWS veterans to join the People for Bernie core was Kat Brezler, a school teacher and former occupier from Yonkers. Her love for the people was palpable, and she cursed like a sailor. For Kat, like many of her Occupy cohorts, there were hard lessons learned following the occupations.

When I asked what those were, she said, "Our tactical errors started by forgetting that there was a government. We should have gotten as many local leaders as we could on our side. We should've organized with them. But we weren't organizers at that time. We were baby organizers. We didn't know how to get everybody on our side. We were just starting to experiment with social media.

We were in a movement based on the false belief that it would never end."

People for Bernie would build on these lessons.

Five years later Kat and her platonic life-mate, Brett Banditelli, a veteran of Occupy Harrisburg, PA—who looked like a young leftist Santa Claus crossed with a long-haired pirate in glasses—became the heart of the People for Bernie's social media operations. Brett worked in the labor movement and was one of the best digital organizers in the game. Brett dressed up as Santa Claus for rallies in July and was ride or die for the 99 Percent. He and Kat worked tirelessly together on social media. With no budget, they outperformed the Clinton campaign on Facebook, Twitter and Instagram almost every day of the primary campaign.

"The initial structure of the People for Bernie was based on fifty former members of the Occupy movement," remembers Brett. "We were looking for people who could run independent operations, such as Students for Bernie. They could do that. The goal within the first month was to have ninety-nine meetups in ninety-nine days for the 99 Percent. We ended up having two or three hundred events. These spawned all the local Bernie groups that we had later, which eventually became Our Revolution."

One of my favorite memories of Brett was during the Bernie 2020 campaign, when he wore a full Santa Claus costume to a Sanders rally in Venice with Alexandria Ocasio-Cortez.

There was also Moumita Ahmed, a small but mighty daughter of Bangladeshi immigrants who understood the struggle of poor working people of color. She hadn't played a big role during the original Occupy, but the camps had inspired her to connect with the community during the first year of anniversary gatherings. She was one of the many millennials who supported and campaigned passionately for Barack Obama in 2008 with the false hope that he would be a true agent of change, only to see him further the neo-liberal corporate agenda, upsurge the war machine and expand the militarized police state.

She would certainly get her chance to make a difference, as the People for Bernie group and everyone who would stand for the Sanders campaign had their work cut out from them.

When the Clintons were in office, they told the staffers in charge of Air Force One that if there was ever an empty seat on the airplane that could have been filled with an influential person, that people would be fired immediately. They were determined to use the office of the White House to become a dominant political force in the world. A project of their foundation, the Clinton Global Initiative, was meetings that acted as a vehicle to leverage their position as power brokers across the world.

Without the organizing efforts of the PDA and the OWS networks it tapped into, history would likely have played out very differently. Sanders's success was driven not by hired professional consultants, but by the collective efforts of his grassroots supporters. This marked the first time in the American experience that a grass-roots movement of ordinary citizens legitimately challenged the corporate state's political machine. The reason that the machine didn't see the whirlwind coming was the same reason they allowed conditions to get so unlivable for poor Americans in the first place: they live in a Beltway Bubble, far removed from the woes of working people.

Even after the convulsions of Occupy, it did not occur to them that millions of Americans were ready to reject the political status quo as embodied by Hillary Clinton. They did not see that people were fed up with the lies and the platitudes, were tired of the wars, angry over the obscene and growing wealth gap, and terrified of climate extinction. The country had reached an inflection point. The left of the Democratic Party had to make a stand.

The stand they took proved that Occupy Wall Street had not been defeated. The Bernie campaign was powered by people who saw the lessons of Occupy as building blocks. They were not ready to return to silence, but continued planning for a political war over the soul of the country.

"We are activists and organizers trying to build a broad, effective movement for democratic change," declared the first People for Bernie letter:

> *The initiators of this letter are veteran grassroots organizers of Occupy Wall Street, and are joined by many energized brothers and sisters we have met along the way. In September 2011, our efforts changed the narrative of American politics, helping to focus it on the issues of our time: inequality, surrender to the power of concentrated wealth, the corruption of our democracy by moneyed interests, and the need for solutions as radical as our problems... We are signing as individuals hoping to kickstart a "small d" democratic movement. People For Bernie won't be a corporate-style, staff-driven, controlled-message, top-down enterprise... We call on all other progressive forces to unite behind Sanders so we can have a united front in this important campaign.*

Most Democratic Party insiders no doubt dismissed the letter, if they noticed it at all. They would soon regret not paying closer attention.

Chapter 3

The Primary That Changed Everything

*The purpose of the media is to inculcate and defend the economic,
social and political agenda of privileged groups that dominate the
domestic society and the state. The media serve this purpose in
many ways: through selection of topics, distribution of concerns,
framing of issues, filtering of information, emphasis and tone,
and by keeping debate within the bounds of acceptable premises.*
-*Manufacturing Consent*, Edward Herman & Noam Chomsky

I met Senator Sanders at the Sister Giant conference held on
March 29, 2015. I went to the event—organized by the author
and transformational leader Marianne Williamson—to try to
connect with speakers and other like-minded people who might
want to collaborate on projects and campaigns in the future. There
was no shortage of people I wanted to meet: the two-day event

featured a number of rousing speeches by people like Dennis and Elizabeth Kucinich, Thom Hartmann, and Keith Ellison.

What had started as a small group of scrappy activists in 2014 had gained significant traction one year later.

Earlier in the first day of the event, the PDA had its biggest event for Bernie, at the Musicians' Union in Los Angeles. In retrospect, it blows my mind to think about the endless synchronicities and connections between those of us who came together to support the Sanders campaign. I didn't know it at the time, but the people I met that day, and others who were throwing an event across town, would become like family to me, and we would share life-defining experiences together.

Russell Greene, a former executive at the Cheesecake Factory and something of a class traitor to the 1 Percent, had convinced Bernie and his team to come to Los Angeles. David Braun was a co-founder of the groups New Yorkers Against Fracking, Californians Against Fracking, and Americans Against Fracking. He was also the grassroots director for the release of *Gasland*, the Oscar-nominated documentary by Josh Fox that had alerted the world to the dangers of fracking. David wasn't able to get the big green orgs on board to ban fracking in New York, so he and other activists on the ground had formed a coalition that included many unlikely bedfellows, including conservative vineyard owners who didn't care to see their groundwater poisoned by the noxious chemicals that seep into the water table during this process.

When Bernie spoke at Sister Giant, the sleeves of his blue-collared shirt, bought most likely from Ross or Costco, were rolled up. *"If billionaires can buy elections, members of Congress will be paid employees of the billionaire class,"* he said that night. *"In order to move this country forward and create the policies we need, we are going to need election reform and increased voter turnout. Democracy is not a spectator sport. They want us to believe that they are too powerful and making change is hopeless. We have struggled for civil rights, labor rights, women's rights, gay rights, and we have won. Nothing is ever won unless millions of people stand up and fight back.*

We are going to do something radical and practice democracy. We might have to get arrested for it."

He was calling for a political revolution.

There are many leftists who suggest that voting for or associating with policymakers is pointless, as all politicians are corrupt. I would counter that the goal of the political revolutionary is to create systemic change that brings peace, prosperity, justice, and sustainability for even the most vulnerable citizens of the world.

There is no systemic change without building legislative power. Without access to the power to write and change laws, such change is seldom possible. Of course, this depends on whether or not the policymakers' fealty to the corporate lobbyists exceeds that of their responsibility to the people and the grassroots activists fighting for fair policies. You can stand outside of a government building with a bullhorn all you want, but unless you are specifically disrupting the life, business or reputation of specific stakeholders or are leveraging resources that will benefit them, they simply won't care. Prefiguratism may be comfortable, but it is wildly ineffective.

The Sister Giant conference was the first of many times I would listen to one of Bernie's speeches on income inequality and the challenges facing the nation. My first impression was that it sounded more like a college lecture than a political speech. For one thing, it was long. At the end of his speech, Marianne came out and asked Bernie if he would run for President. The crowd shouted, *"Run, Bernie, run!"*

No doubt there were many in the audience who had been following the PDA's campaign to push Bernie to run.

In his unmistakable Brooklyn accent, he responded, "Look, there's no point in me running for president if there isn't a grassroots movement behind me, to do the things that we would set out to do to get this country back on track." At that point, Marianne turned to the audience and said, "If you're going to stand behind Bernie when he runs, please stand up."

There was a pregnant pause. Time seemed to slow down as the Senator stood on stage facing a silent crowd. Everyone was now standing.

Everyone except me.

Standing alone on the stage, Bernie looked exposed. His face suggested that this demonstration of love and support was difficult for him to take in. It was as if his humble nature and lifelong career as an outsider were suddenly being confronted by the possibility of a task that had previously been outside of his wheelhouse, if not his comprehension. I've heard stories that Bernie was not popular in Congress. He often ate lunch alone, as his colleagues spent every waking moment in the pursuit of power, money, and influence.

His vulnerability was certainly very powerful, but to me this wasn't the type of executive presence that I associated with someone who would be the Commander-in-Chief. His hands were awkwardly crossed, as one hand clutched the opposite wrist. I didn't join the crowd in standing because the thought had crossed my mind that I couldn't imagine him possessing the boldness to sit across the table from Vladimir Putin.

Consider that I, like many Occupy activists, did not put my faith in any elected official easily, especially after the last five years of watching the Obama administration give a pass to the bankers that had crashed the economy in 2008. He'd even appointed some of them to his Cabinet. We'd watched him fake-sipping Flint water to assure people it was okay (it is not okay to this very day, as of 2022). We watched him celebrated as a Nobel Peace Prize winner, while he spied on Americans and waged drone warfare. He had allowed shocking police violence and suppression of our Occupy Movement. The irony of it all is that without Occupy Wall Street, Mitt Romney might have won the presidency in 2012. The Obama campaign used the aftermath of OWS to brand Romney as the candidate who was the living embodiment of the 1 Percent.

Maybe ten seconds had elapsed after Bernie's speech concluded when the crowd erupted in applause. Still I remained seated, unconvinced. Marianne then invited everyone from the audience to convene in an adjacent room for an unscheduled fundraiser for Bernie. The ask was a minimum donation of a hundred dollars, but a donation of any amount would grant access to the Senator.

This was a stark contrast to the invisible primaries that were taking place in the billionaire summer homes of the Hamptons, where the Democratic candidates are selected, not elected.

At the fundraiser I met Thom Hartmann, one of the most impressive speakers I'd ever seen. Every Friday Thom Hartmann hosted a nationally syndicated radio show called "Breakfast with Bernie," which had amassed Sanders a loyal following.

My introduction to the man whose decision to run for president would alter my destiny and the course of the nation was anticlimactic. I was used to a certain amount of glad-handing by politicians, but Bernie was outright surly when I shared my bona fides.

"Yeah, yeah, good kid," he said dismissively in his thick accent and kept walking, probably assuming I was some wannabe politico.

Knowing what I know now, I would have led with talking about my grassroots experiences with Occupy.

He simply gave no fucks about glad-handing and politicking, and escaped the fundraiser as soon as possible. I was taken aback by the exchange. For the next couple of weeks, I would occasionally contemplate the experience, unsure what to make of it.

Then I came across an old video of Bernie lambasting the late chairman of the Federal Reserve and icon of free-market economics, Alan Greenspan.

Sanders seemed to be breathing fire as he confronted Greenspan about his role in deregulating the banks, saying that Greenspan simply "did not know what's going on in the real world," and that "country clubs and cocktail parties are not real America."

It was at that moment that I *felt the Bern* for the first time.

These feelings were deeply personal. I was born in a trailer park in Rawlins, Wyoming. My family moved back to Massachusetts after my grandfather died so that my father could finish college. At the age of twelve and throughout high school, I worked on cucumber and tobacco farms to earn extra money. We had enough for our basic needs, but money was a constant cause of violence in our household. I made the choice to drop out of college at nineteen to live on my own because I knew that student debt would be a prison sentence—a mountain of quicksand from which few Americans escape to pursue their dreams. As a result of this, I would have to scrape by for almost two decades, subsisting on low-paying jobs. I never had health or dental insurance until I was in my late thirties, so the idea of a candidate fighting for a living wage and Medicare for All was a revelation.

For all my personal struggles, I was still born a white guy in America, which comes with substantial advantages. Nonetheless, for much of my life I have known the constant anxiety and humiliation of *extreme* poverty. In my early 20s, I would sometimes steal food from the restaurant I worked at because I was so hungry and broke. I carried shame about it for many years. Poor people carry a lot of shame. We live in a society that tells us we're only valuable if we're famous, wealthy, or able to consume or be hyper-productive. I don't regret my past, but I often wonder what I might have achieved if I'd had access to the free and affordable education that the baby boomer generation was given. I was never able to earn a degree, and I haven't had healthcare for most of my adult life.

When I realized Bernie understood all of this, everything fell into place. For the first time in my life there was a viable presidential candidate who had somehow remained honest in a crooked political system, and had always fought to change it where he could.

Poor and working-class people know who's for real and who isn't. We know our lives are not going to change significantly with another feckless centrist president who'll continue to shore up the war economy, ensuring that the military remains one of the only pathways out of poverty. We know who's been arrested for civil disobedience, who's stood on the picket lines fighting alongside unions, and who's only made fine but predictable speeches.

Nothing can quite describe the feeling of that first *Bern*. It was like falling in love with someone you think might be a soul mate, except it's with a seventy-year-old politician from Brooklyn. So many of us had never felt anything but disdain for, mistrust of or indifference to politicians—and here, finally, was a candidate who was really one of us, who had fought for our values his entire life. And now millions of people were coming together to support him. There was an immediate feeling, a connection and solidarity with anyone else wearing some type of Bernie swag. It was like a shibboleth, or a secret handshake of sorts. Your eyes would meet with a total stranger and you would both just nod at each other, in the understanding that you were fighting for something important, that you were a part of it.

I soon discovered that for just about every single important societal issue of the last forty years, there was a video of Bernie trying to fight on the right side of it. On one famous occasion, he railed against the first Gulf War to an empty chamber in Congress.

In my research, I discovered that he had been an organizer in Chicago for the Civil Rights Movement. He had been arrested protesting segregation at the University of Chicago. It was the first time I'd ever seen a presidential hopeful who had been arrested for organizing. Perhaps one of the most important paradigm changes of the last decade was the way Bernie made it cool again for middle class kids to get arrested.

Frontline activists have been arrested doing non-violent civil disobedience actions for decades, but after that photo of a youthful Bernie in cuffs broke through into the popular culture, the number of people willing to put their bodies on the line increased dramatically.

This would be reflected in the Democracy Spring actions led by Kai Newkirk in April of 2016, and then again during the Indigenous-led movements at Standing Rock.

As a peace activist, I had spent the better part of a decade watching the Democrats celebrate Obama as a hero while he served the interests of Wall Street, bailing out the bankers who'd crashed the economy while leaving millions of working-class people to pick up the pieces of their shattered lives and dreams. Obama and the then-Secretary of State Hillary Clinton had sold fracking around the world on behalf of their fossil fuel industry benefactors. They were the main proponents of the regime changes that had seen United States-led NATO forces drop thousands of bombs, killing up to six thousand innocent civilians in airstrikes across the Middle East.

Libya had once had a standard of living not unlike a European country. The Obama policy reduced it to rubble, making it a failed state, a home for ISIS and a haven for modern slave trading.

That's right. Actual slavery. This was their legacy.

The Obama administration also provided military support to the Saudi genocide in Yemen that would lead to the death from starvation of more than fifty thousand children, and put more than 20 million civilians at risk of famine.

At home, Obama was known as the "Deporter in Chief." Two and a half million undocumented citizens were deported under his leadership—more than under any other sitting president. More bombs were dropped in more countries than under any other administration. He invoked the Espionage Act to prosecute whistleblowers like Edward Snowden—again, more times than under any other sitting president.

Domestic NSA spying programs were expanded without the knowledge of the American people. The National Defense Authorization Act of 2012 enabled the indefinite detention of American citizens. Despite his campaign promises, Guantanamo remained operational throughout his eight years. Hillary's State Department transacted 165 billion dollars' worth of weapons sales to brutal dictatorships (many of which had donated tens of millions of dollars to the Clinton Foundation). Nineteen billion dollars in commercial arms were personally brokered to the Saudis by Secretary Clinton—weapons used in the campaign of Yemeni genocide—a fine tribute to the gods of war. You can imagine the disbelief we felt when the Clinton campaign went on to falsely smear Bernie as a shill for the NRA, despite his D-minus record with the lobby.

The Obama regime's foreign policy, largely influenced by Secretary Clinton, was also fighting a proxy war in Syria funding militant groups. At one point, Department of Defense-funded militants were actively fighting CIA-funded militants.

If this sounds insane to you, that's because it was.

The Democratic Establishment assumed that the base would simply accept Hillary Clinton as the "inevitable" nominee.

Millions of Americans would not quietly accept the status quo and the same old meaningless platitudes. They would not stand by while another darling of Wall Street, another war-mongering chicken-hawk, and another member of the ruling class was selected to shore up the bottom line of the super wealthy and send poor kids to die in stupid wars.

If wages for the 99 Percent had increased at a commensurate rate with productivity and corporate profits, the minimum wage would have been $22 per hour instead of $7.25. Democrats had long since sold out the unions and working class, shifting their ideological fealty to that of a technocracy. Meanwhile, the conservatives and libertarian billionaires had been waging war on labor organizing for years with "right to work" union-busting legislation.

To make matters worse, the human race was facing possible extinction scenarios due to the climate crisis, and the Obama-Hillary regime was solidly in the bag for the fossil fuel industry. Clinton was not only a continuation of this regime, but represented an escalation of the rightwing corporate elements of the Democratic Party.

The Trans Pacific Partnership was the largest trade deal in American history. It was thousands of pages long, and written in secrecy largely by global corporate conglomerates. Think of a mutant, next-generation NAFTA, five-thousand-page piece of legislation that would allow corporations to sue the twelve sovereign nation signatories for losses if there was legislation that might diminish projected (not actual) profits. For instance, if a country wanted to put a warning label on cigarettes, Phillip Morris could sue that country in secret tribunals for the money they would have made. This was a nightmare for climate activists trying to fight for policy changes to laws governing the environment. It would undermine internet freedoms and give Big Pharma a monopoly on drug patents for life-saving medications, and if passed it would be virtually impossible to undo.

We had reached an inflection point. We had to make a stand.

No—Occupy Wall Street had not been defeated. It was just taking a different form, that of a political war for the soul of the Democratic Party (if it ever had one) and the country, the likes of which had never been seen.

Occupy the Rose Bowl Parade

It was a sunny morning in Pasadena on New Year's Day, 2016, when I joined around 250 Berniecrats in a park across from the Rose Bowl stadium. The big game of the same name was scheduled for that afternoon, and the streets were lined with onlookers in folding chairs who had gotten up at the crack of dawn to observe the spectacle.

It was my ninth month working to promote Bernie's candidacy, but this was my first direct action. It was the brainchild of Carlos Marroquin's affinity group, The Bernie Brigade. Carlos was an OG Occupy Los Angeles organizer, and when he wasn't working as a friendly neighborhood mailman, he remained one of my favorite compatriots in activist spaces.

He had an indefatigable will and the uncanny ability to create community wherever he went. Post-Occupy LA, Carlos helped organize the Occupy Fights Foreclosures movement, which fought for homeowners facing predatory banks to keep their homes. My friend Michael Mowgli and I had gotten zero sleep the night before, having attended the Dead and Company's New Year's Eve show at the Forum, but the energy of the action was enough to sustain us.

The plan was to follow the ten-mile parade route in Bernie regalia and be seen by roughly a million bystanders. But not just any bystanders: one of the teams playing that day was the University of Iowa, and the thousands of Hawkeye fans formed an ocean of black and yellow. We wore Bernie T-shirts and had prepared floats to join the official parade toward the end.

When the last float rounded the bend, we all ran out at maximum speed, pushing our Bernie floats to catch up with the official parade as one would imagine a group of soldiers would when charging a castle door with a battering ram. A band of riot police stood between us and the main parade as we marched and waved just like we were any other Rose Bowl parade floats—to anyone watching we were a formidable addition to the cavalcade.

The all-important Iowa caucuses were exactly thirty days away. This made it an opportune moment to demonstrate the love, commitment, and ingenuity of Bernie supporters to the thousands of Iowans who had traveled to California in support of their team.

As we prepared for the day's work, the symbolism of the red rose emblazoned on the stadium across the street was not lost on us.

The red rose has been a symbol for socialism and social democracy since the late nineteenth century. Marxists in Germany wore red rose pins in the 1870s to signify their political and ideological commitments. After the Kaiser banned the pins in an attempt to suppress the Social Democratic Party, simply wearing the emblem had landed members in prison. German socialists that immigrated to the US had imported the red rose sigil and popularized it in the wake of the Haymarket affair of 1886 as an emblem of solidarity in support of the anarchists falsely convicted of a political bombing. By the turn of the century the red rose became the international symbol for socialists and social democracy.

I personally don't identify as a Marxist, or a Socialist, because I am not an ideologue. I focus on vision, strategies and solidarity, not ideologies, which I believe are inherently limiting and divisive.

But I digress.

The great challenge of civil actions like the Rose Bowl Parade is to present a compelling and easily understandable message. Football games are like the *bread and circuses* of ancient Rome, which the state used to keep social order by distracting the common man from social problems and from the senators who might be blamed for them. Something similar is at work in the modern world, where people turn to sports for a bottomless source of distraction and succor. Our modern day gladiators wear football helmets instead of riding chariots. (There is a reason that the Department of Defense pays millions of dollars every year to the NFL and works to condition in the minds of fans the connection between the flag, the anthem and the military.)

The spectacle we'd prepared for the unsuspecting fans was the work of a local artist named Alex Schaefer: a fourteen-foot hand-sewn Bernie puppet that towered over the people below and required three people to operate. A sound system, meanwhile, would blast revolutionary slogans like "Power to the People!" Alex and the other Sandernistas marched for five miles that day in the Pasadena heat. Big Bernie, as we called him, would become an inspiring sight at a number of events during the primary.

The crashing of the Rose Bowl Parade was a guerrilla action. The campaign had had no role in planning the stunt, but Becky Bond, a senior advisor to Bernie 2016, flew out to meet with us before the action began. She was blown away by the DIY ingenuity of the stunt and the passion of the participants.

It was emblematic of the self-funded, grassroots, out-of-the-box thinking and tactics that activists were bringing to Bernie's candidacy, to capture the imagination of potential supporters while also taking control of the media narrative.

If such a campaign had existed before in American politics, nobody could remember it.

The Rose Parade Feels the Bern, like the growing Bernie movement, was full of music. My friend Alex Ebert, the singer for Edward Sharpe and the Magnetic Zeros, had written an original song called "Feel the Bern." I passed out copies of the lyrics to the marchers with one of my oldest friends by my side: Michael Mowgli, a brilliant songwriter in his own right and former front-man for the Venice band The Mowglis. This was the latest in a long line of adventures that I'd shared with Michael over the years. As we prepared for the parade, I was reminded again that the greatest gift of organizing is the love, experiences and comradery we share with each other. The memories are as priceless and enduring as the endless ripples our deeds create through time and space.

Music was an important part of the campaign. There were almost always musical acts opening up at the rallies. When I saw Bernie speak in August 2015 to a packed stadium at USC, the line to get in was like entering a music festival or a sold-out Rolling Stones concert. People sold T-shirts and merchandise outside. Even his ninety-minute lecture on income inequality and oligarchy was received as if it was a greatest-hits list by our favorite band. Many even followed Sanders around the country, like fans of the Grateful Dead, and like the Deadhead scene we would see and recognize one another—campaigning in the next big primary state by day and rocking out at the rallies by night. Bernie supporters coded DIY apps for rideshares and places to stay.

Bernie had the coolest swag, by far. The grassroots made DIY merchandise of every imaginable kind: Bernie figurines, onesies, endless T-shirt designs. Most used the sales to fund campaign efforts. It was punk rock in the best and truest sense, and many of us amassed quite a selection of DIY wearable merch. This was important, because supporters wearing paraphernalia in public are walking billboards that generate free-earned media.

Ben Cohen, co-founder of Ben & Jerry's Ice Cream, came out as a Bernie surrogate. He had previously been a Dennis Kucinich supporter in 2004. Ben debuted a special ice cream flavor called "Bernie's Yearning" on January 25, 2016. The flavor, released under the brand Ben's Best, consisted of plain mint ice cream covered by a solid layer of mint chocolate. According to Cohen, "The chocolate disk represents the huge majority of economic gains that have gone to the top 1 percent since the end of the recession."

Along with Alex Ebert, Killer Mike from the rap duo Run the Jewels was one of the first big musicians to endorse Bernie. Killer

Mike was one of the boldest, edgiest, most popular and most influential artists, rappers and activists in pop culture. He did an interview with Bernie at the SWAG barber shop in Atlanta on November 23, 2015.

I knew his endorsement would open the doors to other vanguard artists and influencers. Because of my past in music and events, I soon found myself at the intersection of Hollywood, Washington, and grassroots political activism. I knew there was a wave coming, though I still couldn't have imagined at the time where it would take me.

Bernie could pack a stadium like the Rolling Stones, but his politics and persona were more like punk rock. He'd gone against the grain for years by fighting for universal health care. When he spoke out against the media, the big banks, and the military industrial complex, it was the equivalent of the Dead Kennedys telling MTV to get off the fucking air.

Bernie was even directly responsible for fostering the seminal punk scene in Vermont in the eighties. When Bernie was the mayor of Burlington, VT, he recorded a folk album called *We Shall Overcome*. He also, together with his wife Jane, opened an all-ages DIY music venue called 242 Main in a 1984 collaboration with local youth leaders. The venue hosted acts like Fugazi, Operation Ivy, and the Misfits, making Sanders the only presidential candidate to ever run an actual punk club. This helps explain all of the Bernie-themed renditions of famous punk logos from Black Flag, the Ramones, and the Descendents, just to name a few. If anyone ever made one with a Sick of It All theme, that would have been especially fitting.

He wasn't trying to act sweet for radio time or make friends in the industry. He'd opposed the Defense of Marriage Act, and had defended LGBTQIA+ members in the military long before it was cool or popular. Punk is about taking on the status quo; it is inclusive to women, queer and trans folk, and people of color. Punk lyrics rail against injustice, consumerism, corporate greed, and war. Sanders had been speaking out about wealth inequality, criminal injustice, free college, and universal healthcare since the eighties.

There was also more than a little punk rock in the campaign. In the seventies and eighties punk rock was defined by its do-it-yourself ethos, known as DIY. Punk rock set out to kill the vapid pretense of the major-label rock god, who in the political context would be the highly paid consultants and corporate-backed candidates. But anyone could play punk rock music, just as anyone could set up guerrilla campaign events with some creativity, some friends, and dedication to a cause. The Bernie movement, like OWS before it, was DIY at its core—powered by grassroots videos, art, reporting, direct actions, and energy.

Punk rockers knew that no record label or big promoter was coming to save them, just as we all knew that no billionaires were coming to save or help us. The Punk crowd had to do it themselves. They made their own clothes, created their own music venues, and even published their own newspapers. The Bernie movement was very much the same. Because of YouTube, anyone could become a political pundit and build a following. Proof was everywhere you looked online: Kyle Kulinski, The Young Turks, Jimmy Dore, Tim Black, The Humanist Report and Chapo Trap House all emerged as voices of the progressive left around this time.

No corporate media outlets would be coming to fairly cover the Sanders campaign. If we wanted accurate political analysis and commentary, we had to do it ourselves.

Big Organizing

People poured their entire lives into the Bernie campaign. Hundreds of thousands of people gave as much as twenty to sixty hours a week to volunteer. Many of these people were also working full-time and fighting to survive.

But they showed up anyway.

These people were the fuel fanning the flames of the campaign. Poor people skipped haircuts to donate small amounts to the campaign. The average amount of these donations—$27—would become one of the most powerful and lasting symbols of the entire presidential cycle.

Organizing and channeling all of this collective energy and its resources required novel means and methods. One of these was an extremely effective and creative social media operation. Bernie groups deployed Slack, Facebook, WhatsApp, Signal, Twitter and other platforms to facilitate and grow organizing efforts and draw new forces into the movement.

Because the majority of the staff came from the grassroots, the official Bernie campaign understood DIY in its bloodstream. If it hadn't it never would have gotten off the ground.

If Sanders was going to make a serious run, he was going to need 'people power.' The first calls to action were conceived by the People for Bernie affinity group in early 2015. One was a call for supporters to plan local GOTV events; another asked that supporters host phone banking events and barnstorms. The campaign provided scripts and how-to guides for organizing these events, and made themselves accessible on platforms like Slack for support and troubleshooting. The campaign was able to scale quickly, mobilizing these new volunteers and collecting emails that were sent directly to headquarters. Many of these second-wave recruits were already accustomed to organizing outside of and against the establishment. The activist energy around the campaign, in other words, compounded fast, especially due to the early efforts of the People for Bernie's Occupy network and the PDA.

It must be remembered how terrified the members of the Washington political establishment were by all of this. Once it became clear that Sanders was not only not going to play nice, fade away, and that he might even threaten Clinton's chances, a coordinated expression of establishment wrath was inevitable. It was known that Hillary Clinton kept a list of those who were obedient and those she perceived as traitors. She even used a numbered ranking system to mark loyalty and treachery. She had lost the nomination in 2008 to Obama.

Losing again was not an option, and she would leverage the full power of the Washington political consultant class.

All of the most experienced and talented consultants were on Clinton's team. Even vendors did not want to risk getting blackballed by the Democratic Party (something that happens a lot). If the primary were a war, the think-tankers would have described it as an "asymmetrical conflict."

In the end, however, this imbalance only reinforced the message of the Sanders campaign. It would also prove a blessing in disguise by forcing the campaign to rely on 'super volunteers' with no prior political experience. They would become its secret weapons.

Claire Sandberg brought over a decade of high-powered experience in grassroots organizing to the campaign's digital organizing efforts. Among her victories was leading the digital campaign to ban fracking in New York State. She and two advisors—Zach Exley and Becky Bond—were put in charge of the forty-six states with no campaign staff on the ground.

"Imagine having to campaign in forty-six states with very little budget and staff," Zach told me years later. "At first, there was no one to answer the phones or emails coming in. The campaign was opposed to this and gave them no money. I paid out of pocket for the software we used for the help desk."

Becky Bond was an innovator working at the intersection of organizing, politics, and technology for over a decade. Becky was also a cofounder of the CREDO Super PAC, named by Mother Jones as one of "2012's Least Horrible Super PACs" for helping to defeat five sitting Tea Party Republican congressmen.

Zach worked as a union organizer before joining MoveOn.org as its first organizing director during the run-up to the Iraq War. No stranger to presidential races, Exley was an early advisor to the Howard Dean 2004 campaign. He later served as John Kerry's director of online fundraising and communications in the 2004 general election, raising more than $100 million online for the nominee. Unfortunately Dean went on to become a shill for Big Pharma, lobbying to keep drug prices high. (Do yourself a favor and search YouTube for "Howard Dean and The Screaming Goats Remix.")

Sandberg, Bond, and Exley were later joined by Saikat Chakrabarti, who had previously worked at the Silicon Valley firm Stripe, to help run the tech side of the campaign, and two very talented organizers from Tennessee named Alexandra Rojas and Corbin Trent. Saikat built a digital tool to take PDF scans from barnstorms, to get lists into the system. "It was like building a startup, but with all volunteers," Zack Exley told me. "We did the barnstorms because we could get them to show up to a livestream, but they wouldn't do voter contact if we asked by email.

The numbers of participants started to decline and the campaign was losing faith in us."

Next to join was campaign volunteer Rapi Castillo, who built Maps.berniesanders.com and helped found Coders for Bernie. As the tech brain trust grew, the resource gap with other campaigns started to shrink.

This small group had their work cut out for them. They had a forty-six state national campaign to run with no money or resources. Traditionally, building a campaign's field operations is a simple matter of renting out offices, and hiring staff to canvass and organize volunteers. Since this was not an option, they would need to rely almost exclusively on the energy, creativity, and dedication of unpaid volunteers. This model, known as "distributed organizing," would end up powering victories in twenty-two primary states, winning 46 percent of the delegates, and netting a record $230 million in small donations from 2.8 million Americans.

In October 2015, the campaign began to invite Sanders supporters to organize the first of what it called *barnstorms*. The team started in Tennessee because Corbin Trent had already done much of the organizing work there on his own. Barnstorming involved traveling to small towns to put on shows and exhibitions and make political speeches. The tradition of barnstorming dates to the early 1800s in New York, when comedy troupes traveled the countryside entertaining the locals in barns. The term connotes an impressive display, one set up rapidly before moving on to the next location.

The first step was to reach out directly to supporters on social media and ask them to canvass, make phone calls, send text messages and knock on doors. It took some trial and error to get the model right, but eventually the Bernie Barnstorm was born. It soon became a big part of the distributed organizing strategy, creating enthusiasm that spread like wildfire across the country.

So many leftists and progressives make premature assumptions about the viability of various strategies, but never operate out of a possibility mindset that demands a clear outcome, iron resolve and the resilience to continue to iterate and innovate until success is achieved. It's much easier to gripe on the sidelines than it is to reinvent oneself on the field—to go through the pain of repeated failure before emerging victorious.

The events enabled the campaign to expand exponentially by design: every event generated follow-up events, by creating space for people to announce other projects to the group, and encouraging them to organize their own and begin working out the logistics. The campaign was able to capitalize on the grassroots energy and enthusiasm generated by the People for Bernie's *Ninety-Nine Events for the 99 Percent*.

It is worth noting that Bernie's barnstorm organizers were operating out of a possibility mindset, as opposed to a fixed one. So often progressives and leftists simply engage the same old tactics without commitment to the innovation that would ensure the desired outcome. Their strategies hadn't worked for months, until finally they discovered the winning algorithm for success— they made sure to hold the microphone and only gave each potential barnstorm host a few seconds to share what part of town they lived in and what would be fun about their event, thus giving the opportunity for those attending the rallies to form hyper-local affinity groups with campaign objectives.

You never know how close you are to success until you iterate. The household cleaner 409 got its name because the two scientists who invented it had failed to get it right on 408 previous attempts. True story.

By the day of the Iowa caucus, the campaign had hosted roughly a thousand barnstorms across the country—650 of them run by volunteers, who together made 85 million calls to potential voters. Before the first vote of the primaries was cast, it was clear the campaign and movement was gaining momentum.

The first results sent shockwaves through the political world. Sanders, the unknown Senator from Vermont, had won by a landslide in New Hampshire, and in Iowa had fought Hillary Clinton to a virtual tie.

Despite all of this, Clinton had already locked up nearly all of the party's superdelegates. The superdelegate disparity was significant, not just for its implications for the convention, but because the corporate media used it as a narrative to justify its ongoing coverage of Clinton as unbeatable.

The corporate media and the Democratic establishment soon decided that this narrative alone would not be enough to stop the Bernie juggernaut. As Bernie's momentum started to grow in the summer of 2015, it started to pair the story of Clinton's "inevitability" with a story of toxic masculinity at the core of Bernie's campaign and its most fervent supporters. This was the birth of the "Bernie Bros": an alleged breed of young, disillusioned, misogynistic white males who looked suspiciously like updates on the "Obama Bros" seen eight years earlier during another Clinton presidential run. The neoliberal establishment uses these narratives to crush dissent against militarism; this is the same tactic as a Palestinian defense being equated with anti-semitism. It is an example of cultural hegemony at work.

Cultural hegemony is a concept proposed by the Italian philosopher and organizer Antonio Gramsci, who theorized that the ruling class establishes and maintains its control over society through the manipulation of its culture. Gramsci was imprisoned by Mussolini's government, who viewed his mind and ideas as a threat.

The term comes from the Ancient Greek word hegemonia, meaning "rule." Traditionally this implies the dominion of an imperial nation over a subordinate nation through the threat of force, but in this context it implies more subtle and indirect mechanisms of manipulating the assumptions and worldview of a population.

It is impossible to understand the 2016 primary election without first examining the influence that neoliberal corporate outlets like CNN and MSNBC have over the Democratic Party base, and second, the extent to which the neoliberal media is entrenched within the party establishment.

This Bernie Bro trope was officially launched in a 2015 Robinson Meyer article in the Atlantic, titled "Here Comes the Bernie Bro." It was then picked up by a raft of centrist Clinton-supporting mercenary journalists: Rebecca Traister, Jude Doyle, Jessica Valenti, and Jill Filipovic would use the term extensively in their writing throughout the primary and the general elections. In 2008, Traister had written a *Salon* piece, "Hey Obama Boys, Back off Already!" that set the stage for her 2015 *New York Magazine* article, "The Bernie Bros vs. the Hillary Bots." A WikiLeaks dump of DNC emails would later reveal that Doyle, Valenti and others were coordinating with the Clinton campaign to push the Bernie Bro concept and other damaging narratives.

Former officials and celebrities within the Clinton orbit also did their part. During a Clinton campaign rally, former Secretary of State Madeleine Albright told the crowd, "There's a special place in hell for women who don't help each other," implying eternal damnation was reserved for female Bernie supporters. (Albright should know something about hell. She once said that the deaths of half a million children in Iraq was a worthy "price" for maintaining sanctions against the regime of Saddam Hussein.) In an interview with Bill Maher, feminist icon Gloria Steinem stated that young women support Bernie Sanders because "the boys are with Bernie." (This was the same Gloria Steinem who called Bernie "an honorary woman" during his 1996 congressional run against Republican Susan Sweetser.) Not to be outdone, *New York Times* op-ed writer Bret Stephens penned a column headlined "Bernie's Angry Bros."

It's a little-known fun fact that Steinem worked with the CIA during the 70s to disrupt leftist ideologies in feminist spaces. Over time one of the most effective tactics of the establishment has been to weaponize liberal identity politics to divide the left.

In truth, young women made up a larger percentage of Sanders's base than men. The polling numbers showed that he was the most popular candidate amongst nonwhite voters, receiving the most donations from the party's growing number of Hispanic voters in particular. Displaying their dexterity for online rapid response, Sanders supporters countered the media myth of the "Bernie Bro" with the hilarious hashtag *#BernieMadeMeWhite* which featured BIPoC supporters riffing on how they expressed their newfound caucasity and white privilege with endless jokes about how they are now wearing boat shoes and taking trips to Martha's Vineyard. The hashtag response made it clear the media was falsely erasing huge swaths of black and brown supporters.

At no point am I suggesting Bernie supporters were immune to sexism and misogyny, or that occasional cyber bullying did not take place. Far from it.

Let's be clear: all men raised in a patriarchal culture have been subjected to misogynistic conditioning. Every campaign must struggle with supporters who do not live up to the purported values of the candidate. This is not an anti-feminist or alt-right position. The "Bernie Bro" narrative was a bad faith and insulting argument, and it erased the majority of women and people of color who made up the base of Bernie's movement. More than 70 percent of Bernie's national staff were women.

The Clinton campaign's online and cable news media boosters were too numerous to recount. But the most shameless standouts included Zerlina Maxwell, Neera Tanden, Chuck Todd, and Chris Matthews. They went after Sanders and our movement like a pack of ravening hyenas attacking a carcass. Lee Fang of the *Intercept* has reported that lobbyists working for Hillary Clinton Super PACS were routinely brought onto corporate news to be presented as unbiased political experts.

Along with the Bernie Bro narrative, corporate media pundits framed the entire primary dishonestly, by suggesting that the superdelegates Clinton had secured prior to the start of the voting gave her an "insurmountable" lead. What they neglected to mention was that Hillary had also had a commanding superdelegate lead during the 2008 primary, but that these party-appointed delegates don't vote *until the convention.*

When Obama took the lead in the 2008 primary, the superdelegates went with him. It is also notable that during every presidential primary in memory, the dominant media narrative has focused on the amount of money that the candidates had raised. The size of the war chest was assumed to be the single most important factor in electability. But when Sanders broke every single campaign fundraising record with small individual donations and without corporate Super PAC money, that theory suddenly and curiously became obsolete.

Bernie's decentralized grassroots army was an online tsunami. This was a problem for Hillary: in the past voters relied on the media to curate information about candidates. Now voters had access to unlimited information and could research and share facts about the candidates on their own.

One of the ways they combated this was through David Brock's Clinton Super PAC, Correct the Record, which spent $1 million on paid troll accounts to spread misinformation about Sanders, and which attempted to silence Hillary's critics.

It was described by the *New York Times* as Hillary Clinton's own 'personal media watchdog.' Progressives repeatedly called foul but somehow this never made the national news cycles. David Brock, by the way, was once the Republican hitman who smeared Anita Hill (the black attorney who testified about being sexually harassed by conservative Supreme Court Justice Clarence Thomas) before he defected to become a Clinton operative.

What a guy.

Super PACs, known technically as Independent Expenditure Only Political Committees, are a direct result of the Citizens United court decision. Justice Anthony Kennedy, the author of the decision, proclaimed that deregulating outside money would have no corrupting effect on candidates, because there would be strict firewalls between candidates and outside groups.

Mr. Brock took full advantage. In September 2015, Brock and Correct the Record published a piece on Bernie Sanders, attempting to link him to Hugo Chavez and his socialist political party. DARVO is an acronym for "deny, attack, and reverse victim and offender." It is a common manipulation strategy of psychological abusers.

The fact that Brock was willing to employ his dirty tactics for Hillary was not so much an indication of personal liberal enlightenment as it was a signifier that the Democratic Party had moved so far to the right that they were in many ways indistinguishable from the GOP of the past.

Brock's troll army was incredibly effective and could not be reasoned with.

Anyone who tried to draw distinctions between Sanders and Clinton was met with venom from people paid to silence and gaslight them. They were paid to be unreasonable and unswayed by small details like facts and voting records. A study was conducted at the University of Illinois at Urbana-Champaign analyzing experiments over two decades. *Anchoring bias* is a term used in psychology to describe the common human tendency to rely too heavily, or "anchor," on the first information that is heard.

"The effect of misinformation is very strong," said co-author Dolores Albarracín, professor of psychology. "When you present it, people buy it." The trolls had a perceptible impact on the culture of Clinton supporters and were effective at setting a tone of meanness.

Brock wasn't the only one. Democratic communications consultant Sally Albright was another one of Bernie's biggest detractors, who was revealed to be using a small army of fake Twitter accounts to amplify claims that Sanders was a fraud, a liar, racist and corrupt, among many other things. In one instance she even tweeted that Bernie's free college platform was racist.

But not even the combined weight of corporate media narratives could derail the Bernie train. What the Bernie movement lacked in financial and media resources, it made up for by inspiring people to get involved and choose their own narratives about the country and its future. Just like OWS, the movement caught fire for Sanders, and millions of Americans began to Feel the Bern. The movement even spread around the world. People in different countries would regularly phonebank for Sanders. Across the pond, Bernie supporters found a kindred spirit in the supporters of British Labour Party candidate Jeremy Corbyn.

Of all of Hillary's flying monkeys, Debbie Wasserman Schultz was by far the most loyal and effective. She was the head of the Democratic National Committee, but had been Hillary's campaign co-chair in 2008. How could one possibly suggest the Democratic primaries were in any way democratic, when the frontrunner's top lieutenant was allowed to run the organization presiding over the contest?

The number of sanctioned televised debates were cut from twenty-six in 2008 to just six. Schultz, or DWS, became an enduring nemesis of Sanders supporters, as her presence was felt throughout the contest—until she was forced to resign in disgrace after leaked emails proved what we had known all along. Then-congresswoman Tulsi Gabbard from Hawaii emerged (for a time) as a progressive hero for stepping down as the Vice-Chair of the DNC on the eve of Super Tuesday in protest of DWS and others putting their fingers on the scales for Clinton and for the war crimes she was responsible for.

Perhaps Bernie's greatest defenders were the dedicated members of National Nurses United, which endorsed Bernie Sanders at their national conference on August 10, 2015. With over 185,000 members, NNU is the largest nurses' union in the country and gave Sanders his first sizable labor endorsement of the campaign.

Having grown up in a family of nurses, I can say with some authority that there are few professions so fiercely committed to the betterment of our collective wellbeing. If you went to any Bernie Sanders rally across the country, you would witness red tour buses and a sea of red shirts waving "Nurses (heart) Bernie" signs.

NNU Executive Director RoseAnn DeMoro explained the

decision to endorse Bernie in a press release, saying, "Bernie Sanders has a proven track record of uncompromised activism and advocacy for working people, and a message that resonates with nurses [and] people across the country. What the Bernie Sanders campaign represents is an opportunity not just to speak truth to power, but to join movements together to change our country."

DeMoro was a true political revolutionary. It is arguable that without her support the PDA would never have gotten off the ground in 2004. Twelve years later, when Sanders was being pushed to run, she was once again at the vanguard, using her union resources to energize the insurgent campaign and bring Medicare for All to the forefront of American political discourse.

It was going to take a lot more support to mount a credible challenge to the presumptive front runner and the establishment behind her. Bernie was going to need a few more superheroes to fight for him and for the 99 Percent.

Chapter 4

Bernie's Avengers

Whatever you can do or dream you can, begin it.
Boldness has genius, power and magic in it.
-Johann Wolfgang Von Goethe

I first met Luis Calderin at a show called the *Art of the Political Revolution*, where my favorite modern poet, Saul Williams, was performing in support of the campaign.

This was very fucking cool.

Luis had been a childhood friend of Bernie's son, and was now serving as the campaign's Art, Culture and Youth Vote Coordinator. He wasn't hard to find; in his signature black-rimmed glasses and fedora, and with his intensely determined expression, Luis looked every bit the part.

As we spoke, Luis explained his plans to create a cultural movement around the campaign. After all, it was Bernie's mandate that artists should play an important part in the political revolution. It was clear that Luis had no shortage of ideas, but it was also clear that the campaign was like a start-up that had scaled too fast to keep up with the growth. They simply did not have the resources and infrastructure to handle how fast they were growing.

It was also clear that if Bernie was going to have any chance against a powerful political machine, he would need cultural firepower that was on another level. There's a reason Breitbart and the conservatives have made such concerted attacks against Hollywood. Entertainers are overwhelmingly influential, with a power that can cut across all dividing lines. True artists also tend to be freethinking and comfortable outside of dominant paradigms and systems. In other words, they are natural supporters of political insurgency.

Not long after we'd met, Luis and I discussed an idea of mine over lunch. I wanted to try and enlist the support of my friends and associates in the entertainment industry. I called the initiative Bernie's Avengers. Luis suggested we were like a team of wizards. And what, exactly, do wizards do?

They make magic.

I had always been enamored by those pockets of time when the stars align to bring extraordinary people together in the same place and at the same time, to be the axis upon which the wheel of history turns. I was enamored with tales of the Romantic Poets, the Algonquin Round Table, the Harlem Renaissance, the Beat Poets, the Chicago 7, the happenings at Haight-Ashbury in 1965, the Bowery in 1977, Seattle Grunge, The Wu-Tang Clan, and so on. I theorized that one didn't have to wait for the fates to arrange this—that this confluence of genius could be engineered by bringing the right people together.

Sun Tzu once said, "All warfare is based on deception. Hence, when we are able to attack, we must seem unable; when using our forces, we must appear inactive; when we are near, we must make the enemy believe we are far away; when far away, we must make him believe we are near."

We decided that Bernie's Avengers would operate in secret so as not to draw unnecessary attacks from establishment consultants, while quietly enrolling surrogates to promote the campaign and execute media initiatives.

There's a reason that brands spare no expense to be represented by celebrities. It's called the halo effect: a cognitive bias that creates a positive mental impression based on association. If someone likes a certain celebrity, and that celebrity likes something, then that person is more likely to have a positive view of that thing.

We knew enrolling famous surrogates would be a powerful tactic to gain critical mass and social acceptance for Bernie— maybe even be a game-changer. I was grateful my career and activism had given me connections to conscious artists.

My first call was to my friend, Angelica "Geli" Cob-Baehler, a record label executive and Ice Cube's manager. She was the brains behind some of the most iconic artists in pop culture, and was one of the most brilliant people I have ever known. She had routinely guided and shaped the careers of prominent acts, including Katy Perry, Thirty Seconds to Mars, Death Grips, and countless others. At one point early in Katy Perry's career her label was going to shelve her record so that it would never see the light of day. Geli stole the master recordings and smuggled them out of the building. She was a punk rock leftist outlaw with a heart of gold.

As a top executive at one of Hollywood's most outstanding music management companies, Geli had access to just about everyone, and she was willing to use this access to help the campaign. She confided to me that she had always felt like she was missing out on her calling to make a difference. We talked about the campaign, our strategy, and how much we felt the Bern. It was very personal to her.

The first official meeting between Geli, Luis and the campaign occurred the day after the Red Hot Chili Peppers' Feel the Bern benefit concert in downtown Los Angeles, shortly after the Iowa caucus. (It had been organized by Rain Phoenix, sister of Joaquin and the late River, and had included a heartfelt political speech by Flea.) This concert was one of the most important moments of the campaign to date, as it was not only a huge endorsement, but it involved a dedicated fundraiser for Bernie. The energy of the event was pure, electric dedication.

Before the concert, I called Luis with a question about a potential big donor and asked the minimum donation for a VIP ticket. His answer was, "Just tell him to give what is in his heart." This was a very different kind of political fundraiser. Usually the goal is to maximize the donation, by hook or by crook.

Also present at the meeting was Scott Goodstein of Revolution Messaging, the firm credited with many of the digital strategies behind the campaign's fundraising success. We agreed that Bernie would win most if not all of the progressive vote. But to win we also needed to win over a good number of suburban liberals who were not moved by Bernie's non-traditional speechifying, full of 99 Percent rhetoric and words like "oligarchy." Unlike the liberal technocrats, he didn't pander with empty rhetoric; he spoke to working-class people as if they deserved the dignity of being treated as intelligent adults.

One of the reasons Donald Trump dominated the Republican Primaries was his intentional use of a fourth-grade vocabulary. He delivered emotionally charged, easy-to-understand rhetoric that connected with the largest number of voters. He oversimplified problems and offered compelling imagery. He was also completely overt about his racism and misogyny, which tapped into the suppressed rage of conservative white voters terrified by a world that was changing faster than they could adapt. He was a vicious caricature of American sexism, xenophobia and bigotry.

Progressives, on the other hand, tend to be high-information voters. They know and care about politicians' voting records. They will research policies and positions. Party loyalist liberals are much more susceptible to following the party line, which is what made them easy marks for Democratic Party-connected troll farms that promulgated baseless tropes against Sanders to deflect substantive criticisms. They care most that a Democrat wins because it somehow makes them feel like a winner by proxy, like a football fan cheering for their favorite team despite never having stepped onto the playing field.

It was as Simone de Beauvoir once said: "The oppressor would not be so strong if he did not have accomplices among the oppressed."

Bernie was the opposite of the liberal-friendly MSNBC candidate. For starters, he was very obstinate. Though this staunch commitment to his principles endeared him to progressives, it could have the opposite effect on liberal voters. One of the functions of Luis's team and of Bernie's Avengers was to compensate for this through the power of art and culture. Liberals would never listen to a ninety-minute speech about oligarchy and income inequality, mostly because they skew in the higher tax brackets and prefer the status quo, even if it means the majority of Americans are struggling to survive.

I suggested the campaign focus on short-form narrative storytelling to personalize Bernie's often abstract platform and show how it would affect suffering citizens. If you wanted to win the uninformed liberal vote, you had to connect with their hearts in a powerful way. They don't care about records but are highly swayed by hopey-changey rhetoric. Ultimately the campaign did produce a series of brilliant short videos, including the personal story of Erica Garner, a Black Lives Matter activist and daughter of Eric Garner, who was murdered by police over selling loosie cigarettes.

Over the course of the campaign, Bernie's Avengers would bring together a number of remarkable people under the campaign's banner—musicians, artists, actors, storytellers, activists, and people who straddled them all. Though I could never do justice to the full list, I would like to record some memories of a few leading Avengers and their incredible work.

★ ★ ★ ★ ★

I would sometimes get a call from Luis about recruiting bands and speakers to open for Bernie at giant rallies. Occasionally, these calls would be frantic.

"Jay—I need someone for New Hampshire *in five days!*"

"I could call Alex from Edward Sharpe and the Magnetic Zeros?"

"Brother, get me Alex!"

We would then go directly to the artists, cutting out the agents and managers who usually try to keep their clients out of politics for fear of alienating fans. In the 60s and 70s, musicians were the bards of the revolution until the suits turned it into a business driven by quarterly reports. Napster, the free music sharing platform that toppled the music industry, is perhaps the single greatest metaphor for the relationship between the Democratic Party and the Bernie Sanders movement in 2016. Instead of adapting to a world that had already changed, like Apple did with iTunes, the record companies fought Napster tooth and nail, and never recovered. The Democrats would suffer the same foolish hubris by attempting to crush our candidate and movement, who represented an unprecedented opportunity to bring in a whole generation of new voters and the greatest fundraising apparatus on the planet to defeat Donald Trump and the Republican Party.

Alex Ebert, the lead singer and ringleader of the band Edward Sharpe and the Magnetic Zeros, never gave a shit what the suits thought. We first met during Occupy LA, where he rode a bike around the encampment as if he were right at home in the punk rock circus. Alex was a superhero in his own right. When he wasn't headlining Coachella or the Hollywood Bowl, he was working with frontline communities in Flint or developing tech for revolutionizing voting and the political process. He was an organizer at heart.

Alex was one of many excellent acts to open for Bernie during the campaign. I always enjoyed these rallies best, as one of my favorite things was hearing Bernie thank bands that we had brought in, which he'd never heard of, in his thick Brooklyn accent: "I'd like to thank Fan-tas-tic Negri-to, and [pause] Chicano [pause] Batman for playing tonight."

At a show and rally in Las Vegas, I got to hang backstage where I met Connor Paolo and his then-girlfriend, Lindsay Keys, who was documenting footage for the campaign. Connor was an actor on several shows I had never heard of (*Revenge, Gossip Girl*), but he was popular among the millennials. You'd never know it because he was so down to earth. We stayed up all night scheming ideas for Bernie at the Flamingo hotel.

It was also at the Flamingo that Luis introduced me to Seven McDonald, one of the campaign's surrogate wranglers. She was the daughter of Country Joe McDonald, famous for performing his "I-Feel-Like-I'm-Fixin'-To-Die Rag" (which you might recognize as the "One, Two, Three, What Are We Fighting For?" song) at Woodstock.

Seven was born into a world of famous people and had a big network to bring into the campaign. She had also managed Johnny Depp's Viper Room nightclub and the Smashing Pumpkins in the 1990s. Her superpower is relationships. We connected because we were both into meditation—we'd later work together at Standing Rock and other events, and see each other every year at the events held by the Indian spiritual leader Amma, known as the "hugging saint."

Connor Paolo made strong contributions to Bernie's Avengers, connecting us with Pantera Sarah and Chris Kantrowitz, who were also super-connectors. Kantrowitz was a tech CEO and one of the first Hollywood wizards to get a BernieSanders.com email address. His superpower was facilitating connections between people that can make things happen.

Pantera Sarah (yes, that was what she went by) was a force of nature for the campaign as a surrogate wrangler. A veteran of the Obama campaign, she'd helped produce will.i.am's Grammy Award-winning "Yes We Can" music video for Obama.

Sarah, Connor, Chris and I worked together to produce a series of public service announcements. Rain Phoenix brought in talented creatives like Ramy Youssef to brainstorm. It blows my mind to think that one day Ramy was just another Berniecrat offering his gifts to the Political Revolution, and then suddenly he was winning awards for his self-titled Hulu show.

It was while filming the resulting PSAs on set that I met Bernie Avengers Kendrick Sampson and Max Carver. Both big contributors to the campaign, they had traveled the country on behalf of the

Political Revolution. Kendrick remained a prominent advocate of the Black Lives Matter movement, but also went to the frontlines at Standing Rock, as did Max.

Kendrick was known for his recurring roles on *The Vampire Diaries* and *How to Get Away with Murder*. Max was known for his roles on *Desperate Housewives* (and later the television series *Teen Wolf*). I think it was lucky in the long run that I hadn't owned a TV or watched network television since 2003, because most of the Avengers were really just other Berners—citizens who cared deeply for the movement and what it represented for the future of our world. What mattered is that they were there. They weren't just tweeting from their ivory towers, they were down in the trenches with the rest of us. We were a wild bunch of road dogs across the country for Bernie and the Political Revolution. They showed up to knock on doors and phonebank. They risked their careers and gave everything for the cause.

Beyond their palpable passion and inspiration, it is definitely a tactical advantage to have an affinity group of dedicated people with influence over mainstream culture. They were at the top of their respective fields, in some of the most competitive industries on the planet. This meant they possessed a very high capacity for executive functioning. There's also a lot less ego involved in working with people who have already achieved some level of professional success, and who are working on a project just to make a differ-ence. They have nothing to prove.

We were going to need every advantage we could get. As of March 2016, we knew Super Tuesday was around the corner and we would have to seriously escalate our tactics if our political revolution had any chance of succeeding.

Chapter 5:

The Clooney Counter-Party

The media's the most powerful entity on earth.
They have the power to make the innocent guilty
and to make the guilty innocent, and that's power.
Because they control the minds of the masses.
-Malcolm X

Never underestimate the power of intention.
In the spring of the 2016 Democratic primaries, I came across an interview in the *Guardian* with George Clooney. He called Bernie Sanders "single-minded" on the subject of income inequality. The piece appeared on the heels of an announcement he was to host a $350,000 per plate fundraiser for Hillary Clinton.

My blood boiled as I read Clooney's smug dismissal. I imagined him offering this statement from one of his five multimillion-dollar mansions, perhaps his summer getaway at the eighteenth-century villa on Italy's Lake Como, where his butler served him lattes and foie gras. This mental picture was immediately followed by more images of hordes of angry villagers scaling the walls of his villa with torches and pitchforks gripped in their teeth, driven by savage intentions of eating the rich.

But what could I do?

The best idea I could come up with at the time was an open letter. Unbeknownst to me, life (and the campaign) was conspiring to set in motion a far more compelling response.

On April 4th, 2016, an LA contingent of Bernie supporters rallied to protest at CNN's Hollywood headquarters.

The influence of OWS was apparent, as the action was called "Occupy CNN." It had been masterminded by activist-producer Eden McFadden, and it proved to be one of the more effective demonstrations of the primaries, attracting upwards of two thousand participants. It also drew a fair amount of attention on social media. Bill Maher even mentioned it on HBO.

Their thesis was proved once again on April 13th, 2016, when Bernie held one of the largest political rallies of all time in Manhattan's Washington Square Park, just ahead of New York's April 19 primary, but it was completely ignored by the corporate media. Special guests included Vampire Weekend, Rosario Dawson, Spike Lee, and Tim Robbins. The campaign was also an opportunity for many leaders to rise to greater prominence. One such case was a Brooklyn-born Muslim human rights activist of Palestinian descent named Linda Sarsour, who also spoke that night as a Bernie surrogate.

Some reports estimated that more than forty thousand people attended. The primary was a major event in the Democratic presidential race, and the seventy-three delegates up for grabs in New York City were crucial to winning the state.

For a moment, all things seemed possible.

It was exactly one year after the Sister Giant conference. A lot had happened since then. It seemed like every week Bernie was gaining more awareness and momentum.

The first big turn was the Michigan primary, where Bernie had been down by twenty-five points but had come from behind to win in a huge upset that had stunned the pundits and the so-called experts. If this was possible, then what else could be achieved? We badly needed these moments. The psychic toll on us was tremendous, watching the media collude with the political establishment to put the heels of their designer boots on the neck of the campaign and our movement.

Behind the numbers was the fact that Bernie supporters were a growing army of organizers and activists.

Sanders had narrowed Clinton's initial sixty-point lead with voters nationally to ten points, and appeared to be gaining on her lead in pledged delegates as he rode the momentum of seven straight primary wins. Shortly before the rally, I'd attended a meeting between Bernie and union organizers in the basement of the Wiltern Theater. I sensed that something had shifted in the senator. He was a different man compared to the one I had met a year before at the event organized by Marianne Williamson. After the winning streak, it seemed as though Bernie himself was starting to believe he might be able to win.

That moment reminded me of Hunter S. Thompson's recounting of his quixotic 1969 campaign to be elected the first drug-addled anarchist Sheriff of Aspen, Colorado, when he wrote in *The Great Shark Hunt*:

"We had nothing to lose. We were like a bunch of wild-eyed amateur mechanics rolling a homemade racing car onto the track at Indianapolis and watching it overtake a brace of big Offenhausers at the 450 pole."

Of course, right on cue, enter the corporate media fuckery. On the day of the rally, CNN and MSNBC broadcast an empty podium at a Donald Trump press conference for twenty minutes. Neither network sent cameras to cover Bernie's historic rally. By the end of the election cycle the networks had given Trump $3 billion in free advertising, according to the data analysis firm mediaQuant.

I met one of my all time favorite Avengers, Kii Arens, at Occupy CNN. He heard the speech I gave at the rally and literally gave me the Bernie shirt he had designed off his back right there and then.

Kii was an amazing artist known for making album and poster art for major festivals and bands like Radiohead and Cheap Trick. He had directed music videos for Queens of the Stone Age, Devo, the Pixies, and Elton John. He wore glasses and his head was completely shaved. He was always dressed in bright pastel colors and his fingernails were usually painted to match. He was a wizard if one ever lived.

A few days after Occupy CNN, Eden McFadden called me to let me know that a man had approached her at the event. Not just any man, but George Clooney's neighbor in the Hollywood Hills. He said he was willing to discuss an action in protest of the upcoming Hillary Clinton fundraiser. Due to her work schedule, Eden said she couldn't take on organizing the protest. She asked if I had any interest.

The opportunity to embarrass Clinton, Clooney, and their oligarch buddies?

The answer was, "Yes. Absolutely."

Now all we needed was a mob of villagers.

The Clooney Counter-Party

★ ★ ★ ★ ★

The man who lived next door to George Clooney was named Howard Gold, an eccentric millionaire with a family fortune and a good heart.

When he first approached Eden, he wasn't fully committed to supporting the Sanders campaign. But he was an enemy of US militarism. He confided to me that upon being notified of the upcoming fundraiser, he'd left an anonymous note on George's mailbox that read: HILLARY CLINTON IS THE CANDIDATE OF THE WAR MACHINE.

This was a man after my own heart.

Howard possessed an uncommon amount of knowledge about foreign policy. We quickly bonded over our resolve to bring accountability and awareness of the fact that recent Democratic administrations had dropped more bombs than their Republican predecessors—in Obama's case, they'd waged war in seven countries.

Howard Gold's family had made its fortune creating the 99 Cents Only chain of discount stores. This past informed our plan for what needed to happen outside of the Clooney-Clinton event: a $27 per plate fundraiser for the 99 Percent. This would starkly juxtapose the two campaigns; one crowdfunded and people-powered, the other run by a junta of wealthy, elite insiders hopelessly removed from the problems of everyday Americans.

The challenge was to plan and execute this action in less than eight days.

Because of Hillary's armed Secret Service detail, there were potentially serious legal issues to consider. If we publicized the action too widely, they might shut down the single access road into the Hollywood Hills for security reasons, which would block access for our participants and the media.

By doing research into Secret Service protocols, I learned that Hillary's Secret Service codename was Evergreen. Bernie Sanders's codename was Intrepid—no doubt a nod to his chutzpah for taking on the oligarchy. Not surprisingly, there is absolutely nothing useful on the internet to help you organize against the Secret Service. In fact, it only served to freak me out a little about what we were up against. Secret Service meant potentially serious consequences.

The target of the protest was a former First Lady, a former Secretary of State, former US Senator, and front-running presidential candidate, having dinner with Hollywood's A-list in a mansion on a narrow, dead-end, one-way street.

No big deal.

Howard was also understandably nervous. It took a few long phone calls to finally put his mind at ease. Eventually he came around to see that this was a once in a lifetime opportunity to make a historic statement. We agreed that we would leave his name out of it and not mention his family's business.

We were organizing guerrilla theater, so no one would be risking arrest. The objective was to co-opt the media, to show the differences between the campaigns. The media was driving the narrative that Clinton was close to Sanders on the issues. The Clooney fundraiser was the perfect opportunity to highlight the distinctions and show the face of Clinton's true constituency.

To execute a *Mission: Impossible* caper of this magnitude, we were going to need help.

Luckily, during the primary there was no shortage of people who wanted to help. Most Sanders supporters were fed up with the Clinton establishment fixing the game at every turn, and it's difficult to capture the lengths those who were Feeling the Bern were willing to go to in order to support the campaign.

The fundraiser was scheduled for the night of April 16. We were able to rally a couple of hundred people to RSVP. Everyone was under strict instructions not to post anything about this on social media so as not to alert the Secret Service. For some reason, when you tell people there's something they can't tell anyone about, everyone wants to tell everyone about it. We had sent out very detailed instructions for the guests, including protocols, suggested attire, and parking info.

The night before, the Clooneys had hosted another fundraiser for Hillary in San Francisco, and were met outside by a small group of Sanders supporters. As George and Amal entered their posh Bay Area apartment, one of the protesters shouted, "You sucked as Batman!"

Tough to argue with that one.

On the day of the big night, guests began to arrive at 11 a.m. One of the first to show up was Frances Fisher, whom you might remember as the haughty socialite mother of the character Rose in the movie *Titanic*. Frances's superpower was being fearless and outrageous. She wasn't afraid to wear one of our "Fuck Politics, Vote for Bernie" T-shirts to speak in front of a crowd of fifteen thousand people and open for the Senator. Frances stood outside of the gate to Howard's estate, holding a giant sign announcing, "Feel the Bern Fundraiser $27." I'd met her first at Marianne's Sister Giant event carrying a little dog. I would have never thought in that moment the woman I was looking at would eventually become a hardcore frontline warrior.

Gaby Hoffmann also joined us. I had met her at the Las Vegas rally, where she'd done a full backwards bend for the crowd. You might remember Gaby from the show *Transparent*, or when she was the most adorable little girl in Hollywood, stealing hearts in classic films like *Sleepless in Seattle*, *Uncle Buck* and *Field of Dreams*. "If you build it, they will come," was perhaps one of the most fitting metaphors for the Sanders campaign.

There was also Alan Minsky, at the time the program director of progressive LA radio station KPFK, and who would go on to be the executive director of the PDA. Alan's activism began in college, with union solidarity work and opposition to US involvement in Central America. Alan was on the ground organizing in the months leading up to Occupy Wall Street and had also helped to organize the PDA launch event for Bernie at the Musician's Union in 2015. So many of our paths had crossed and intersected, like countless tributaries flowing into the same ocean—an ocean that on occasion would rise into tidal waves crashing over the American political landscape.

Outside of Howard's we had asked guests to dress business casual so as not to be categorically dismissed by the media. It was also important to not be seen as angry or bitter. You can't be angry or bitter if you're having a good time at the cooler party next door. We'd learned well during OWS how the media would target supporters that were easily dismissed as unrealistic hippies or mentally unstable indigent people. The signs we held were meant to communicate our message. We also invited the local media trucks to come early and park in Howard's driveway. They did some interviews with us before the action started, which admittedly could have been Feds or consultants doing oppo research.

Throughout the course of the morning and early afternoon, somewhere between a hundred and fifty and two hundred people came to Howard's house to participate. Many of the local LA organizers and 'super volunteers' were present. Howard had gotten about five hundred signs printed that had been designed by Kii Arens.

They read, "Big Oil for Hillary, we fracking love you!" and "Wall Street is with her," and other salty slogans.

Then the Clooneys' guests began to arrive.

Clooney and Howard live on a narrow, dead-end street on the valley side of the Hollywood Hills. The sun was shining—a perfect sunset. It took hours for the big donors to arrive, as fancy cars filled up the lot. They had no choice but to drive right past us. It was a little tense, a little uncomfortable, and completely glorious. They had nowhere to go, no choice but to sit there and read the signs.

Most of the time, they were sitting in a long cavalcade of cars that barely moved, surrounded by a hundred or more Berners on either side who stared at them with disapproving eyes and waved cheeky signs reminding them that they were spending tens or hundreds of thousands of dollars to support a candidate in bed with Wall Street, the fossil fuel industry, and the war machine.

More reporters started arriving. Cary Harrison, a progressive television and radio personality, made significant contributions to this action, and fast became a ride-or-die Avenger. He'd brought in a Hollywood publicist named Ilene Proctor, who was able to get a writer from *The Hill* to show up. Her blog post quickly racked up fifteen thousand shares in less than an hour.

Then the black suits entered the scene. They pushed us back to either side of the road, which wasn't very effective since the road was so narrow. Then one agent walked to the far side of the street, grabbed a random woman sitting casually on the ground, picked her up and dragged her across the street to incite us to engage, and thereby grant them a justification to shut us down before the Secretary arrived.

The Bernie supporters began shouting and engaging the suit as the guests continued to arrive. Appropriately, it was like a scene out of the movies. Some of our people began approaching the agent, incensed, yelling for the man to unhand her. I raised my voice, loudly enough so that everyone could hear, and said,

> "WE ARE HERE TO REPRESENT BERNIE!
>
> DON'T GIVE IN AND LET THEM
> MAKE YOU LOSE YOUR PEACE.
>
> SHOW THEM THAT WE STAND HERE
> FOR BERNIE WITH LOVE!"

It seemed to work. If there's any lesson I've learned from direct action protest and event organizing, it's that there's a time for governance by group consensus, and there's a time for making command decisions.

Hillary's arriving benefactors were a parade of A-listers: Jeffrey and Marilyn Katzenberg, Steven Spielberg, the biggest talent agents, studio executives, technology and finance people, Ellen DeGeneres, Twentieth Century Fox Chairman and Chief Executive Jim Gianopulos, and Sony Pictures Chairman Tom Rothman, just to name a few. If we'd been angry and shouting, that's all the media would have shown. Our goal was to demonstrate that the Bernie party was a different party, the better party. It was a metaphor for what America could be.

The stakeholders of the establishment however had no intention of letting go of their absolute power without a fight.

There was an intense feeling of anticipation when the Clinton motorcade finally arrived. Howard, me, and two others had fistfuls of small bills in hand. No one else knew what we were about to do. My old friend Will Celestine had brought a phantom-powered sound system which was stationed by the side of the road. When the motorcade turned the corner onto George and Howard's street, we started playing "Hail to the Chief" before transitioning into "The Gold Diggers' Song (We're in the Money)," sung by none other than Rosemary Clooney, the aunt of George Clooney. As the black SUVs got closer, the old-timey horn section rang out in the ragtime melody, "We're in the money, we're in the money…"

The convoy charged toward us at a pretty good speed to get past the crowd as fast as possible. Just as they passed by, we threw fistfuls of money into the air, amounting to $1,000, showering the SUVs as they drove by. One of the speeding cars had no less than five assault rifles pointed at us from the opened windows as we hurled the cash at the air above the former Secretary of State and First Lady.

When the cars turned into Clooney's mansion, the DJ changed the tune to the 1964 Martha and The Vandellas' classic, "Dancing in the Street" at maximum volume. The agents and police postured to keep us contained on the lawns. Without missing a beat, Frances charged them with arms in the air in celebration, dancing as she ran. All two hundred Bernie supporters followed suit, cheering as an impromptu dance party in the middle of the street ensued. An agent with male pattern baldness bullied a young woman as he tried to hold back the tide of people closing in on both sides. It was at once comical and futile.

The merriment continued for about ten minutes. The local news cameras captured only our victory dance; the national progressive media would tell a different story.

(Yes, we picked up all the money.)

Howard and I intended to raise awareness about Clinton's record as a warmonger, so I approached the CNN reporter on the scene and attempted to introduce myself. His name was Dan Merica.

"Hi I'm Jay Ponti, and I'm the lead organizer of this event. Would you like to know why we are doing this?"

Without missing a beat he barely turned his head to acknowledge me, said "Not really," dismissively and then continued to film the action.

The next day, the corporate media went berserk with the story, running it 24/7. Our Clooney Counter-Party was the stupid thing of the week in the 24-hour news cycle—for four days running. CNN and MSNBC went into high gear to spin the stunt as an act of misogyny. They suggested that by throwing money, we were implying Hillary Clinton was an exotic dancer or a prostitute. They played the Dan Merica footage minus the Rosemary Clooney song (which they failed to mention).

Chris Hayes organized a panel discussion. Rebecca Traister, a *New York Magazine* writer and progenitor of the Bernie Bro trope, asserted that the act was inherently misogynistic. I don't know what music they play in strip clubs, but I find it hard to believe they're playing musical theater numbers from the 1930s. It didn't matter that the money-throwing tactic was used by Abbie Hoffman in the sixties when he threw a fist full of money onto the floor of Wall Street to watch the traders scrabble for it like wild animals. In 2015 comedian Simon Brodkin showered money over FIFA president Sepp Blatter to bring attention to his corruption. If they had played the original footage with the Rosemary Clooney song, no reasonable person would ever have thought that our actions were suggesting Hillary was a sex worker.

We experienced first hand being the victims of fake news.

Jimmy Dore and Cenk Uygur from The Young Turks were the only outlet to call out the media for their hypocrisy.

Why couldn't they see the obvious, that we were bringing attention to the disgusting amount of money required to gain access to and influence with a Democratic candidate for president? I mean, couldn't they have just read one of the two hundred signs we were holding?

The Avengers Barnstorm at Howard Gold's House

In the aftermath of the Clooney Counter Party, spirits were high. The previous months had been rough, watching the Clinton campaign, corporate media and the Democratic Establishment put the screws on our candidate and movement on a daily basis. To make matters worse, things on the ground in our own community were turbulent.

Political revolutionaries love to fight. We love to fight The Man. We love to fight so much that very often we end up fighting everyone, including those who are in the trenches next to us. This was very prevalent throughout the Southern California Bernie groups.

There was the Bernie Brigade, Team Bernie LA and Los Angeles for Bernie. There were also organizers and free agents putting together events, rallies, and marches independently. There were media makers like Shane Barbera making full-length multi-episode animated parodies of *Star Wars* called *Bernie Sand Wars*, which was amazing. The storyline featured many of the personalities involved in the political primaries as Star Wars characters. Debbie Wasserman Schultz was portrayed as Jar Jar Binks. Which of the two was more despised, it would be difficult to say.

The path to victory was as thin as a razor's edge. Super Tuesday had been a bloodbath, because Sanders was still relatively unknown to voters at the time. The primaries are by nature much easier to control by the two political parties of the duopoly. Traditionally Super Tuesday exists to favor the selected candidate with the biggest national following. The problem is that the outcome of the Democratic primary is greatly influenced by the voting of red states that will have no impact on the general election. This gives right wing "centrist" candidates with the backing of the party a huge advantage.

This was also a great disadvantage for Bernie, whose numbers always skyrocketed when he had the chance to campaign in any given state, bringing giant rallies, his ground game and cultural influencers that could generate enthusiasm. This, combined with the superdelegate lead, meant the corporate media never failed to mention that if Bernie and our political revolution was to succeed at winning the nomination, Sanders would need to win 70 percent of the votes in California. This meant that the Golden State was going to be the decisive battle of the contest (though I use this word loosely due to the fact that the word "contest" implies a fair competition, which this certainly was not).

To my mind, if we were going to make it to 70 percent and keep the dream alive, it was going to require all of our forces working together. I thought if we could just bring everyone together and align on a vision of unity we might have a chance. It was a nice idea, anyway.

We called everyone together for a meeting at the Howard Gold mansion. It was an invite-only barnstorm on how to recruit entertainment industry professionals committed to evening the odds in advance of the primary. It was a long shot, but we were all-in. So many hopes and dreams hung in the balance.

I put the word out to some of the key organizers in Los Angeles, as well as asking all the Avengers to reach out to their networks to bring in more heavy hitters who could help get us over the finish line. The meeting that followed at Howard's was very powerful. During the opening introductions, I invited everyone to share their superpowers as we went around the room.

Two of the most powerful additions to Bernie's Avengers that day were Ann Kleinhenz and Shailene Woodley.

Shailene Woodley is a Hollywood actress, but has a lot more in common with her character in the *Divergent* series than people might realize. Shailene's superpowers are her massive social media following and indefatigable positive energy. She also has a visionary spirit. She might be an actress by profession, but deep down she is really a hippie with the heart of a warrior.

Ann Kleinhenz is a producer and a damn fine organizer. Her superpower is to create extraordinary projects with her besties, Shailene and Rosario Dawson. She was also great with on-the-ground management and logistics. Despite consistently generating big wins, she always remains humbly in the background.

Looking back on that moment, it's incredible to think about the journey that would await all of us. Shailene was so humble and understated, you'd never guess she was a movie star. Little did we know that in just a few months, she'd become a frontline warrior at Standing Rock and one of Bernie's fiercest surrogates.

Mikki Willis, the founder of Elevate Media, also attended. I had known him for years through the conscious media community. He was once called the Greatest Dad in the World because of a viral video in which he spoke to the prejudices around assigned gender roles as his son picked out a doll in a toy store. His superpower was keeping love in the conversation. Mikki was one of the people I could call on for advice when things got tough or personality conflicts arose. (Years later, we would have a falling out and he'd gain online infamy for directing a viral conspiracy video called *Plandemic*, but we will come to that eventually.)

There were upwards of eighty people at the meeting, and it produced some powerful magic. There is tactical, goal oriented, strategic organizing, and sometimes organizing is simply bringing people together. One thing I have found that is true about embarking on a big *holy shit*-type mission is that you can't do it alone.

There is also a psychic shift that happens when you get a bunch of badasses in a room together. As each goes around the circle, introducing themselves and who they are in the world, something happens where the full magnitude of our collective power and potential becomes real. It is a premise I had been experimenting with for years. One cannot predict what will emerge from the connections made. Part of the fun is seeing the ripples that continue long after the first rock is cast into the water.

It is foolhardy to think that anyone can own or control these ripples. When you try to be a gatekeeper and control the process, (or indeed, anything) you kill the magic. As an organizer, you may set things into motion, make connections for people, and create possibilities that would never have existed. There were people whose lives were changed forever because of the connections they made in that room. Some will not appreciate you or the sacrifices you make. They may even try to project bad motives onto you, spread gossip about you or work to undermine your efforts. If you are going to set out to make a difference it is important to be prepared for this. It helps to have mentors or therapists with whom to process these challenges. Take the problems and negative feelings to your confidential advisors and the solutions back to the movement.

We closed the meeting with a giant solidarity circle, all of us arm in arm. For a brief moment, we achieved unity in our Los

Angeles Bernie community. We all left that meeting with a renewed sense of possibility and solidarity, as well as some strategic plans for creating media campaigns, art, and guerrilla marketing. There was a sense of power, matched by the ominous, sobering realization of the monumental task that lay ahead.

What could be done?

Bernie's Coffee Shop

Howard had mentioned in the course of our conversations about the Clooney Counter-Party that his family also owned the famous Johnie's Coffee Shop. It was a historic landmark that most people know, even if they don't know that they know it. It's the place where Walter says to the Dude, "You want a toe? I can get you a toe, believe me. There are ways, Dude." It's the place where Mr. Pink gives the speech about not tipping the waitress. It was also at one of the busiest intersections in Los Angeles, on Fairfax and Wilshire, where almost a hundred thousand cars pass every day.

Curating the murals and art that would transform Johnie's into Bernie's Coffee Shop was a job for Kii Mutha Fuckin' Arens.

Once Howard had given the thumbs up, I called Kii, who brought in street artist Dionisio Ceballos to paint a psychedelic Bernie mural on the side. It was brilliant. It took time but he opened up to the idea that we might create a not-so-secret headquarters for the Avengers, a central location for all of the unofficial Bernie and grassroots groups to come together, work past our differences, and join forces.

This was going to take an ace crew. We had met a lot of good people at Howard's house, and the interest in the community was high to get on board and to turn Johnie's Coffee Shop, a dilapidated orange and turquoise 1950s Googie relic, into a working campaign center. The place was a wreck, though; it had been decades since it was used in a film. There was no electricity, no running water. Thick grime covered every surface. There were no working bathrooms. Getting it into shape was going to take a small army.

If we could get enough of a posse together and enough hands on, we could pull it off. We had run ops for the Clooney Counter-Party almost entirely on Facebook Messenger threads. Everyone broke off into specialized teams. Team Bernie LA was particularly eager to take a leadership role in coordinating the clean-up effort, and I was happy not to have to shoulder the full responsibility.

My original intention was for Johnie's Coffee Shop to be a place that could bring us together—to heal the divisions in our community and unite us. My favorite idea was to invite superdelegates to the diner for private lunches. Our celebrity surrogates would show up as their servers, bring them milkshakes, and lobby them on Bernie and the issues.

We opened on May 27, 2016, with a big launch event that attracted the local press. Kii designed signage for the tall glass front window that read "OPEN 27 HOURS." It all looked very legit. The Young Turks ran a terrific segment about the opening.

We had turned the iconic Hollywood landmark Johnie's Coffee Shop into a Bernie-themed center for grassroots activism and campaigning, replete with psychedelic murals. If the left is going to reclaim control of the government from the current corporate conservative regime, we are going to need to think outside of conventional politics. The extreme makeover of Bernie's Coffee Shop had been just one example of Sanders's supporters rising up and creating much-needed inspiration with our gumption and DIY inventiveness.

It was around the time of the opening that I met Josh Fox, a filmmaker who brought tremendous vision and enthusiasm to the Avengers. Josh was an official Bernie surrogate known for the black glasses and New York Yankees cap that he wore for his Oscar-nominated anti-fracking film *Gasland*, famous for a scene where a man lights his tap water on fire.

Josh was in LA for the premier of his documentary *How To Let Go of The World and Love All the Things Climate Can't Change*, the third movie in his *Gasland* trilogy. It was about what people around the world, who were already suffering the fallout of the impending climate crisis, were doing to resist. I had always been pro-climate action, but for some reason it had never been a central issue for me. The first-person narrative storytelling about people on the frontlines of the climate crisis who had no choice but to fight forever lit the flame of climate action in my heart.

Josh had also been a regular at Zuccotti Park during Occupy.

It included top climate scientists and activists, and finally landed for me the brutal reality that the human race has already crossed the Rubicon with respect to carbon levels, and that there was nothing we could do to stop the impending devastation except to attempt harm-reduction.

Mikaele Maiava, a Samoan activist, flew in for the premiere with flower leis for everyone. He was the founder of the Pacific Climate Warriors, who battle oil tankers with indigenous dugout canoes and perform a dance like the Maori Haka dance while shouting, "WE ARE NOT DROWNING, WE ARE FIGHT-ING." They say this because their islands are disappearing due to rising sea levels. The film shows him paddling out with Josh to the island where his father was buried, only to discover that it has disappeared under water.

Josh's superpower was being a force of nature. Josh and the journalist Nomiki Konst were inseparable in our group. They had first met at a party for *Gasland* in New York in 2011. Winnie Wong from the People for Bernie affinity group used to call Josh her Italian grandmother, a joke referencing his strong-willed combination of Jewish and Calabrese heritage. Josh and Nomi became powerful leaders of the Avengers, especially when we had to rapidly respond to the endless dumpster fires happening in the national narrative or the fuckery being perpetrated within the Democratic Party.

Josh also brought in Armand Aviram, a viral video content creator for *NowThis*, the millennial-focused media platform. He was instrumental in telling stories from the frontlines that the mainstream media never covered and generating millions of views in the process. Armand would later do an exclusive interview with Bernie, who had been very smart to lure him away from *NowThis* and bring his style to the campaign's digital efforts. I didn't know it at the time, but he had covered the Clooney Counter-Party for *NowThis*.

We also met YahNé Ndgo that night, a brilliant black organizer from Germantown, Philadelphia. She had come to Los Angeles, like many others, for the big showdown in California.

Show Me the Ballots

The run-up to the California primary was full of ominous events. In New York, two hundred thousand New York Democratic primary voters were mysteriously stripped from the rolls in Bernie's home borough of Brooklyn. It was later determined to be an act of fraud. New York Attorney General Eric Schneiderman would reveal that two hundred thousand New York City voters had been illegally wiped off the rolls and prevented from voting in the presidential primary.

Was it any coincidence that Brooklyn was one of the biggest strongholds for Bernie voters?

The Bernie love was so strong there that Clinton supporters had to create safe spaces in the NYC borough. Benari Poulten, a comic who worked for Comedy Central's *The Nightly Show with Larry Wilmore* said, "You can't just roll out of bed and walk into a Bernie event [to find fellow Clinton supporters], you have to take two trains and a bus and an Uber and a Lyft and, like, talk to somebody at the door, who's like, 'Do you really want to be here?'"

Considering the dismal crowds that Hillary's rallies attracted, there was a lot of truth to this statement.

In October of 2017, the city's elections board quietly settled the lawsuit by admitting it broke federal and state election laws.

The Arizona primary on March 22nd, 2016 was another fiasco.

Carlos Marroquin, one of the all-time great super volunteers, had organized six buses to shuttle Angelenos out to Phoenix to knock on doors for the campaign. We spent a few days canvassing in the Arizona heat, and on election day at about 7 p.m. we received word that voters were expected to wait up to seven hours in line to cast their ballots. Bernie supporters responded by bringing crates of bottled water and snacks to pass out to voters in lines that would put any Disney ride—on a weekend during peak season—to shame.

I brought my guitar and we sang songs to entertain people. There had been a great deal of tension between various supporters of different candidates. All of that melted away as the people continued to stand, refusing to be disenfranchised by a state that had cut the number of polling places. The news announced that the lines were up to five to seven hours long, which I'm sure discouraged many poor working people from casting their ballots. Imagine being a single mother coming home from working long hours and perhaps multiple shifts, seeing those lines on the news and having to decide whether or not to exercise their sacred franchise.

With the California primary only weeks away, Shailene hosted a picnic with Kendrick Sampson and Black Men for Bernie in Simi Valley. Black Men for Bernie had been started by Bruce Carter. He drove across the country in a touring bus with images of Bernie and the name of the group wrapped around the side. Both the bus and Bruce made a statement wherever they went. That day was no exception, especially since African Americans represent only 1 percent of the population of Simi Valley. The local news covered the event, including Shailene's appeal to her fans and her hometown's voters to support Bernie.

Michelle and Taylor from TYT were also there, whom I had originally met at the Occupy CNN action. They consistently made the highest quality short-form videos of the notable events of our movement. As things were wrapping up, Michelle mentioned some concerns she had in conversation. Michelle and Taylor weren't just journalists, they were activists at heart. They Felt the Bern as much as any of us did; maybe more. She suggested we had a serious problem. It was all coming down to California voters and there were indications that there would be serious election fuckery to contend with, just as there had been in the New York primary.

Bernie supporters had been organizing to knock on every door. We were at a disadvantage because early voting by mail would heavily favor party stalwarts. We were feverishly texting, phone-banking, face banking, and generally pulling out every possible stop to close the gap and win the California primary. We could feel the dream slipping away, somewhere between a dissipating mist or a mother clutching for her child as it slips off of the top of a ledge.

It was the last chance for Bernie to get enough delegates to win the nomination, or at least make an arguable challenge at the convention in Philadelphia. Michelle had been in contact with civil rights attorney Bill Simpich and Election Justice USA. They shared her serious concerns about the California Democratic Party rigging the game for Hillary. California was a semi-closed primary and Bernie needed to win that 70 percent of the vote.

Everything was on the line at this point; the pathway to victory was the width of a razor's edge. The main concern was Independent and crossover voters being able to cast ballots. Voters were either not informed, or the instructions were confusing. Bill was part of a team of lawyers that filed suit against then-Secretary of State Alex Padilla for voters to be able to have more time to request a Democratic presidential crossover ballot.

Bill and Stephen Jaffe had filed the suit on behalf of Bernie Sanders supporters as well as the Independents who would be shut out of the primary process. At the time, Simpich was on record as saying, "Independent voters who have stated No Party Preference (NPP) may not be able to vote in the June 7 primary because of the confusion over how to obtain a party-based presidential primary ballot. Those ballots are not automatically mailed. They must be requested by the voters. That has not been made clear in the instructions sent."

This even happened to me when I attempted to cast my ballot.

Collaborating on the lawsuit was Election Justice USA, a national election integrity and voting rights organization, which had already made international news with its suit over the voter roll purges prior to the New York Primary. Bill uncovered that the registrar of voters handbook specifically instructed poll workers not to inform voters of the Democratic crossover ballots and that their NPP ballots might not be counted.

Our plan was to make an informational video for The Young Turks informing No Party Preference voters that anyone who did not specifically request a Democratic crossover ballot might not have their votes counted. Michelle and I met Susan Sarandon at Bernie's Coffee Shop to get a soundbyte. Little did I know how this meeting would, in just four months, change my life with a campaign we would create together called *#BankExit*.

As part of our *Show Me the Ballots* production we drove to City Hall in the Black Men for Bernie tour bus to film a stunt in which we asked city officials for the location of Democratic crossover ballots. It would have all gone to plan had it not been for a white woman with Team Bernie LA showing up uninvited, bursting onto a bus full of black men with a clipboard in peak white-lady fashion to announce that she was now in charge. Michelle Boley and I looked at each other with mouths agape as she proceeded to badger staffers.

Grassroots populist movements have historically struggled to find a healthy balance in terms of racial dynamics. The women's suffrage, labor, and anti-war movements were all plagued by paradigms of white supremacy. Being progressive or leftist does not make one immune to cultural conditioning. The Occupy and Sanders movements also had their challenges with white supremacy, patriarchy, colonialism, and so forth. It takes deep inner work to heal and transform the assumptions rooted in our unconscious minds.

And when I finally showed up at the polls to cast my ballot for Bernie Sanders, sure enough, I discovered that my status had been changed to NPP.

The Clooney Counter-Party

★ ★ ★ ★ ★

Two days from election day, Luis called me to inquire about opening acts for a large rally in San Diego. I immediately looped Michael Mowgli into the email chain in hopes he would be able to help secure talent. The response caught me off guard.

"I'll do it," he replied.

I forgot that I had already pitched the Mowglis to the campaign, but Michael had since left the band. I didn't consider that Luis would be open to him doing a solo set. I also didn't consider that Michael, the wizard that he is, would put together an eight-piece band in two days and ask me to join—but it made perfect sense. He had a wild head of curly blonde hair, a mischievous twinkle in his eyes, and his animus was very much that of a trickster coyote.

On the afternoon of the rally, Tulsi Gabbard, Shailene, Dr. Cornel West, and Josh Fox all gave rousing speeches. Mikki Willis filmed the event. Our impromptu band, which we were calling Michael Mowgli and the Altruists, opened up for Nahko and Medicine for the People. I had brought Nahko and his band into the fold with the campaign after meeting him at the Lightning in a Bottle festival. I was able to convince Jesse Flemming, one of the event's co-founders, to let us play a recorded address by the Senator to the crowd, which was to air before Nahko and Grimes.

It was a dream come true.

In my former rock n roll life, I had played with great musicians like Slash, Jerry Cantrell, Kenny Wayne Shepherd, and others, but at no point had I ever considered the remote possibility that I'd get a chance to open for the Senator at a rally.

It once again proved the theory that the most magical things happened around the Bernie campaign. If you haven't been there, it is impossible to explain, but I think it comes down to this: when you have so many people focusing their intentions with single-minded purpose on a common goal, the matrix of life itself bends to your collective will. As Paulo Coelho once said, "When you want something, all the universe conspires in helping you to achieve it."

One example of this was when a bird landed on Sanders's podium at the Moda Center in Portland on March 25th, 2016. Of all the places this could happen, Portland was fitting, given the classic skit from the comedy show *Portlandia* in which Fred Armisen repeats, "Put a bird on it!"

The audience went crazy.

"I think there's some symbolism here," he told the capacity crowd at the Moda Center. "I know it may not look like it, but that bird is really a dove asking us for world peace."

Even Rachel Maddow couldn't deny how magical it was.

It was a simple notion, but it hit home for me as an anti-war activist and it inspired me as we prepared for the rally in San Diego. It was only days before the final votes would be tallied in California on June 7th, and it was going to take a miracle for Bernie to win.

This was perhaps magical thinking, but I remembered the bird and it gave me the crazy idea to say a few words to the crowd and lead them in an impromptu guided meditation after we played our songs. When else was I going to have an opportunity to experience something like this, and who knows, maybe I also had something to say. Bernie's message was that real change comes from the bottom on up. Michael was on board with the idea, so we cleared the speech with Rania Batrice, the director of surrogates. There had been a few instances where the campaign got bad press for speakers going off script at rallies. Luckily, she loved the message and gave the green light to us backstage.

Michael performed before fifteen thousand people outside the Qualcomm Stadium. He was brilliant. The lyrics to his songs rang out as we sang in eight-part harmonies, "We are, we are, we're the ones we're waiting for. We are, we are, we are our only hope. The Revolution will happen in your heart."

After we finished the final song, I stepped up to the microphone and cleared my throat.

"It is a profound honor," I said, "for all of us to be here today, and to see over the course of the last year how many people have sacrificed to make this movement stand behind this great man, Bernie Sanders. They said it was impossible and yet look where we are. I want to invite all of us right now to hold the vision of Bernie Sanders together. I want you to look around, I want you to look at each other and remember what you've been through, but know that this is only the beginning, because this is not just a political revolution. This is not just a campaign. This is a prayer for the whole world."

It was one of the greatest moments of my life.

It was only possible because I had been focused on serving others and serving the cause. We are raised in a culture that tells us that the only things that matter are our own needs, wants and desires, that tells us not to give or sacrifice for others or something larger than ourselves. The message we receive is that our value is based only on what we consume and our ability to produce. In my experience, all of the greatest experiences and opportunities I have received are because I showed up to be of service to something greater than myself. When we give to life, life gives back to us in greater measure.

We closed the rally with all of us singing "This Land is Your Land." I even got a turn to sing a verse. I wasn't aware then that this Woody Guthrie classic was also a colonizer anthem, but at the time this was everything.

The next day we all went back to Los Angeles for the final rally. The week before, Luis had called us frantically asking for help to find another venue after an LA City Councilman named David Ryu had canceled the Sanders Campaign permit on the Greek Theatre at the last minute so that Hillary could do her event there. Kii Arens and I had a plan to fly a single-engine plane over the outdoor venue and drop about ten thousand printed glow-in-the-dark ping pong balls with Bernie's face and a caption that read "VOTE YOUR HEART" printed on them. We found a vendor that could turn around the job and rush the shipment in time. Unfortunately, we couldn't find a pilot willing to risk flying over a federally restricted airspace due to Secret Service protocols protecting the former First Lady.

Later that night, we gathered for one last hurrah at a giant airplane hangar at the Santa Monica Airport. There was electricity in the air amongst the crowd of thousands. "We are going to fight hard to win the primary in Washington, DC, and then we take our fight for social, economic, racial and environmental justice to Philadelphia," Sanders told the crowd. "I am pretty good at arithmetic and I know that the fight in front of us is a very steep fight," he said. "But I will continue to fight it. The struggle continues!"

Little did we know what lay in store for us.

Chapter 6

See You in Philly

Every battle is won before it is fought.
-Sun Tzu

As of 2016, the Associated Press had been syndicated by more than thirteen hundred newspapers and broadcasters. The venerable agency operated 263 news bureaus in 106 countries. And yet somehow they made the rookie error of announcing Hillary Clinton the winner of the California primary before a single Californian had cast their ballot at the polls.

Of course, it wasn't a *rookie error* at all. It was another example of what the campaign was up against. The Bernie Movement had to deal with the corporate news media bias on a daily basis.

As soon as the premature AP results went out over the wire, the Avengers chat started blowing up. One of the advantages to having so many influencers on one thread is the ability to rapidly respond to the events of the day. And there was never a shortage of dumpster fires. Our group would have emergency calls and then take to social media. I dream that one day the real left will not just react to the tactics and narratives of the establishment but will strategically control the narrative.

Hillary did end up winning California. It felt like a gut punch, but the fight was far from over. Bernie had not been mathematically eliminated, and he promised that the progressive insurgency would take the political revolution all the way to the convention in Philadelphia and that he would revive the old tactic of the brokered convention. In other words, there was going to be a floor fight. Sanders and his delegates would challenge Clinton for the nomination.

The last time a Democrat successfully won the presidency at a brokered convention was FDR in 1932. The historical echoes with FDR, and the Chicago Convention of 1968, set the stage for an epic showdown. Even though most Berniecrats would acknowledge that the math didn't look good, we would usually sign off our conversations with the battle cry—"See you in Philly."

But before the Democratic National Convention was to take place, the two candidates and their chosen appointees were scheduled to negotiate the party rules and the platform document outlining the policies that the winner would pursue for the next four years.

Between June 9 and 11, National Nurses United sponsored a progressive convention in Chicago called the People's Summit. I was planning on driving cross country from Los Angeles to the east coast for the convention, so Josh Fox hired me for his national tour of grassroots rallies, which would bring local activists together for screenings of his new documentary. I also supported launch strategies for the film's premiere on HBO. By coordinating with influencers who possessed millions of social media followers, we were able to trigger the algorithms to make Josh trend nationally for almost four days.

This is a strategy I call the "Harambe," named after the gorilla in the Cincinnati zoo who was unjustly killed in May of 2016, sparking widespread outrage. This was a significant phenomenon because it was one of the early examples of citizens mobilizing online to real world effect.

It was also relevant because Donald Trump had amassed millions of social media followers with his television career and his bombastic rhetoric. He was a master at making wild, inflammatory statements and posting tweets that would dominate the media. Trump's strategy was shock and awe. He had annihilated an entire field of seasoned Republican candidates in the primaries, even though he had zero experience campaigning for office. It was like a frenzy. It was clear that Trump's brand of leadership, or lack thereof, was chaos. There was an overwhelming sense of fear amongst the Democratic base that Trump represented a clear and present danger.

Trump threw a brick through the Overton Window on day one of his campaign announcement by calling Mexicans rapists. In a sane world, his run would have been over that same day, but the corporate news networks stood to make a killing off of Donnie's crazy-time circus and the Democrats needed an opponent with lower net favorability numbers than Hillary's. He publicly stated that he would use nuclear weapons. He was blatantly racist and misogynistic, even suggesting Megyn Kelly's interview with him went badly because she was on her menstrual cycle. When activists disrupted his rallies, he called for them to be punched in the face or carried out on stretchers by his dull-eyed, brown-shirt cult followers.

The Democratic base was obsessed with Trump. The Clinton campaign and establishment saw this as a boon and focused their rhetoric on being "not-Trump," so as not to promise any substantive policies that might make life better for the poor and working class. Hillary's campaign used the high stakes to their advantage, arguing that Clinton was a continuation of the Obama-era status quo and that running in the general election on Bernie's "radical agenda" would alienate too many people, despite the overwhelming popularity of programs like Medicare for All.

The problem was that the status quo had stopped being enough a long time ago for working people. They were arguing this while Trump had risen in popularity like a meteor, with one of the most radical platforms in history. What had been utterly disregarded was that in times of populist outrage, the political rhetoric either focuses its ire on the super wealthy and income inequality, like FDR, or on xenophobia and scapegoating minorities, like Hitler and Mussolini.

A populist was always going to win the 2016 election; the only question was what kind.

The People's Summit

This was the big question going into the People's Summit. There was a screening of Josh's film and a Q&A after the event at the convention. I had a car full of posters and hand flyers for Josh's film and it was a thirty-hour drive from Los Angeles. I got delayed leaving LA and pulled the last fifteen hours of the haul in a single shot. If I refilled gas like a goddamn Nascar pit crew, according to my GPS I'd make it just in time for the end of the movie. Josh's film ends with the Beatles classic, "Ob-La-Di, Ob-La-Da," and he would lead the entire audience in a giant conga line around whatever venue they were screening in.

I drove, my knuckles white, clutching the steering wheel of my PT Cruiser the whole way. I pulled up within five minutes of the convention center in Chicago and was on track to make it just under the wire when I heard loud clunking and grinding noises coming from the motor. The engine gave out completely as I coasted into the loading zone of the convention hall.

I left the car in the loading zone of the convention, grabbed a box of flyers and posters and ran for the auditorium. The McCormick Place convention center was fucking enormous. It seemed like I was running forever and I must have looked absolutely ridiculous, but I was still on track to arrive just as the film was coming to an end. I finally reached a large auditorium with stadium seating where the film was to be screened, only to find it completely empty. I let the box drop from my arms unceremoniously, stood in disbelief and tried to get Josh on the phone, but there was no answer. Apparently, someone had called in a bomb threat and the film had been canceled.

I felt utterly dejected and was beyond exhausted.

Luckily, I ran into Winnie Wong in the lobby of the hotel. She was working with RoseAnn DeMoro and the nurses' union to organize the People's Summit. National Nurses United and The People for Bernie Sanders were the lead organizers of the progressive summit, but other organizations contributed, including Democratic Socialists of America, Food & Water Watch, Our Revolution, and Progressive Democrats of America.

Winnie helped me find our crew, who were in Rosario Dawson's Penthouse suite having a very intense "Where-do-we-go-from-here?" type of meeting.

The room was full of what 60s anti-war organizers used to call movement heavies. Some of our Bernie's Avengers cohorts were there, including Josh, Frances Fisher, Max Carver, YahNé Ndgo, Ann Kleinhenz and Kendrick Sampson, as well as some future members of our crew. Bruce Carter, who owned the Black Men for Bernie tour bus, was also there, though he had never joined the team.

We were meeting to discuss upcoming key events at the Democratic Platform Committee and the convention in Philly. It was here that I first met Kai Newkirk; he was a serious dude. Kai had launched an organization called 99Rise in 2012. Their first action was to march 480 miles from Los Angeles City Hall to the State Capitol building in Sacramento, California and call for legislation to get money out of politics. Kai had studied social movement building back in my old hood of Pioneer Valley at Hampshire College. In his full beard and flannel shirt, he looked like a cross between a male model and a lumberjack who'd gone to private school. He had generated national media attention by disrupting Donald Trump during one of the Republican primary debates.

99Rise later changed its name to Democracy Spring, and earlier that April had organized one of the larger direct actions in US history with over twelve hundred people arrested outside the Capitol Building in Washington, DC. They had marched for two days all the way from the Liberty Bell in Philadelphia. Rosario and Cenk Uygur from The Young Turks both got arrested in the action with Kai.

Kai was a solid addition to the Avengers as he was very grounded in the inside-outside theory of movement building. He understood how to use the power of nonviolent direct action to pressure legislators into making policy reforms.

I also met Desiree Kane, an Indigenous organizer and member of the People for Bernie group. I met Anthony Rogers-Wright, who was a grassroots climate policy advisor for the campaign. I also met Sameera Khan, a former Miss New Jersey turned Sandernista. All would join our Avengers crew.

That night in Chicago, we debated the path forward for several hours in Rosario Dawson's penthouse suite. The vibe was heavy and often contentious, as there was a wide spectrum of ideologies represented. Afterwards, to break the tension, Rosario and the gang got very festive while enjoying their share of libations. We concluded the meeting around 2 a.m. and I knew that if I didn't sit for my daily meditation, then I would be in danger of missing a day of meditation for the first time in eleven years. I'd driven non-stop for fifteen hours, my car had broken down, and then I'd immediately attended a super-intense movement meeting for several more hours. My car was still parked in the loading zone outside. I must have seemed like a freak to the others for meditating while everyone else was partying to loud music, but I couldn't really concern myself with that. Character is the ability to follow through on a resolution, past the emotion that inspired it, regardless of feelings or circumstances.

The highlight of the evening for me, however, happened just as I was finishing my ninety-minute meditation. On two separate occasions, security had come to ask us to turn the music down. On the third occasion, two security guards showed up at the door and knocked loudly so as to establish that this time they were really serious.

The guard postured aggressively, using an authoritative tone to convey that we had gone past the limit and that the party was over. But he was not able to finish his sentence as YahNé and Frances greeted him at the door. Without saying a word, Frances put her arms around him, and kissed him squarely on the lips. He stood wide eyed and speechless as Frances, again without a word, closed the door in their faces and locked it.

We roared with laughter, the music started playing again and the party was back on. From the highrise, we watched the sun climb over the Chicago horizon as it danced off of the waters of Lake Michigan. The rest of the weekend was full of epic keynote speeches from Nina Turner, Tulsi Gabbard and Naomi Klein, as well as breakout training sessions. This was the first time I'd met Nina and the then-Congresswoman from Hawaii, who'd also joined the Avengers squad.

We met up with Gaby Hoffmann—whom I hadn't seen since the Clooney Counter-Party—the next night, as she, Frances, Rosario, Max, Kendrick, and Wallace Shawn (whom you might know from his roles as the Sicilian in *Princess Bride* and *My Dinner with Andre*) performed "The People Speak" in front of a capacity crowd of several thousand people, where each took turns reading passages from Howard Zinn's *A People's History of the United States*. It was powerful medicine for our weary souls. Little did we know that, even after almost a year of hard campaigning, the most intense battles that our fellowship were to face were yet to come.

Standoff at the Democratic Platform Committee

On July 8, I picked up Josh and Nomiki from the train station to drive us to the final session of the Democratic Platform Committee in Orlando. It was definitely not going to be a trip to Disney World. We were headed into the heart of an ideological battle for the soul of the left.

Josh didn't want to fly from New York because of the climate impact of the airplanes. By this point, I had driven about four thousand miles from Los Angeles, to Chicago, to New York, to Massachusetts, to Washington DC, and then straight to Florida.

The back seats were out of my car so Josh had to recline in the back. Both he and Nomiki live-streamed to their followers as we drove. The advent of this new form of livestream activist journalism, first popularized in America during Occupy Wall Street, allowed progressives to get an inside look at what was happening in the trenches—a look that had previously been reserved for insiders. Everyone could follow the events in real time and feel like they were a part of the action.

The California primary had been our last hope in terms of the delegate count, but we still held out hope of winning by pushing the party to adopt Bernie's policy agenda, which was the agenda of his grassroots allies and campaign leaders. Josh had been instrumental in introducing the fracking ban to Bernie's agenda, so this was very personal to him. Nomiki had been a member of the party her whole life and was taking a hard stand to save it from shifting too far to the right. It was by now painfully obvious that this was going to be a difficult task.

A showdown of ideas and agendas was turning into a civil war within the Democratic Party. The party platform itself was simply a document outlining the Democratic Party's policy priorities and positions on domestic and foreign affairs. Sanders had won 46 percent of the delegates in the primaries and caucuses, so he could nominate the same percentage of delegates, who would then determine the direction of the party for the next four years.

This was a crucial battleground for the political revolution. Many of us had learned a lesson from Occupy, that there is no systemic change without building both inside and outside power in order to change the laws that govern the system. For those who understand climate science, this caucus was in a very real way to us the fight for the future of humanity, due to the enormous influence the Democratic Party has on policies that govern fossil fuels.

Not only would the outcomes of the Democratic Platform Committee influence the direction of the party, it would create a concrete set of declarations that grassroots organizers could use to hold the party accountable. For this reason, we knew we would meet with substantial resistance from corporate influencers.

In the early nineties Newt Gingrich transformed American politics when he shifted the GOP strategy from politicking in congressional districts to just focusing on raising corporate dollars. Nancy Pelosi and the Third Way Dems followed suit. There is an HBO documentary called "The Swamp" that unpacks this history and the paradigm shift of our broken system.

In 2016, Sanders nominated the most impressive grassroots leaders, academics, and policy advocates from movements for racial, health, and climate justice. They constituted a *Who's Who* of progressive heroes such as Josh, Cornel West, Bill McKibben, Deborah Parker, and Ben Jealous, who at the age of thirty-five was elected the youngest president and CEO of the NAACP. This was the embodiment of everything we had been fighting for. Bernie had used his power to give progressive grassroots leaders a real seat at the table.

It was in Orlando that I first met one of my all-time favorite Avengers. David Braun was a relentlessly passionate spiritual warrior, who had helped lead the charge to ban fracking in New York State alongside Josh. He had also helped build the Californians Against Fracking coalition. You might say he was the Reverend of the climate movement. His superpower could summon fierceness for the cause and compassion in equal measure. He always held space in his heart for forgiveness.

For all the trauma we were experiencing, we were going to need plenty of those qualities to emerge as whole, healthy beings. And not all of us would come through unscathed.

Bend the Knee

Clinton had won a 54 percent majority of the pledged delegates, which gave her squad a decisive advantage. The platform committee wasn't even a binding document or piece of legislation, and still they fought us on everything.

Hillary's foot soldiers included Neera Tanden from the neo-liberal think tank Center for American Progress, and Howard Berman, a lobbyist for Covington & Burling, LLP, a firm which boasted having aided fossil fuel companies in navigating lawsuits, so they could continue drilling in the Gulf of Mexico. Hillary's whips, Carol Browner and Wendy Sherman, both worked for the Albright Stonebridge Group. Collectively, the delegates' firms represented pharmaceutical companies, fossil fuel companies, Wall Street financiers, big banks, Silicon Valley titans, foreign governments, defense contractors, Coca Cola, Walmart, and Dow Chemicals.

The platform document itself was drafted over four two-day sessions on June 8 and 9. The Bernie delegates anticipated an uphill battle, but it was even steeper than expected. In the third session, Bill McKibben proposed measures to combat climate change, challenging the Hillary wing to go beyond posturing and embrace bold leadership. The results (as Bill McKibben published in his *Politico* article):

> *"A carbon tax? Voted down 7 to 6.*
>
> *A ban on fracking? Voted down 7 to 6.*
>
> *An effort to keep fossil fuels in the ground on federal land? Voted down 7 to 6.*
>
> *A measure to mandate that federal agencies weigh the climate impact of their decisions? Voted down 7 to 6.*
>
> *A plan to keep fossil fuel companies from taking private land by eminent domain? Voted down 7 to 6.*

All measures were voted down by Clinton, who held the majority of delegates. The only success: a unanimous vote in favor of building more bike paths."

The committee delegates chosen by Hillary Clinton and Debbie Wasserman Schultz also voted down amendments advocating Medicare for All, a $15 minimum wage, several proposals to halt climate change, a call to denounce the Israeli "occupation" of Palestine, and an amendment explicitly opposing the TPP trade agreement.

Let's be honest. A $15 minimum wage is laughable if you are trying to support a family, especially in a major city. And yet the federal minimum wage has remained at $7.25 per hour for over ten years. If wages had increased commensurately with productivity and profits for corporate America, the minimum wage would have been $22 per hour.

The Clinton delegates voted down just about everything, but the Sanders squad came in ready for battle, and Bernie still had a few tricks up his sleeve.

From 1995 to 2007, Bernie Sanders had been dubbed the "Amendment King" of the House of Representatives. Getting bills passed in a bipartisan government is extraordinarily difficult, but he was the most effective member of Congress at getting amendments added to legislation, passing ninety out of 491 during that time period.

This was also the strategy Bernie and his accomplices used at the platform committee: adding language to the existing platform, beyond vague platitudes and empty promises. These amendments would involve very specific policies that the grassroots could organize around. Jeff Weaver was on site, and the lead delegates were in constant contact with Bernie as the events unfolded.

The party platform is only a written document that outlines the Democratic Party's policy priorities and positions on domestic and foreign affairs. It has no binding impact on democratically elected officials or candidates.

The first day was painful at best.

Anthony Rogers-Wright and I sat in the general public section behind the delegates. We'd met up with his friend Jimmy Betts, a fellow climate activist, Korean by birth and raised in Nebraska. Other Bernie supporters shouted from the back, waving signs denouncing both the TPP and party support for the Israeli occupation of Palestine. The liberal intelligentsia and party hacks were not used to this open scrutiny from the unwashed masses.

Bruce Carter and the Black Men for Bernie tour bus were also on site, which was always a spectacle.

One after another, the majority of amendments proposed by the policy advocates and grassroots leaders appointed by the Sanders campaign were voted down by the Clinton delegates. They made impassioned pleas that explained why the language would address serious problems facing the nation—but to no avail. Inevitably, some party insider would argue that the additions would hurt Hillary's chances against Trump. Each time a vote was called, Carol Browner, the whip, turned her thumb down like a Roman emperor to signal to the Clinton gang that the amendment was to be killed.

Boos and shouts rang out from the crowd in the back.

Nomiki railed on the microphone, calling out elected Clinton delegates who had been under investigation by the FBI for bribery. Dr. West spoke of justice for the Palestinian people in a resounding voice that boomed with moral clarity. His words rang out with a lyrical timbre of holy fire that could have been delivered from any pulpit of a Southern Baptist church. None of it mattered in the end. Hillary wouldn't allow the People's agenda to get in the way of her relationship with AIPAC.

There were, however, a few bright spots. Nina Turner led the charge to win a victory in the fight for a $15 minimum wage, and Ben Jealous won amendments for criminal justice reform. It was clear to many of us that Nina represented the future of progressive leadership.

But these victories were not enough. The Clinton wing of the party seemed to revel in refusing to give an inch. Their message was clear: "Bend the knee. Kiss the ring. We're in charge. Your little insurrection is over."

At the end of the first night, I was having a conversation with Bill French, who was one of Bernie's foreign policy advisors. The party hacks were stalling on procedures; they were employing dirty tactics to wear down the Sanders delegates. No coffee or water had been offered. Delays had kept the committee up until 1:30 a.m. with little progress. Everyone was tired and frustrated. Donna Brazile came in to break the ice and offered to bring Jägermeister shots.

In the middle of our conversation, a stout bald man in a very expensive suit and wire rim glasses sat down next to us.

He listened to our conversation for a while before breaking in. He introduced himself as Marc Elias. He was senior counsel for the Clinton campaign.

Frustrated by the long day and months of heartbreak, I asked him rather harshly if he knew he was letting Trump win. He took off his glasses and rubbed his nose like he was being forced to explain something difficult to a child. In lockstep with the rest of the Washington political establishment, and completely out of touch with the rest of the country, he condescendingly informed me that their "data [was] clear, and everyone [was] gonna come around to supporting Clinton."

I told him that the election was going to ultimately be decided by the working class, angry white guys that had been fucked over by NAFTA in the Rust Belt and that they were going to need to fight for every vote. It was going to be a horse race until the end of September, then the real numbers would come in during late September, and they would realize too late that they were losing to a reality show hack.

My voice was strained as I went on a tirade. My finger was pointing at him aggressively as I tried to get him to understand that we progressives were the most energetic left-wing voters in the country and that they couldn't win without us; that it wasn't just the numbers, but the enthusiasm and the campaigning that were vital to victory. I ended by telling him they were already losing and didn't even know it. He just said, "Good luck," dismissively and walked away.

What we didn't know at that time was that Marc Elias was senior counsel for Perkins Coie, LLP, and had been involved in a secret deal that would put the entire DNC under the control of Hillary Clinton and her campaign. This was later revealed in Donna Brazile's book *Hacks: The Inside Story of the Break-ins and Breakdowns That Put Donald Trump in the White House.*

Almost 1 billion dollars went to four consultancies, including Perkins Coie, LLP, which represents the DNC, DSCC, DCCC, Hillary for America, Media Matters, Correct the Record (remember David Brock's troll farm PAC?), and the Joint Fundraising Committee. They lit a billion dollars on fire to give campaign strategies like, "Hey, let's not have Hillary step foot in Michigan or Wisconsin!"

Donna Brazile's book revealed that, a full year before the primary, the Clinton campaign had signed an agreement called the Hillary Victory Fund, undertaking that it would raise money to refill the party's coffers in exchange for control over the hiring, operations and key data.

Obama left the party $24 million in debt—$15 million in bank debt and more than $8 million owed to vendors after the 2012 campaign—and it had been paying that off very slowly. State parties were broke because of the 2012 presidential re-election campaign.

Here is a passage describing what she'd learned from a conversation with the CFO of Hillary for America, Gary Gensler:

> *"He described the party as fully under the control of Hillary's campaign, which seemed to confirm the suspicions of the Bernie camp.... Individuals who had maxed out their $2,700 contribution limit to the campaign could write an additional check for $353,400 to the Hillary Victory Fund—that figure represented $10,000 to each of the thirty-two states' parties who were part of the Victory Fund agreement—$320,000—and $33,400 to the DNC. The money would be deposited in the states first, and be transferred to the DNC shortly after that. Money in the battleground states usually stayed in that state, but all the other states funneled that money directly to the DNC, which quickly transferred the money to Brooklyn (Clinton campaign headquarters)....*
>
> *"Wait," I said. "That victory fund was supposed to be for whoever was the nominee, and the state party races. You're telling me that Hillary has been controlling it since before she got the nomination?"*

Wait, there's more.

The agreement—signed by Amy Dacey, the former CEO of the DNC, and Robby Mook, with a copy to Marc Elias (senior counsel for Perkins Coie, LLP)—specified that in exchange for raising money and investing in the DNC, Hillary would control the party's finances, strategy, and all the money raised. Her campaign had the right of refusal of who would be the party communications director, and it would make final decisions on all the other staff. The DNC was also required to consult with the campaign about all other staffing, budgeting, data, analytics, and mailings.

Remember the $33,000 and $353,000 per plate fundraiser we protested outside of George Clooney's that was also supposedly going to fund down-ballot candidates? This was the truth behind the scam.

If Americans are already governed by a two-party system, and those parties completely subvert the democratic process, then how can we possibly pretend to be living in a democracy? We can't. At the time of the 2016 elections, Americans were already living in an oligarchy.

The DNC's handling of the primary only exacerbated the sentiment that the party and its already wildly unpopular candidate were rigging the game. This was a metaphor for our entire economy. Not exactly the best strategy to encourage voter enthusiasm.

The delegates finally concluded at 1:30 a.m. Bill, Anthony, and I joined David Braun and Nomiki in her hotel room. We enjoyed some libations and licked our wounds. David joined the Avengers and became an inspiring force within the team.

After losing on amendments for Palestine, the TPP free trade pact, Medicare, and others, we entered into the final day with a greater sense of resolve. There was still the climate change portion of the platform to come, which could have been the standard to rally around for the next four years.

Bill McKibben, Russell Greene, Jane Kleeb, and Josh Fox negotiated fiercely with Carol Browner and Hillary's lieutenants. They were constantly on the phone with Bernie discussing strategy for inserting significant clauses into the platform document with specific measures to halt fossil fuel extraction.

The Bernie delegates would give speeches when the amendments were proposed. Anthony and I hatched a plan to prepare Bernie supporters to rush the barriers and occupy the stage. Jimmy Betts helped us round up about fifty people to stand at the ready should the Clinton delegates vote down the climate revisions. The security was minimal and in no position to stop us, though the laws in Florida were draconian and it is definitely not the most optimal state to get arrested in. C-SPAN cameras were covering activities in the ballroom for the next two days. We were going to give them a show like they had never seen before.

Russell Greene and David Braun gave two of the most impressive and heartfelt speeches I'd ever heard. Russell, a long time friend of the Senator, and David had both been part of the big PDA event at the Musician's Union in Los Angeles in 2015. Russell seemed to be able to communicate in a language the corporate centrists could hear. He gave a sermon about the future of the planet worthy of the ages.

David's voice trembled with such love, power, and vulnerability that even the coldest hearts were touched. He shouted, "Mother Nature is angry with us!" and within three beats a crack of thunder reverberated throughout the hall. On that amendment, he was able to enroll even the most unfeeling members of the opposition. Sometimes the best strategy is to speak straight from the heart. When Trevor Houser and other Clinton delegates began speaking against the climate measures, we began to move closer. Tensions mounted. The Clinton delegates shifted nervously as the pitchforks assembled behind them. We were ready to make our move.

Suddenly, Nomiki came running out, hands extended, motioning for us to stop. She told us to stand down because Josh and McKibben had struck a deal with Carol Browner and the Clinton campaign.

After the votes came in, the Bernie delegates assembled to announce the victory. A consensus had been reached. Cornel and Josh gave rousing speeches. It was a glorious moment that we'd all badly needed. There had been so much losing of late. We had all sacrificed and suffered for Bernie's platform and candidacy. We had been fighting like our lives and the future of our country depended on it—in our minds, they did—and it was our platform, our better vision for America.

But for all that "unity," Clinton did a fundraiser with the fracking lobby just days after the Platform Committee. It was clear that Hillary had no desire to work with the grassroots on substantive people-centered policies nor did she care about our support.

Bernie or Bust

For weeks I had been working with Angelica "Geli" Cob-Baehler (one of our first Avengers, whom you might remember was Ice Cube's former manager), and YahNé Ndgo, on a Bernie or Bust strategy that would give Bernie and the delegates leverage at the Democratic Convention. There are very few people who would argue with the assertion that Geli Baehler was perhaps the greatest marketing mind in the entire music industry. A true wizard.

YahNé had emerged as the de facto leader of the Bernie or Bust movement after a powerful television appearance as a member of a voter panel on CNN.

Black women voters were supposedly the backbone of the Democratic Party, so Yah dropping truth bombs about the actual bombs Hillary Clinton was responsible for as Secretary of State caused a great deal of commotion. She was brought back on for follow up interviews on CNN where she calmly dismantled her interrogators on Hillary's record concerning regime change in Honduras and Libya, and her role in suppressing the minimum wage for Haitian workers. "It's her history that we simply do not like, it's not just the Colombian free trade agreement," she said. She went on:

> *It's what the State Department did under her leadership going into Haiti. And when they went in to raise the minimum wage for the Haitians from 24 cents an hour to 61 cents an hour, they negotiated down to 31 cents an hour. It's the regime change in Honduras. It's the mistake of the Iraq war. It's the mistake of Libya. So now she's saying new things that are popular. Suddenly she realizes the importance of Black Lives Matter because of the Black Lives Matter movement, and these things don't seem genuine. They seem like what she needs to say in order to get elected. We don't trust what she says, and we don't like what she's done. So for those combined reasons, we won't vote for Hillary Clinton.*

Statements like this were causing liberals to lose their minds as they realized that not everyone would fall in line behind Clinton, and would instead choose to stay in bed on election day. (Liberalism is the worldview of the status quo.) David Brock's hired troll farms set the tone of vote shaming and gaslighting to browbeat progressives and leftists into voting for the Democrats.

We planned to use their fear to our advantage.

The strategy was to launch a campaign where we would collect signatures from Bernie or Busters who were committed to leaving the Democratic Party if Sanders was not nominated at the DNC. We would then leverage these numbers to drive the narrative through the Avengers surrogates and progressive media that Hillary's nomination would cost the Party too many members.

Sanders had told his followers in several speeches that he intended to take the fight all the way to the floor of the convention. Throughout his campaign Bernie had been compared to FDR, and so there couldn't have been a more fitting narrative leading up to a battle in Philadelphia—as Roosevelt had been the last president to be nominated in a floor fight at a brokered convention.

At the Platform Committee we heard that Bernie, instead of fighting on, was planning on conceding to Clinton before the convention. Nomiki and I hunted Jeff Weaver down to desperately try to plead with him to talk Bernie out of it. He wasn't aware of all of the phone calls and meetings that had taken place in preparation for the final showdown in Philadelphia.

It didn't matter.

Little did we know there had already been a meeting between Sanders and Clinton a month prior in Washington, DC, where Hillary's campaign manager Robbie Mook and Weaver had stayed for two hours afterwards conspiring together about the path forward.

They had been talking daily since then. A regular bromance.

Mook had even traveled to meet Sanders at the Farmhouse Tap and Grill in Burlington, where they continued plotting the end of our resistance over craft beers and farm-to-table fare.

The 2016 Sanders primary campaign ended with Bernie and Hillary holding a joint rally in New Hampshire on July 12. "Let me begin by thanking the 13 million Americans who voted for me during the Democratic primaries," began the speech that crushed the dreams of millions of Berniecrats. "Our campaign won the primaries and caucuses in twenty-two states, and when the roll call at the Democratic National Convention is announced, it will show that we won almost nineteen hundred delegates."

Ultimately, *#BernieOrBust* was meant to be a strategy to rally registered Dems to leave the party, if the superdelegates didn't exercise their power to try and avoid the train wreck that was to be the Clinton vs. Trump campaign by nominating Bernie Sanders. He would clearly be a much stronger candidate in the open general elections. The whole point of superdelegates in the first place was to have "grown-ups" in a position to save the party from the tyranny of the unsophisticated, unwashed masses who might select a losing nominee in the primaries.

Only in this case, we were the grown-ups.

In 2016, Hillary had a net-favorability (likability) rating that was lower than Bob Dole's in 1996. She was the face of NAFTA, which had decimated the Rust Belt. She was an establishment candidate in a populist race. The GOP had demonized Hillary for decades and there was no opponent that would fire up the conservative base like her. She was the candidate of Wall Street corruption and illegal wars. She was under FBI investigation for her emails. She had alienated the entire Millennial Generation and could barely draw a crowd.

Bernie on the other hand was packing stadiums, had an entire grassroots army, and the single greatest fundraising apparatus in the history of American politics. His brand was synonymous with honesty and integrity. His net favorables were as high as Barack Obama's and he had a policy vision that transcended partisan politics.

He was the stronger candidate by every metric to face Trump.

But the machine politics of Democratic primaries have nothing to do with nominating the strongest candidate.

The history of superdelegates goes back to the 1968 Democratic National Convention. The war candidate Hubert Humphrey was nominated for the presidency despite not running in a single primary election. He lost to Richard Nixon.

A commission headed by Senator George McGovern and Minnesota Representative Donald M. Fraser met in 1969 and 1970 to make the composition of the Democratic Party's nominating convention less subject to control by party leaders and more responsive to the votes cast in primary elections. The Democratic Party made changes in its delegate selection process to correct what was seen as the "illusory" control of the nomination process by primary voters.

The rules implemented by the McGovern-Fraser Commission shifted the balance of power to primary elections and caucuses, mandating that all delegates be chosen via mechanisms open to all party members. As a result of this change, the number of primaries more than doubled over the next three presidential election cycles, from seventeen in 1968 to thirty-five in 1980.

When Bernie conceded, I told Yah that it was over, unless she still wanted to use the "Bernie or Bust" slogan to build her list. The Trots (short for Trotskyists, the faction of the left that believe they represent the purest form of socialist ideology, like members of the Bread and Roses Caucus of the DSA) and Greens had co-opted the message at that point, and it was being used as an expression of anger.

"Bernie or Bust" became *#DemExit*. Some believed that if you simply bled the Democratic Party of its membership it would fall and give way to something more progressive, like the Green Party. The problem is that there is no theory of change there

In a duopoly, destroying the Democratic Party simply empowers the Republicans. Both parties serve the corporate state, but the Democrats at least pretend to care about social justice and equality. This narrative makes it possible to primary-challenge these corporate Dems, and elect progressives who live those values and are beholden to the people they serve instead of wealthy donors.

It's an inside-outside game.

Maybe one day we will see the rise of a real American Labor Party.

It broke my heart when Bernie endorsed Hillary, but in hindsight it was the correct political calculation. Otherwise, he would have been blamed for Trump. They certainly tried to blame him anyway, but it didn't stick because it wasn't true.

A small fraction of disillusioned Berners gravitated to Jill Stein and the Green Party. If one could understand and empathize with the experiences they had endured throughout the primary, this was totally understandable, even if it was another example of prefiguratism. Then again, most voters make their decisions out of emotion rather than logic.

At the Democratic National Convention, Sarah Silverman famously said, "To the 'Bernie or Bust' people, you're being ridiculous," as Al Franken (soon to be disgraced after a series of sexual harassment allegations) jeered next to her.

Really?

Was it ridiculous for poor working people—who had worked harder than they had worked for anything remotely political in their lives—to be angry as they watched helplessly while the Democratic Establishment used all of its power to crush their dreams of a presidency that would serve their interests?

What was ridiculous was the notion that people living on Main Street would rally around a candidate that was clearly the champion of Wall Street, and the very embodiment of the corrupt Washington Establishment that had long since abandoned them.

Sarah Silverman had been an early adopter and ardent Bernie surrogate. I'm not gonna lie, it was painful to watch her stand next to Al Franken and shame the crowd for chanting Bernie or Bust. She sounded like the teacher's pet trying to shout down her rowdy classmates. At the end of the day, though, Sarah in that moment embodied the base Democratic voters who were panic-stricken in the face of the reality that the general election was going to come down to a Wall Street war hawk versus Orange Hitler.

And they weren't wrong to be terrified.

Chapter 7

The Not-So-Democratic

Party Convention

Those who make peaceful revolution impossible
will make violent revolution inevitable.
-John F. Kennedy

Bernie had been expected to hold his last big rally the Sunday before the convention. We were all looking forward to it as a much-needed catharsis. Then I got a call from Josh. I was in Atlanta, driving up from Orlando on the way to Philadelphia.

"Bernie canceled the rally," he said.

"Fuck," I replied, already suffering from exhaustion.

"But it's okay. Here's what we're going to do—we're going to put on the rally."

He would get this sing-song quality to his voice every time he was about to convince us of one of his wild ideas. In truth this meant that Kyle Cadotte, his managing director, and I were going to be turning ourselves inside out to make this rally happen.

"In eight days?"

"Yes."

"We're going to do the Climate Revolution rally." Josh had a vision to continue the tour he had launched the previous January to screen his film *How to Let Go* with live concerts and rallies. We had pitched the idea to NextGen, Tom Steyer's organization, but hadn't heard back. Josh was calling it the "Let Go and Love Tour" after the first leg, but I suggested that the Climate Revolution might be more emblematic.

Because that is what the world needs.

"Where are we going to get the money?" I asked skeptically, knowing full well the magnitude of what he was proposing.

"We'll get the money," he replied. It was also going to be Josh's birthday that day.

At any other time, in any other situation, it would have been lunacy to even consider it, but it was the calm before the storm. Thousands of Bernie supporters were converging on Philadelphia.

On July 4th, Shailene made a big organizing call-to-action, to invite Berniecrats to join her in Venice, California and drive cross country to the final showdown in the City of Brotherly Love at the Democratic National Convention. The vision was to have two caravans departing from Los Angeles and Portland, crossing states eastward and meeting in Philadelphia. Each night they were to have community meetings with organizers from frontline communities and hear about what was troubling them.

Mikki Willis and his company Elevate Films made a promotional video featuring Shai in fast motion, creating a badly-drawn map of the United States and the paths of the caravans converging on the DNC.

"There's a lot of confusing events that have occurred in this election, like 1 million ballots still uncounted in California, and mainstream media's questionable 'reporting.' A lot of it just doesn't make sense. But what does make sense is the people in this country using their voices to say ENOUGH IS ENOUGH! From every corner of our nation, Americans have stood together with strength and resilience. It is easy to feel lost, defeated and unheard, and a lot of us are wondering, 'What's next?' In order to make a movement move, we must stay activated, engaged and unified. We must show up! Imagine doing something that has never been done before. A cross-country caravan all the way to the DNC."

The Up To Us caravan was making their way east, so the plan was to combine the Climate Revolution rally with the Up To Us caravan when they reached Philly. Along the way, they met up with a band of young Indigenous people from Standing Rock who were running on foot from their reservation to the White House at Obama's request to raise their concerns about the Dakota Access Pipeline. No one at that moment fully understood the power and scope of the movement these youth runners would create, but we will come to that later.

The Up To Us caravan would be showing up to support the direct actions outside, and also the fourteen hundred pledged Sanders delegates (of whom Shailene was one) who would represent Bernie and the movement at the convention inside. It was expensive to be a delegate, so many were doing a GoFundMe to attend.

There were so many meetings and conference calls leading up to the convention. On July 4, Josh invited everyone to his cabin in the woods in Pennsylvania.

We just couldn't pull it all together in time to organize something well orchestrated. There was too much chaos, there were too many cooks in the kitchen. We had also tried to strategize actions that would mobilize the thousands of Berners sleeping in FDR Park, across the street from the Wells Fargo Center, to stage direct actions that would draw media attention. Incidentally, there couldn't have been a more fitting scene for the drama to unfold than the juxtaposition of a park full of disaffected populists named after New Deal hero Franklin Delano Roosevelt, and the corporate party establishment convened in the Wells Fargo Center across the street.

In any other time or place, the notion of trying to pull off a production of this magnitude would have been insanity. One thing had been made clear in the previous six months—where Bernie Sanders and his revolution was concerned, anything was possible.

At the time I was also trying to de-escalate a Twitter war Josh was having with Jill Stein and the Green Party. I knew Dr. Stein from a leadership training session I had organized and facilitated that she had flown in for in 2014. There was a clear divide amongst the progressive Democrats and the more radical leftists. For Josh and some of the climate activists, there was concern that the Green Party was going to try to capitalize on Bernie's dropping out by courting his followers, thus potentially setting in motion a chain reaction that might lead to a Trump presidency.

They weren't fighting for Hillary Clinton or the Democratic Party by any stretch of the imagination. They were fighting for the hard-won climate platform that would be a standard for the movement to organize around. The Clinton regime would of course have fought tooth and nail but they, unlike Donald Trump, at least acknowledged that climate change was real and not in fact a hoax put on by the Chinese. Diplomacy wasn't always one of Josh's defining traits, so I attempted to de-escalate with Jill's campaign manager.

Philadelphia was YahNé's city, so naturally she was consulted on what the location might be for the event. YahNé was a community organizer in Germantown, so that's what we decided on.

Germantown was the birthplace of the American anti-slavery Abolitionist Movement, so it was a fitting site for the official launch party of the post-campaign political revolution. There was a feeling of struggle and beauty in equal measure.

The week was madness as expected. Normally a production of this magnitude, which included over thirty speakers and performers and a movie screening, would take months to organize. Kyle Cadotte and I worked around the clock to mobilize and promote.

Even though the trip from Center City and FDR Park was only twelve miles, it was about an hour's journey to Germantown through the convention gridlock. This presented a significant problem. Over the years I had learned that the key to a successful event was collaboration.

One of the goals behind YahNé's hard fight to organize the event in Germantown was to bring business to the predominantly-black local community.

Kyle and I worked frantically to get all the production elements into place. As it turns out, it is not that easy to find a giant inflatable outdoor movie screen to ship into Philadelphia at a moment's notice. When it finally arrived, we discovered when they tried to blow it up that it didn't fit in the park in the proximity of the stage.

As if transporting a little slice of Venice Beach to Philadelphia, the Up To Us caravan rolled into Vernon Park singing and banging drums just as we were scrambling to finish setting up the stage, giant LED monitor and sound systems.

Never make assumptions that everyone knows the plan, is on board and committed. There are levels of commitment. This is very, very important to understand. The best way to know how committed someone is is to ask them directly.

Unfortunately, I didn't ask this question of some of the members of Team Bernie LA, whom I had invited to participate in the DNC as stage managers in an olive branch gesture to heal past wounds. They were in FDR Park selling Bernie's Coffee Diner T-shirts with Kii's design (without his permission), and showed up three hours after their call time. But we made it all work.

YahNé was the main emcee. She'd brought in a number of local artists to perform. Anthony Rogers-Wright and I co-hosted the event at times.

I thought it would be cool to have a DJ playing in between speakers and bands, which became a trend later at grassroots rallies. Rallies can be tedious. It's a good idea to bring in music to keep the energy high. We also booked Amy Goodman to talk about the media's role in society. Most of Bernie's heaviest hitting Avengers came out to speak: Susan Sarandon, Danny Glover, Kendrick Sampson, Nomiki, and Cenk all stood to fire up the troops.

The Up to Us caravan had been started to keep the movement going beyond the Bernie primary campaign. When Shailene gave her speech, she highlighted the difference between protesting with anger versus showing up with love and solidarity. Shai yielded most of her time on stage to bringing up Indigenous activists Calina Lawrence and Chase Iron Eyes.

Chase was running for Congress in North Dakota and spoke about a struggle brewing on Indian land to stop the Dakota Access Pipeline. He and his community were drawing allies from around the country and the world to come to the Standing Rock Sioux Reservation. This was the first time that thousands of the most passionate and committed Sandernistas were introduced to the

NoDAPL struggle. At that moment, the Standing Rock Youth runners were running from North Dakota to Washington D.C. to deliver a petition to President Obama. The movement started with Occupy Wall Street, ignited Bernie's Political Revolution and was about to evolve to join the biggest pipeline fight in history.

Tim DeChristopher, who was one of the featured interviews in Josh's film, was one of the surprise highlights. He had been to prison for protesting the Bureau of Land Management's auctioning off of 116 parcels of public land in Utah's red rock country by successfully bidding $1.8 million on 22,500 acres of land being leased for oil and gas drilling. He had zero intention to pay, so Tim was removed from the auction by federal agents and taken into custody. He faced a maximum sentence of ten years in prison and $750,000 in fines. Alex Ebert recorded a music video of the public protests in Salt Lake City that were organized in his support.

Tim served twenty-one months for his commitment to the people and the planet. If more people shared even a fraction of Tim's commitment, courage and resolve, humanity would have a shot at saving itself from the climate apocalypse.

We put a house band together. Richard Vagner played violin and I sat in on guitar with local Germantown musicians. Richard had been a part of Michael Mowgli's band when we'd opened for Bernie at the San Diego rally.

The speakers finally finished just as the sun was setting.

That the giant inflatable movie screen didn't fit in the main stage area of the park really worked out, ultimately, because at the end of the movie almost a thousand people danced together in a giant conga line back to the stage for a DJ set by Tommie Sunshine and an all-star jam. Josh grabbed his banjo. Nahko and I took turns singing verses of "This Land is Your Land."

It was our last waltz.

To paraphrase Dr. Hunter S. Thompson, we had been riding the crest of a high and beautiful wave and with the right kind of eyes you could almost see the high water mark—Vernon Park was the place where the wave finally broke, and rolled back. We concluded the Climate Revolution Is Up to Us rally the same way the tour began in Venice, the same way we concluded our barnstorm at Howard Gold's house months before: together, holding hands in a giant loop encircling the commons of the park.

In ancient cultures, rains descending from the sky signify renewal, rebirth, and the grace of God, to bring life. New beginnings. In our final moments together, just as the final hands were joining to complete the circle, the rain fell like a benison, or a baptism. It was the end of one era and the beginning of another.

I sat on the steps after the rally ended with Winnie Wong. She'd always presented a tough front, but began to cry when the music stopped. She wasn't the only one.

A Tale of Two Conventions

By the time the Convention came around, the Avengers fellowship had begun to splinter. The ideological divides had started to become apparent. The less successful people were the biggest problem.

It's just as well, because the 2016 Democratic National Convention in Philadelphia was a sham, a total shit show. The day after the Climate Revolution Is Up to Us rally, we headed over to the Wells Fargo Arena.

I was absolutely exhausted.

When I finally arrived at the stadium, the first thing I saw when I walked up to the perimeter of the arena was hundreds of people lined up around hundreds of yards of twelve-foot black barricade fencing. A row of people stretching at least fifty yards across were pounding on the fences like a scene out of a prison movie.

Instead of shouting "At-ti-ca!" they clamored, "Hell no, D-N-C, we don't want no Hill-ar-y!" as their palms pummeled the tall barricades. And it wasn't just angry white dudes. There were angry Americans of all colors, genders and ethnicities.

I couldn't help but remember Hillary's lead counsel Marc Elias telling me that Bernie's supporters would come around for Clinton. At the time it was impossible to reconcile this idea with the rage and disillusionment we were all experiencing. And now here was the proof.

Only a week prior, the Wikileaks info had dropped. Everything that had been obvious to Bernie supporters was finally revealed to the public. The leaks revealed that Debbie Wasserman Schultz, as head of the DNC, had done everything possible to give Clinton a decisive edge.

Everyone knew this.

She was the living embodiment of the corrupt Democratic Establishment and perhaps the most despised opponent of Berniecrats nationwide. And yet despite being forced to resign in disgrace, she was immediately rehired by Hillary's campaign. It was yet another fuck-you to Bernie supporters on the eve of the convention, all the while they were crying unity.

The DNC had been colluding with both the Clinton campaign and CNN to put their thumbs on the scale against the Sanders campaign. People were both vindicated and enraged. Many of us had never cared so deeply about a cause. It was an odd mixture of deep love and deep desperation, like a scream without a mouth.

There was a solid month of conference calls with delegates and organizers planning actions inside and outside of the convention. FDR Park just adjacent to the arena was still a veritable encampment of thousands of Berniecrats looking to storm the Democratic dog and pony show with pitchforks in hand.

For all our planning and big ideas, we didn't stand a chance of breaching the perimeter.

Police had placed blockades strategically hundreds of yards away. Due to an elaborate series of security measures, the chance that any dissidents without tickets might challenge the festivities or its attendees was close to zero. The image of the disaffected Sanders supporters was a nearly perfect snapshot of the divide between progressives and the Democratic Establishment.

There was a standing army and a long series of security checks between us and the inside action. In retrospect, we could have started with a diversion at the main entrance on Broad Street. If we'd had a bunch of ladders, we could have run en masse with massive numbers at the SW corner of the park and used them to clear the high barricades like a medieval army storming a fortress. On the other hand, we still would have had a lot of the parking lot to cover to make it to the arena, and a lot of stormtroopers to potentially intercept us.

In reality, we could never have achieved the level of alignment and planning necessary to really effectively disrupt the convention from the outside, due to all the egos involved. There were too many personality conflicts and too much infighting amongst the so-called organizers. There was talk of some of them being infiltrators. It can be difficult to find a balance between creating a safe security culture and snitch jacketing (publicly calling out people as infiltrators).

We had done our best to arrange conference calls with other organizers planning actions inside and outside the convention. When we'd been at the People's Summit in Chicago the month before, Max Carver had had the amazing idea of creating a fire pit or a paper shredder that looked like a ballot box and we could stage an action where people lined up to destroy delegate credentials before the press, symbolizing the charade that had taken place for primary voters.

We had had strategy calls with some of the Bernie delegate whips and other organizers leading up to the convention. The idea had evolved into a potential delegate walk out, converging with demonstrators outside the convention as a media stunt, but we couldn't get it together in the end.

I'd managed to get tickets because every day Chris Kantrowitz or Calina from the Up To Us crew would leave a pair for me and Anthony Rogers-Wright.

If you were watching the convention on television, you didn't see the riot police or the fires set outside of the barricades.

Lee Fang of *The Intercept* broke the story in October 2015 that Debbie Wasserman Schultz had convened a meeting with dozens of lobbyists to plan the convention in Philadelphia.

Obama had placed restrictions on lobbyist donations, but as soon as it was clear that he would no longer be leading the party, the vultures had returned in their numbers. The DNC had quietly repealed the lobbyist restrictions so that corporations could feast on the rotting corpse of democracy.

Amongst the attendees of Debbie's fundraising meeting were employees from Capitol Counsel, a Washington lobby firm representing companies like Chevron, Comcast, Exxon Mobil, JP Morgan Chase, Lockheed Martin, PhRMA, and Walmart, who represented both Democrats and Republicans.

Of course party loyalists don't read *The Intercept*, and neither MSNBC nor CNN had any intention of covering this.

It was perfect that the convention was being held in the Wells Fargo Center. Daniel Hilferty had been named Host Committee finance chair for the Convention. Hilferty was CEO of Independence Blue Cross, the insurance industry lobbying group that had led the charge against Obamacare.

Fang also reported that David Cohen was the special adviser to the Host Committee. He was serving as the executive vice president of Comcast, overseeing the company's lobbying and regulatory strategy. In addition to being a "Hillblazer," one of Hillary Clinton's bundlers who had raised $100,000 or more, Cohen had been a vicious opponent of net neutrality, the principle that all internet traffic must be treated equally. And despite hosting fundraisers for Clinton at his home the previous summer, Cohen had spent heavily to help elect a Republican Congress.

This was the crew that had funded and organized the Democratic National Convention, which was supposed to be an institution of democracy, not corporatocracy.

According to Craig Holman, an expert on ethics and campaign finance with Public Citizen, "Party bosses have always preferred a Wild West when it comes to fundraising. If party bosses had their way, we would have no restrictions on campaign contributions to the parties and a return to the days of Tammany Hall."

The Tammany Hall reference was a callback to the Democratic machine politics of New York City in the late 19th century, a period synonymous with open graft and corruption.

The scene inside the convention was surreal. One would never have known that the populist barbarians were quite literally at the gates, so to speak. The nationally televised broadcast could not be depended on to give any indication of what was really happening. Glassy-eyed party loyalists mindlessly chanted *"U-S-A, U-S-A, U-S-A, U-S-A!"* It might as well have been the Republican National Convention.

On the Monday night of the convention, the lineup of speakers included First Lady Michelle Obama, Keith Ellison and Elizabeth Warren, but there were a few moments more heartbreaking and beautiful than when Bernie finally took the stage on Monday night.

Before Bernie could start his speech, the Wells Fargo Center erupted in thunderous cheering. The deafening applause and shouts of *Bernie! Bernie! Bernie!* couldn't be quelled. The arena pulsated with emotion. It was like a tidal wave of love. All of the love and pain and desire of the previous year that had been pent up exploded inside the arena for three full minutes. He intermittently tried to quiet down the roaring crowd, but no one would listen. Some people broke down and cried, others cheered. Bernie himself was visibly moved, trying to hold back tears.

The sentiment wouldn't last.

We'd smuggled in No TPP signs for the Bernie delegates. Chris Kantrowitz handed me a stack to distribute. By all accounts the California contingent was the rowdiest and most dissident. What people saw on network news was very different from the war happening between party officials and Bernie delegates. Keep in mind that these delegates had been elected by the people to represent them and be their voices.

A variety of tactics were used against them, including but not limited to having signs ripped from their hands, and their assigned seats taken from them. Each state had its own section, but very often if Bernie delegates attempted to leave, convention workers escorted paid seat fillers to take their place, hired from Craigslist.

Keep in mind, these delegates were elected party members, most of whom had raised the thousands of dollars required to be able to afford attending the convention on GoFundMe pages.

So much for the Democrats being the "big tent party."

Outside the convention, it continued to resemble some dystopian, futuristic nightmare like in *Escape from New York*, only set in Philadelphia. The crowd continued to press against the barricade and beat their fists on the cold black metal. Crowds of people marched up and down the street. At one point, the demonstrators managed to tear down one of the barricades and began an attempt to breach the perimeter.

Kai Newkirk and Democracy Spring organized direct actions. The disruptors wore white armbands. Sameera Khan wore hers on her head like a Rambo-esque Hindi action film star. Her oversized Gucci sunglasses tied together the whole outfit as she straddled the top of the black twelve-foot-tall barricades with her fist in the air, before disappearing over the other side amongst riot cops with zip ties who had been arresting anyone that broke through the line.

People broke out into shouting, repeating in unison the old Occupy chant, "THE WHOLE WORLD IS WATCHING."

But unfortunately, they weren't watching. They were watching the bread and circus event happening inside the Wells Fargo Center.

You might ask yourself, "How could this all have happened?"

How did we end up with Hillary vs Trump in the end?

The truth is, people wanted to be fooled.

Why do people love magicians? Why did we watch *Game of Thrones*? Why do we yell at our televisions? Why do we go to Disneyland when it is a complete fabrication? Why do we interact with sock puppets and ventriloquist dummies as if they were living beings?

We love to be fooled.

You have most likely watched *The Apprentice*, or seen some clips from it. Did you think that it was a real boardroom and not a set? Conservatives are well aware that Donald is full of shit. They know he is an adulterer and nothing resembling a Christian. C'mon, for Christ's sake, the man can't conjure a single Bible verse. They know who Trump really is.

No one really believed that Mexico was going to pay for Trump's big stupid wall. They don't care, because he is their guy. Social media algorithms, corporate news, and the two-party system have turned the "political football" into rank tribalism. Neither side is willing to admit when they are wrong.

The average citizen has seen the American Dream turn into a nightmare. The planet is on the verge of being uninhabitable due to climate change. No one ever really believed that smoking cigarettes was safe. Even now that it has been proven to cause cancer, people still smoke. We are irrational beings.

There is a term from professional wrestling that perfectly explains this, called *kayfabe*. This refers to the willing suspension of disbelief of the audience, that the scripted performances are in fact real. There are the Faces, hero-types showing humility, patriotism, a hard-working nature, determination, and reciprocal love of the crowd. Then there are the Heels, the archetypal villains who are the raging, narcissistic egomaniacs that the crowd loves to hate. This was an act first made famous by Andy Kaufman. If there is ever a moment when the entertainers fall out of character, it is called "breaking kayfabe."

Donald Trump even appeared as himself on WWE Wrestling.

Trump won because he understood that WWE is America. Democrats love to look down on conservatives as dimwitted, backward, racist simpletons. But to these rank and file conservatives, the "virtue-signaling" left were the Heels who condescended to them while their jobs kept disappearing. Finally, a man had emerged who represented everything they'd been taught to love. He didn't shy away from being a wealthy, racist, misogynist white male. He celebrated it, and he wasn't afraid to say to the Democrats and the liberal media everything they secretly felt. He made it okay for them to be themselves, prejudice and all. So it really didn't matter to them that he was a compulsive liar, a bully, a bigot, or even that he was caught on tape bragging about sexually assaulting women a month before the election.

We may think we are so different, so much more evolved—but in the arena of American politics, Donald Trump is your Heel. Only instead of a wrestling arena, the stage is everywhere. We can't stop talking about him. He is the one we love to hate.

Centrist Democrats missed the point because they were busy being fooled by their own Faces. Under President Obama and Secretary Clinton, the US dropped more bombs than under George W. Bush (over twenty-one thousand per day), and they expanded our foreign wars to seven countries. They did not prosecute one Wall Street executive for crashing the US economy in 2008.

They persecuted whistleblowers and expanded the surveillance state. Without the Snowden leaks we would never have known, not that it has mattered in the slightest. They backed corporate coups in Honduras. They created a failed state in Libya. They tried to do the same in Syria and started a proxy war with Russia over a (wait for it) natural gas pipeline. Did you ever stop to wonder why Russia tried to intervene in a US election? Guess who was right in the middle of this proxy war and called for the no fly zone that could have escalated into a World War.

They railed against Susan Sarandon, not just because she refused to fall in line behind Clinton, but because she broke kayfabe and told the truth. Occupy Wall Street and the Bernie campaign also held a mirror up to the American Dream and revealed a deep betrayal.

The problem was that Hillary and the Democrats tried to run on how great America already was because of Barack Obama's presidency, and the numbers just did not add up. Julian Assange and Wikileaks broke the kayfabe when it revealed that the Democratic Party was not run according to anything resembling democratic principles.

Prelude to Trumpageddon

The next night the mothers of Eric Garner, Trayvon Martin, Michael Brown, and Sandra Bland shared heart-breaking messages about their children who had been murdered by police. It was utterly bizarre and a little inappropriate to juxtapose these brave women's tragedy with the darlings of the white out-of-touch liberal intelligentsia, like Debra Messing, Minnesota Senator Amy Klobuchar, Nancy Pelosi and Chuck Schumer. The Democratic Party often uses identity politics as a shield, but offers no meaningful policy reform to improve the lives of black and brown people economically or to strike blows against systemic racism. Because of this they were poised to suffer the biggest upset in the history of the United States.

The fourth-ranking Democrat, New York Congressman Joe Crowley, also spoke. At the time he had no idea that he would be unseated by a young bartender from Queens named Alexandria Ocasio-Cortez.

Other vapid old white dudes who spoke that week included Vice President Joe Biden, who shouted incoherent American exceptionalist rhetoric, and billionaire Michael Bloomberg, the former mayor of New York City and nemesis of Occupy Wall Street. The one upside of the speech of the Democratic Nominee for Vice President Tim Kaine was that it gave me the chance to take a nap in my seat. He was like a vortex, sucking charisma and enthusiasm out of the arena, which is definitely not the quality you want to have on the ticket for the presidency, especially running against a bombast like Trump. They had the opportunity to unite the party by inviting Sanders to join the ticket, but they had no intention of doing anything to diminish the absolute power of the oligarchy.

The DNC and the political consultant class had the opportunity to unite at the Convention, or with their vice presidential pick. Instead there was no discussion of any campaign promises constituting policies that might help the millions of citizens scraping to get by. It was all rhetoric about Trump.

The entire line-up was a slap in the face to Sanders supporters. We were somehow expected to cheer for our abusers, like Neera Tanden, who were given center stage in the national political spot-light. There were no Bernie surrogates, except for Sarah Silverman. There was a big opportunity to heal the divide by uplifting Bernie's message and platform, but just like the Democratic Platform Committee, the message was to 'kiss the ring' or shut up completely.

The only piece of Bernie merchandise available was a T-shirt bearing an antisemitic caricature of Sanders, strongly reminiscent of Nazi propaganda which had likened Jewish people to rats.

When the DNC Wikileaks dropped, it was around the time that this internal conversation between the CEO and CFO of the DNC was published:

"It may make no difference, but for KY and WA can we get someone to ask [him] his belief," Brad Marshall, CFO of the DNC, wrote in an email on May 5, 2016. "He had skated on having a Jewish heritage. I read he is an atheist. This could make several points of difference with my peeps. My Southern Baptist peeps would draw a big difference between a Jew and an atheist."

Amy Dacey, CEO of the DNC, subsequently responded "AMEN," according to the emails.

The biggest fuck-you came when Nina Turner, one of our greatest heroes and perhaps one of the finest orators alive, was bumped from the speaking line up. I caught up with her just as she was leaving the convention and walking outside. We walked together for a minute as I tried to offer words of consolation for the indignity she had just suffered.

The one bright spot in all the hoopla was Reverend William Barber's powerful speech. He offered moral clarity in the face of those that would corrupt the teachings of Christ under the guise of greed and racism. He referred to Jesus as a brown-skinned Palestinian Jew, and called for a revival of the heart of our democracy and a transcendence of partisan politics to fight for a $15 minimum wage, public education, and free health care. I still wonder if Rev. Barber went completely off script that night.

Nina's snubbing and the treatment of the Bernie delegates would not go unanswered. On the last day, 1,250 elected delegates walked out, en masse, in protest of the wholesale corrupting of the democratic process by the media and the DNC and the unconscionable treatment they'd received.

Outside, protesters carried a white wooden coffin with DNC stenciled in red and blue paint with dead donkey symbols on the side. The crowd feverishly chanted, "HELL, NO, DNC, WE DON'T WANT NO HILL-AR-Y!" It passed through the sea of hands like someone crowd surfing at a concert until it was tossed symbolically over the barricade at the feet of a row of cops casually observing.

I wonder what the mainstream narrative would have been if the media had broadcast these events and informed the public about the truth.

It's impossible for democracy to exist without an ethical, independent news media. A few years after Jeff Bezos purchased *The Washington Post*, the outlet changed their motto to "Democracy Dies in Darkness." Their motto has remained more of a mission statement than a slogan.

There were thousands of Bernie Supporters marching and holding rallies outside the arena in FDR Park, being kept at bay by riot police. The imagery was reminiscent of the 1968 Chicago convention. Shit was on fire. People were being arrested.

I went back and forth between the inside of the convention and the war zone outside. I met up with Dr. Jill Stein outside to march together. It wasn't all bad. I got to hang with Vermin Supreme, who had first filed to run in the Democratic presidential primary and then switched his affiliation to the Libertarian Party. Vermin had donned a giant gray wizard beard, and wore a red cape and a two-foot tall black rubber boot on his head. He was running on a platform of dental hygiene and free ponies for all, which made about as much sense as anything else at the convention had, or would in the general election to come.

Every once in a while the Up To Us caravan hippies would show up singing, "We are in this together!" which was a nice breath of fresh air in the midst of the apocalyptic scene.

Take that Frackenlooper

The Avengers crew was blowing off steam at a downtown Philly pub after the soul-crushing convention, when Anthony came to alert us that there was an emergency meeting happening outside to discuss a potential direct action. As it turned out, Clinton's "energy advisor" (code for fracking lobbyist) Trevor Houser was doing a panel at a *Politico* event with then-Governor Hickenlooper, whom Colorado activists call "Frackenlooper," for enabling the fossil fuel industry there.

David Braun was going to sneak in with a big banner hidden under his suit coat. It was important that we dressed well to fit in with the modish consultant class and reporters, so as not to arouse suspicion.

I was able to make a few strategic contributions to the plan. We hadn't got to occupy the stage at the Democratic Platform Committee, so this seemed like a good opportunity to follow through on that intention. In addition to this, I thought one disruption would be cool, but what if there were multiple agitations?

The first round went off without a hitch. Our fracktivist comrades brought the panel discussion to a halt when David pulled out his banner and began shouting at Houser and Frackenlooper, "YOU GUYS ARE LIARS, FRACKING CANNOT BE MADE SAFE, AND I HOLD YOU PERSONALLY

RESPONSIBLE FOR POISONING AMERICA!!" Security began dragging him out of the building, but he would not be taken without finishing what he came to say. Anthony and the rest of the gang casually walked up on stage until they too were escorted out of the building.

The panelists and guests were a little shaken, but laughed nervously and carried on with the event, casually trying to dismiss the disturbance. Little did they know, Desiree Kane and I are waiting in the audience wearing our Sunday best and ready to let them know how we feel. Desiree stood up and made an impassioned plea to her home state governor to ban fracking, while I rushed the stage shouting about fracked gas and the climate crisis.

As they ushered us out of the building, the moderator said, "Well, that was the proverbial curtain dropping," signifying that the panel event was going to end early.

Politico was livestreaming the proceedings, but specifically edited out the disruption. Luckily, we brought our own media coverage. Jimmy Dore showed up to report for *TYT Politics*. He and Jordan Chariton had joined the Avengers thread just before the Convention.

This would be our last hurrah for the Bernie 2016 presidential campaign, but our journey was far from over. Shailene set up a conference call with the Avengers to support her Indigenous friends who had formed a resistance camp to shut down the Dakota Access Pipeline. We didn't know it at that moment, but the fight of our lives was about to begin.

The Aftermath

Instead of reaching out to Bernie supporters in conciliation, the DNC demanded obedience. Anyone watching at home would never know that, however, because the television presented a total fabrication.

Hillary would go on to lose.

She did not step foot in Wisconsin to campaign. She called Trump voters "a basket of deplorables." Trump's campaign reinvented politics with Cambridge Analytica and psychographics while the Democrats lit a billion dollars on fire to use the same old tactics they had been using since 2004. The Democratic Establishment's biggest idea was to bank on Hillary being so conservative she would appeal to conservatives.

"For every blue-collar Democrat we lose in western Pennsylvania, we will pick up two moderate Republicans in the suburbs in Philadelphia, and you can repeat that in Ohio and Illinois and Wisconsin," was a thing Chuck Schumer actually said out loud.

She and her supporters had done everything possible to alienate progressives and offered no substantive policies for working people.

Despite the fact that Bernie supporters would show up to vote for Clinton in greater percentages than Clinton supporters showed up to vote for Obama in 2008, they would still blame and gaslight us for losing what should have been the easiest presidential victory in history.

We tried to tell them, but they wouldn't listen.

The Political Revolution would not die in Philadelphia that July. Sanders supporters would go on to fight for a new cause in North Dakota at a place called Standing Rock.

And, for the record, the most important thing to remember about the 2016 general election is:

BERNIE WOULD HAVE WON!

PART TWO

Chapter 8

Bury My Heart at Standing Rock

It's not that we were free, not
really
But on a clear day
we could see what
freedom looked like.
-Mark K.Tilsen, *"Camp Life"*

I t all started with thirty Indigenous youth and an old Lakota prophecy. The legend said that one day a giant black snake named Zuzeca Sape would try to cross the land of the people. If that happened, the world would end.

Then in June of 2014, Energy Transfer Partners (or ETP) announced its plans for a North Dakota pipeline to carry Bakken crude oil twelve thousand miles across four states to Illinois. The Dakota Access Pipeline (or DAPL) was projected to cost $3.8 billion, and was originally slated to run ten miles outside of the state capital of Bismarck.

There was one big problem: Bismarck was where all the white people lived.

At the time, according to the US census, the demographics in Bismarck were roughly 1,700 Hispanic people (1.5%), 700 African Americans (0.5%), 500 Asian people (0.6%), 4,400 Native Americans (4%), and a whopping 105,000 white people (92%).

Energy Transfer Partners (now operating as Energy Transfer LP) owns Sunoco brand gasoline. Sunoco pipelines have experienced 257 pipeline leaks since 2006, which resulted in deaths, hospitalizations, or property damage of $50,000 or more. These 257 incidents collectively resulted in $46 million in property damage. In terms of number of incidents, Sunoco had the worst safety record out of 1,518 active pipeline operators.

It wasn't a question of *if* the Dakota Access pipeline was going to break, but *when*. This is a really big problem if the state capital is where all the white people live. The decision was then made to reroute the pipeline through Indian country.

There has been a long history of racism and genocide taking place between the white colonizers of the Dakotas and its Indigenous populations. It's important to frame the events at Standing Rock within this historical context, and to assess its implications for the shape of environmental racism to come, in the age of climate crisis.

Three hundred miles away from Bismarck was the Pine Ridge reservation, where in 1890 the Wounded Knee Massacre took place. The snowy, frozen ground was painted red with the blood of three hundred Lakota men, women, and children, who were shot down in cold blood by the 7th Cavalry, Custer's old regiment. Many were babies. White people in the Dakotas still celebrate the outfit by wearing their uniforms in the Veterans Day parade. Happy Meals in North Dakota still sometimes come with 7th Cavalry dolls inside of them for children.

The US Army Corps of Engineers determined that it wasn't safe for the pipeline to run through Bismarck, but that it was fine for it to be routed through the Standing Rock Sioux reservation. They determined no environmental impact statement would be needed despite the fact that the Dakota Access Pipeline would run across the Cannonball River, a tributary of the Missouri. Downstream, the pipeline would potentially endanger over 17 million people.

The proposed site of the drill pad was on top of Turtle Island, a sacred burial ground for the ancestors of the tribe. Four hundred and fifty thousand barrels of crude would flow through the pipeline every day, threatening their only water source, as well as the surrounding habitat.

ReZpect Our Water

It's impossible to separate the gravity of the Standing Rock pipeline fight from the backstory.

On June 13th, 2014, President Obama came to Cannonball for the 45th Annual United Tribes International Powwow. This event left a powerful impression on the people as Obama was the first president to visit the reservation in fifteen years. After attending the cultural gathering, he invited some of the young members of the tribe to come to the White House for a visit.

"I love these young people. I only spent an hour with them. They feel like my own. And you should be proud of them, because they've overcome a lot, but they're strong and they're still standing and they're moving forward," Obama said.

He and Michelle even took them out for pizza and burgers afterwards on Capitol Hill. You can imagine how much that must have meant to these kids.

In that meeting, he heard their concerns about the pipeline, and promised he would help if they made their voices heard. One can only ponder the hope this experience would have inspired in these young people. The youth of Standing Rock couldn't have imagined just how strong they would have to stand—nor the revolution they would ignite.

Two Indigenous youth named Joseph White Eyes and Jasilyn Charger would become frontline fighters in the campaign against the Keystone XL pipeline. According to interviews, Jasilyn had previously worked on the production team of the local Fox News affiliate. She'd quit after her boss made one too many "Cowboys and Indians" jokes in response to Natives being gunned down by the police.

In April 2016, Charger and the Indigenous youth leaders created an affinity group called the International Indigenous Youth Council to organize efforts to block the DAPL. They worked with LaDonna Brave Bull Allard and other Indigenous women mentors to establish a small prayer camp just off the Dakota Access route, on the north end of the reservation. LaDonna was an official historian for the Standing Rock Sioux and she offered her land for the camp. Veteran Keystone XL pipeline fighter Joye Braun traveled from her home in Eagle Butte, South Dakota to be the first to build a teepee at the Sacred Stone Camp.

Obama had told the youth to make their voices heard, so they did just that. In May, they launched the ReZpect Our Water media campaign, and with the help of celebrities like Leonardo DiCaprio they collected 160,000 signatures for a petition to stop the pipeline. Shailene became one of the leading voices uplifting this campaign, and in June brought this to the attention of our Bernie's Avengers group.

As both a spiritual offering, and a tactic to generate public awareness, thirty young people in their teens set out on foot to run across the country from North Dakota to Washington, DC. The intention was to demonstrate their commitment to their water, to their land, to the wildlife, and to their people, by suffering the elements and delivering the petition by hand to the White House.

Speaking in an interview with *Truthout* in June 2016, Tokata Iron Eyes, a twelve-year-old Lakota girl, one of the lead youth organizers in the campaign, said:

> *"The role of Indigenous young women coming together in this campaign has also been paramount, signaling the enduring strength of Indigenous women's leadership in questions of tribal governance. Women were the people who held the tribe together and they were the willpower of the tribe and its strength. So, just knowing that we come from such powerful genes makes us feel strong inside."*

Tokata was the daughter of Chase Iron Eyes, who was running for Congress at the time. We met him for the first time at Josh Fox and Shailene's The Climate Revolution is Up to Us rally in Philadelphia during the Democratic National Convention, when thousands of Berniecrats first learned about the plight of Standing Rock. Bernie was, not surprisingly, an early supporter of the water protectors.

Most grown adults couldn't fathom running a single twenty-six-mile marathon, and yet these intrepid youth, still in their teens, undertook the grueling crucible of running two thousand miles. This is the equivalent of seventy-five marathons run consecutively. But it was not just an endurance run; it was a sacrifice for their land and people, and an act of spiritual austerity.

Imagine their feelings when they finally arrived in Washington, only to find the doors of the White House closed to them. Their pleas fell on deaf ears. The promises made by President Obama in Standing Rock would not be kept.

ReZpect Our Water was denied a meeting at the White House even after the Obamas had welcomed the Standing Rock youth to the Oval Office in November 2014 with promises to protect them.

Shailene brought national attention to Standing Rock when she was arrested on September 7th. It was clear from Shai's livestream footage that the Morton County Sheriff's Office had sought her out and targeted her for arrest to intimidate and send a message to any influencers that would have the audacity to use their platform to broadcast what was happening on the ground.

"I was strip-searched," Shai later reported to the press. "Like, 'Get naked, turn over, spread your butt cheeks, bend down.'"

Our Bernie's Avengers team was able to respond rapidly by pushing the story out to media outlets. Our media contacts also proved useful a month later, when Josh's producer Deia Schlosberg was arrested for committing heinous acts of journalism. Her crime: filming climate activists protesting the tar sands oil pipelines by turning unguarded valves and shutting off the flow of crude as a solidarity action with Standing Rock. This was deemed by authorities to be a criminal act.

Edward Snowden observed in a tweet that Deia faced more years in prison (forty-five to be exact) than he did for leaking secret documents about the NSA's mass surveillance program in 2013.

"This reporter is being prosecuted for covering the North Dakota oil protests. For reference, I face a mere thirty years," he wrote.

For the Bernie's Avengers and thousands of Sandernistas that flocked to Standing Rock in solidarity for *#NoDAPL*, this was only the beginning. We were in for the fight of our lives.

We Are Water Protectors

The term water protector is sometimes attributed to Dallas Goldtooth, who was an organizer with the Indigenous Environmental Network.

His father, Tom Goldtooth, was the founder of IEN. Father and son were prominent leaders in the fight to stop the Keystone XL pipeline as well as DAPL. Dallas organized the Keep It In the Ground campaign and was also known in some circles for his Indigenous sketch comedy. There was nothing funny, however, about the livestream footage he shot capturing the brutality of the Morton County Sheriff's Office and the hired mercenaries against the Indigenous leaders' direct actions outside pipeline construction sites.

He brought an equal balance of gravity, disbelief, and irony to his coverage and commentary in the media about the events that transpired; events that it was hard to believe were taking place in America in 2016. Dallas would later land a featured role in the Hulu comedy series *Reservation Dogs*, playing the role of Spirit, a horseback spirit guide who appears to one of the Indigenous youth.

The last time there was such a highly publicized Indigenous event was in 1973 at Wounded Knee. Leonard Crow Dog was one of the spiritual and organizational leaders of the action. What ensued was a seventy-one-day standoff between the FBI and the American Indian Movement when they occupied the small town on the Pine Ridge Indian Reservation in South Dakota. The AIM members controlled the narrative by maintaining that they were not occupiers, since it was their land to begin with.

#NoDAPL "*Mni Wiconi!*"—"*Water is life!*"

These became the battle cries of those who stood in solidarity to obstruct the construction of the Dakota Access Pipeline.

Mni Wiconi (pronounced "minnie weechoni") in Lakota means Water is Life. A friend and mentor of mine named Wolf Wahpepah, also a water protector, often joked when people refer to this as a symbolic saying. "You can go without a symbol and nothing will happen, but try going a week without water … you'll die. Water is not symbolically life—it is literally life."

Water was not considered life to the executives at Energy Transfer Partners.

On September 4th at least six people, including a child, were attacked by guard dogs on leashes held by hired mercenaries from the private security agency TigerSwan, contracted by Energy Transfer Partners.

This incident was yet another chilling example of the corporate state, the supreme confluence of the government and private sector coming together to wage war on Indigenous people for the greed of an oil company and its stakeholders—North Dakota Governor Dalrymple, the Morton County Sheriff's Office, the Bureau of Indian Affairs, National Guard troops, private mercenaries, and the Army Corps of Engineers. Just like during Occupy Wall Street, the government, police state and corporations were teaming up to quell popular resistance to corruption with mercenary force.

The agents of the corporate state used rubber bullets, bean bag pellets, LRAD sound devices, and water cannons.

LRADs (Long-Range Acoustic Devices) were developed to deter pirates and can damage one's hearing even through ear plugs.

Also known as "sound cannons," LRADs had been designed as a military weapon after the 2000 attack on the *USS Cole*, and they blast a directed beam of sound waves at decibels so intense they can cause eardrums to burst. They also come fully loaded with a "pain ray" feature which fires a beam of skin-heating microwaves at a range of over 750 meters. LRADs have also been used all over the country against Black Lives Matter demonstrators.

TigerSwan had an estimated 350 employees, and maintained offices in Iraq, Afghanistan, Saudi Arabia, Jordan, India, Latin

America, and Japan. They were the perfect choice to try to stop the water protectors, who were in turn trying to stop the pipeline from being routed through their own land.

TigerSwan was created by retired Army Lt. Col. James Reese during the height of the war in Iraq. Reese was a former commander in an Army special operations unit known as Delta Force. Their job description included missions like hostage rescue and counter-terrorism, small-scale raids, ambushes, sabotage and special reconnaissance against high-value targets.

This is who we were up against.

Reese founded TigerSwan to compete with Blackwater, the private security mercenary firm you might remember for killing fourteen Iraqi civilians in Baghdad.

TigerSwan's internal reports and the intelligence briefings shared with law enforcement named dozens of water protectors. They had infiltrators who reported on the dynamics at camp, potential direct actions and who was infighting with whom.

And there was always plenty of infighting.

Leaked documents revealed a "persons of interest" list, photographs, license plate numbers and other databases of intel. One report indicated that TigerSwan had met with the North Dakota Bureau of Criminal Investigation, "regarding video and still photo evidence collected for prosecution"—which meant that private mercenaries hired by an oil company were colluding with state agencies to build legal cases against unarmed demonstrators on sovereign land.

TigerSwan's reports described conversations between the company's operatives and FBI agents on multiple occasions. There was a DAPL helicopter that provided live video coverage to police agencies that included state and local police and FBI, DHS, and BIA agents.

In one email, National Security Intelligence Specialist Terry Van Horn of the US attorney's office acknowledged his direct access to the helicopter video feed. He wrote, "Watching a live feed from DAPL helicopter, pending arrival at sites."

TigerSwan compared water protectors to jihadist terrorists, and characterized them as "ideologically driven insurgent[s] with a strong religious component." A report dated February 27, 2017 reads, in part:

> *"[The anti-DAPL movement] generally followed the jihadist insurgency model while active, we can expect the individuals who fought for and supported it to follow a post-insurgency model after its collapse. While we can expect to see the continued spread of the anti-DAPL diaspora, aggressive intelligence preparation of the battlefield and active coordination between intelligence and security elements is now a proven method of defeating pipeline insurgencies."*

In other words, they were framing their strategic approach to countermeasures against our peaceful demonstrations on sovereign Indigenous land the same way they counteracted the Taliban in Afghanistan.

Let that sink in.

Buffalo Run

On October 27, I got a call from my friend Greg Gallup. He was a veteran I had met while building a coalition to support Rep. Tim Ryan's Veterans and Armed Forces Health Promotion Act in 2014.

When I picked up the phone, I heard, "Ponti! The buffalo are running!"

He told me he was coming to pick me up in LA and drive us to Standing Rock.

I told him to give me a couple of days to sort out my affairs in LA and that I would meet him there. I booked my flight as soon as we hung up the phone.

One of the water protectors who'd supplied vital counter intelligence via drone footage, named Dean Deadman, was on Myron Dewey's Digital Smoke Signals livestream when the buffalo appeared.

The herd of buffalo running was seen as an auspicious omen. At that moment, hundreds of police descended on the frontline camp that stood directly in the path of the Dakota Access Pipeline, forcibly evicting residents and arresting 142 people. Most of us could only stand by helplessly and watch the events taking place on livestream.

A week later I would arrive at the Oceti Sakowin Camp.

Violence Toward the Water Protectors Escalates

Throughout the course of the day, elders in prayer were being thrown to the ground; LRADs blasted piercing sounds to incapacitate their targets. The Morton County sheriffs moved in a line with batons in hand. The protectors stood with hands raised in the air, beating their hand-held ceremonial drums and singing prayer songs.

A small independent investigative journalist outfit called *Unicorn Riot* captured the chaos. Screams filled the air as the police moved in. One water protector stood still, his eyes and face beet red from the tear gas, as an overweight riot cop grabbed him from the crowd, pulled him into the line of cops, and threw him to the ground unprovoked.

A TigerSwan contractor driving towards camp in a pickup truck was rammed off the road by a crew of water protectors. The man pulled an AR-15 assault rifle on them. They talked down the armed infiltrator and sent him away.

The police and media constantly tried to drive the false narrative that the water protectors were violent, when in fact at every turn it was the oil company's associates who were the armed mercenaries.

The will of the water protectors would continue to be tested, to hold to their commitment of prayerful non-violent civil disobedience in the face of unspeakable brutality.

Bank Exit, Defund DAPL

On Thursday, November 3, over five hundred clergy—including over fifty Unitarian Universalist clergy—answered the call to come to Standing Rock in solidarity, prayer, and to take action with the Sioux Nation and the water protectors. The goal of the peaceful interfaith witness was to increase awareness of the situation and to advocate for elected officials to take action to end the construction of the Dakota Access Pipeline.

On the same day, I launched the *#BankExit* campaign to defund the Dakota Access Pipeline, with the support of Susan Sarandon and other activists. The idea first arose three weeks earlier: Lakota activist George Funmaker was speaking at the Indigenous People's Day rally about the Dakota Access Pipeline and decolonization, and asked the crowd raising his hand in the air, "Does anyone have an account at Wells Fargo? Am I the only one?"

In Los Angeles, we had been working hard to stand in solidarity with frontline resistance at Standing Rock, with local direct actions, coalition building, and media support. We had been looking for solutions to forward this urgent cause. George's speech reminded us about Bank Transfer Day, a call to action that had happened during Occupy Wall Street on November 5th, 2011. It had challenged people to take their money out of the Bank of America in protest of their announced intention to raise ATM fees to $5 per transaction. It had worked; Bank of America had caved and reversed the policy.

This was basically the same concept.

The seeds planted during Occupy were now in full bloom.

It was a big ask to challenge people to make such a commitment and lifestyle change, but the idea itself was simple and sure to resonate, especially after years of resentment growing against the big banks. Divestment had also worked to end apartheid in South Africa in the 80s, and it was the only long term strategy that would not force us to rely on the better angels of our elected officials, who had proven to be corrupt or willfully indifferent. Just like Occupy, the Oceti Sakowin encampment would come to an end no matter who was elected. We had seen this rodeo before. It was clear that the people we were up against had no empathy or concern for life. We had to hit them in the one place it would hurt—their money.

I spent the next few weeks talking to progressive and environmental activists to suggest that a divestment strategy targeting the banks and financial institutions funding the pipelines be taken on with full force, and using all our resources. It was met with limited enthusiasm.

Finally, on November 1, Jordan Chariton from The Young Turks sent some drone footage from the frontlines through our

Avengers Whatsapp thread showing that the pipeline had indeed finally reached the river. All that had been sacrificed to stop the "Black Snake" from crossing the river was in imminent jeopardy, as there had been no indication that the oil company would obey the court injunction and desist from drilling under the Missouri, the only water source for the people of Standing Rock.

I decided to try for a few Hail Marys and urgently reach out to as many major influencers and organizers in our network as I could. I sent a group text to Shailene and to Susan Sarandon. They were friends, and we had all worked together on the Climate Revolution events and other Bernie-related projects. They both responded enthusiastically. Susan said that she was already planning on divesting from Chase for their role in financing this and other pipelines, and then publicizing it. She agreed to a strategy call the next day. Susan was an extraordinary woman—a fierce valkyrie for equality and justice who gave zero fucks about what people thought about her using her platform to support causes like Occupy, Bernie, Syrian refugees or Standing Rock. On the phone she was a very impressive person. Smart, fearless, no-bullshit and straight-to-business.

My original plan was to travel to Standing Rock to submit the plan to Indigenous leadership, and then ideally to film them petitioning people to divest their money. Next we would engage our network of influencers and supporters to kick-start the campaign in response to the call to action.

After Susan committed to the conference call, it was easy to rally people to join. When I checked in with her the morning before the call, I told her my proposed plans.

She said that it sounded good, but that she had already booked herself on the BBC, CNN, and The Young Turks. So much for best laid plans. She asked me what we were calling the action.

"Hashtag BankExit," I said.

"Good name," she replied coolly in her unmistakable voice.

Now I had two hours to put together a campaign that I would ordinarily need weeks to prepare.

On the call, the various luminaries offered strategies, support, and a detailed list of talking points for Susan. We unpacked everything, from the complex legalities to the history of the treaties being violated, so that she would be well prepped for her interviews. Several Avengers signed onto the call, including David Braun and Alex Ebert.

Dennis Kucinich also joined us. Could he possibly have dreamed of the chain of events he would set into motion when he ran for president? How the PDA and the People for Bernie group would spring forth from his campaign, which would set into motion such an impossible confluence of events to bring us to that very moment? We were all but the pawns of some Divine Director, like players in a drama—were we all compelled by the forces of our destiny or by gravity or by some other mystical force?

It sure seemed so.

Oscar-nominated documentary director Matthew Cooke, whom I'd met directing PSAs for Bernie, offered to film and edit his own process of withdrawing his money from his bank and opening up a credit union account.

True to his word, Matthew completed the entire video by the end of the next day, which in itself was a tremendous feat. He edited in the shocking footage from the frontlines, which made a very compelling piece. Kyle Cadotte, Josh Fox's managing director and my Climate Revolution comrade in arms, suggested I contact Xiuhtezcatl Martinez and his foundation, Earth Guardians.

They had contacts at Care2, the largest petition platform in the world, and convinced them to feature the petition I had typed in Susan's name on their front page. They also agreed to pay for a PR campaign and send multiple emails out to their list of 6 million people. The petition would collect over 50,000 signatures or commitments in four days, and would collect 115,850 signatures throughout the life of the campaign.

The idea caught on like wildfire.

Susan's television appearances generated considerable controversy as both CNN and the BBC pressed her about her recent Jill Stein endorsement in the heat of the Trump race, to which she famously retorted, "I don't vote with my vagina." She did a great job of bringing the interviews back to her talking points, despite them persistently baiting her to shift the conversation away from the DAPL to the election. The DAPL had received almost no mainstream media attention, despite the shocking police violence involved.

With no time, no infrastructure, and no money raised, the campaign generated at least 20 million impressions that we can quantify, within four days. Matthew's video was posted on Facebook by Anonymous, and on a number of other large platforms. It received over 10 million views. I left for Standing Rock two days later as the hashtag took off and the campaign took on a life of its own. A month later, DefundDapl.org was launched by Caleb Buchbinder and Adam Elfers, who had been part of Shailene's Up To Us tour. We merged the two efforts, and the divestment campaign continued to grow. People were looking for ways to support the cause remotely and would do direct actions targeting banks all over the country. They set up teepees in banks to disrupt business. Indigenous activists in Seattle took the idea to a whole new level and petitioned the City Council to divest billions from Wells Fargo.

It was clear that the government would not act. Therefore, the time had come to not just say, "Enough is enough," but to *do* something about it.

Beyond the fight to Defund DAPL, the divestment movement would continue to inspire activists in other cities to push their local governments to take billions in tax dollars out of the big toxic banks (as we will discuss in the following chapter).

Media Blackout

It probably shouldn't have come as a surprise, but despite the levels of shocking violence, there was almost no news coverage of Standing Rock outside of independent media outlets like Amy Goodman and *Democracy Now!* Amy had been a speaker at our Climate Revolution is Up To Us rally with Chase Iron Eyes, but she has always been a journalist of integrity who uplifted the important stories from the grassroots. *Democracy Now!* coverage showed DAPL mercenaries attacking water protectors with dogs and mace.

North Dakota authorities (a dubious moniker for sure) issued warrants for Goodman's arrest for committing unspeakable acts of journalism (the actual charges were *criminal trespassing* and *attempting to incite a riot*). The *Democracy Now!* team returned to North Dakota undaunted to continue to cover the events, when a judge ruled that the charges were baseless.

Bernie surrogates supported Indigenous-led actions in New York, Washington, DC and Los Angeles. We maintained comms on the daily on our WhatsApp thread.

Be The Revolution

There were demonstrations outside of CNN Los Angeles, and though the fourteen-story building was full of so-called news professionals, not one of them pointed a camera outside of their window, or turned their attention to cover events at Standing Rock.

The corporate media was completely consumed with the political football of the 2016 presidential general election. There was too much money to be made on campaign advertising to cover one of the biggest occupations in American history.

Leading up to the 2016 race, corporate news ratings were declining fast. In a time when most people were turning to social media for their information, Donald Trump was like a gift from on high—or below as the case might be. Throughout the course of the election cycle, the networks gave him over $3 billion in free advertising. You might remember that they even broadcast an empty stage and podium for half an hour at a Trump press conference while Bernie Sanders was simultaneously addressing a record crowd of forty to fifty thousand people in Washington Square Park in New York City.

CBS CEO Leslie Moonves said about Donald Trump and the 2016 election, "It may not be good for America, but it's damn good for CBS. The money's rolling in and this is fun."

He wasn't wrong. The cable news election-year haul nearly cracked $2.5 billion.

Moonves would never pay for this dereliction of journalism directly, but he would later be forced to resign in disgrace (as we will eventually discuss).

There was once a time when journalists were an integral part of the checks and balances that kept the people informed and able to make decisions based on facts. In 2016 the media was but one of many of the so-called democratic institutions that failed us. Not only did they lie to us to keep the money train going, but they laid the groundwork for Trump's post-fact world and his famous diatribe of, "Fake news."

Hillary Clinton could have generated an enormous amount of voter enthusiasm if she had publicly endorsed the water protectors at Standing Rock. This should have been an easy layup, but true to form she refused to take any meaningful stand on the issues.

People around the globe followed every day on livestream and on independent progressive media outlets like The Young Turks.

NoDAPL had its own media wizards, people like Myron Dewey, who elevated the fight at Standing Rock using his platform Digital Smoke Signals. Myron was able to bring together the worlds of technology, spirituality and frontline resistance with the balance and power of a master. He'd once worked as a wildland firefighter for the Black Mountain Hotshots, and was one of the drone operators that presented valuable counterintelligence to the Standing Rock Sioux and general public, capturing atrocities and tracking both the progress of the pipeline and the movements of the opposition.

Army Corps of Engineers

Like Occupy Wall Street and Ferguson, Standing Rock featured a network of activists who utilized new platforms and technology to break through the corporate media silence. They had direct action trainers and legal experts. Unlike Occupy, and other uprisings like Ferguson, they also had pre-existing hierarchical structures like a tribal council government. It provided central leadership, though it is debatable whether this aided or hindered decision-making.

On July 25, 2016, the US Army Corps of Engineers approved the route for the pipeline crossing the Missouri River on Standing Rock's sacred land. They intentionally did hundreds of half mile assessments to avoid doing a full environmental impact statement. This occurred on the opening day of the Democratic National Convention and just one day after Chase Iron Eyes spoke at the Climate Revolution rally.

A 1,261 page Army Corps report, announcing the approval, said of the public review process that "no significant comments remain unresolved," despite the fact that there was no environmental impact statement. It did not matter that an EIS was required by the National Environmental Policy Act. Corporate influence trumped policy, as well as the treaties granting the Standing Rock Sioux sovereign land that were supposedly upheld by the US Constitution.

The Omaha district commander, Col. John Henderson, wrote, "I have evaluated the anticipated environmental, economic, cultural, and social effects, and any cumulative effects of the river crossing, and found it is not injurious to the public interest." Apparently, destroying sacred Indigenous burial sites or threatening the only water supply of the Standing Rock Sioux did not meet the requirements.

This was a prime example of the interests of big business being protected by the power of the state, as well as environmental racism.

On November 15th, 350.org in tandem with local Indigenous leaders staged actions outside of Army Corps of Engineers offices across the country. This was yet another example of what Becky Bond and Zack Exley might call "big organizing."

Bernie came out to make a surprise speech at the Washington, DC rally in front of the White House. "The issues are very clear," he said. "For hundreds of years, the Native American people in our country, the first Americans, have been lied to, have been cheated, and their sovereign rights have been denied them. And today we are saying it is time for a new approach to the Native American people, not to run a pipeline through their land. And we are demanding that the sovereign rights of the Native American people be honored and respected."

Susan Sarandon and I showed up at the downtown Los Angeles Federal Building to support SoCal 350.org and Indigenous-led action, to promote the *#BankExit* campaign strategy.

It was a powerful day to share with water protectors standing in solidarity together across the country.

Camp Life at Oceti Sakowin

A couple of days after we launched the #BankExit campaign I got on a plane to North Dakota.

The Oceti Sakowin Camp was a historic gathering of over five hundred Indigenous tribes. Driving in from Highway 1806, you could see the many colors of their flags lining the main road into the camp. There were flags representing various unions and organizations, like Black Lives Matter, also there in solidarity.

Oceti Sakowin was the largest assembly of tribes since the Battle of the Little Bighorn or, as the Sioux refer to it, the Battle of the Greasy Grass. *Oceti Sakowin* means "Seven Council Fires," and is the name for all who belong to the Great Sioux Nation.

The original Sioux tribe was made up of seven factions, comprising individual bands representing seven different regions.

This was the first time that over five hundred tribes had united under a single banner in over a hundred years. The aftermath of open war with the colonizing forces of the US Government had divided and sequestered the Lakota, Dakota and Nakota Sioux onto reservations for over one hundred and fifty years.

The "Horn" was a symbolic name for the circle of tribes and their placement within the Oceti Sakowin.

The layout of the camp was reminiscent of Burning Man, except without all the drugs and nudity. Believe it or not, there was even a geodesic dome that had long been a fixture of Burning Man's Red Lightning Camp, brought in by an old friend of mine named Brad Nye. They held briefings in the dome every morning. (Unlike Burning Man, cultural appropriation was less of an issue.) Like Brad, many of the non-Indigenous supporters had a big learning curve negotiating the Native protocols and customs.

The frontline encampment consisted of many smaller enclaves. There were small camps made up of members from unions, Black Lives Matter, and the five hundred tribes.

Though the corporate media would not cover the events at Standing Rock, the numbers grew by the thousands as people watched the violence escalate. At its height, over ten thousand people occupied the area near the DAPL drill pad, making it the biggest pipeline resistance camp in history.

There was a massive upswell of support from Bernie supporters, who were left without a cause to fight for as the 2016 election hype rose to a fever pitch without their champion as the nominee. In truth, though it is awful to admit, Standing Rock was in a way a blessing for the Bernie movement. Without Standing Rock to galvanize us and give us something to fight for, our young movement would have quickly descended into factionalism and infighting. This is what proved to happen following the 2020 primary.

Upon entering camp, you were greeted by security at the gate on walkie talkies. Friendly at first, yet far from trusting. You could tell by the thousand-yard stare and the subtle tone in their voice that communicated clearly, "We are watching you."

Standing Rock was no stranger to TigerSwan infiltrators.

On my first trip to camp, Greg picked me up at the airport in Bismarck. We drove to Oceti Sakowin, where Evan Duke had us set up to stay at the Occupy/Veterans for Peace camp. Pulling up to the camp for the first time I had an immediate feeling of comfort and pride, knowing that we were representing the Occupy movement at Standing Rock. Driving in from Highway 1806, you could see the many colors of their flags lining the main road into the camp.

They stood tall on wooden poles rapping in the North Dakota wind.

Veterans For Peace had been founded in 1985 in response to the global nuclear arms race and US military interventions in Central America. Veterans' causes had long been close to my heart, so the close alliance of Occupy and VFP made me immediately feel at home.

Evan Duke was a tall surly fellow whose voice had a deep gravel to it. He always wore a Palestinian Keffiyeh around his neck and a short-billed Castro cap.

I'd met Evan back in LA and we'd immediately hit it off. We'd taken a road trip to Las Vegas to meet up with Josh Fox and Nahko as part of the Climate Revolution Tour. Evan was an Occupy OG and had participated in the Battle of Seattle back in '99.

This was one of the most significant trigger events in modern movement history. It took place outside of the Seattle convention center to shut down the World Trade Organization.

Lisa Fithian told me over six months went into planning for the mobilization that included an inside-outside strategy. The process for organizing was highly democratic, which created deep trust and solidarity.

Most Americans had never heard of the WTO before. Organizers from unions, environmental groups and other movements came together with one of the most sophisticated and effective tactical responses in modern movement history, to shut down a gathering that represented the heart of neoliberal globalization.

John Sellers, a protest leader and former director of the Ruckus Society, recounted some of the events of the day:

> *"And so, in the predawn darkness November 30th, 5,000 direct actionistas marched through the streets of Seattle toward their targets. Each individual action had its own logic and narrative. Each would have stood on its own as extraordinary. When connected together, they became unstoppable.*
>
> *The action frame we chose was carnival-protest. Outside the stodgy corporate meeting, a giant dance party broke out, complete with marching bands, dancers, theater troupes, giant puppets, radical cheerleaders, a phalanx of 300 turtles and even Christmas carolers."*

Thousands of people created blockades around entrances and intersections, preventing delegates from entering or exiting. As the demonstrations continued to escalate, Seattle police responded with a violent barrage of tear gas and pepper spray. The impact of Seattle was enormous. It launched the global justice movement and showed that a people's victory against global capital was possible.

In my mind, The Battle of Seattle was the gold standard in direct action organizing, so I was very keen to work with people who had been there.

Evan had been at camp for about a month before I arrived. Throughout my time at Standing Rock we were mostly inseparable. He was a true brother and a leftist pirate if ever I had met one.

Due to his status as a veteran and an organizer, he had gained the trust of JR American Horse, one of the leaders of the Native Veterans, who held a lot of clout at camp. The warrior spirit is deeply rooted in the Indigenous culture. A greater percentage serve in the armed forces than any other ethnic group.

Standing Rock had its own name for those they considered warriors.

Akicita. Pronounced "ah-kee-chee-tah."

There was one member of the *Akicita* I met at our Occupy/ VFP camp who I found to be very impressive. His name was Michael Markus, and his Lakota name was Mato Tanka, meaning *Big Bear*, but everyone called him *"Rattler."* He certainly reminded me of a bear, one with a face that looked like it was carved out of granite, hardened by the merciless Pine Ridge winters. He was stoic and fearless, but also held a deep, quiet, and humble wisdom. Rattler was a Marine, a veteran, and a Sundancer—which means performing a sacred dance in the hot sun for four days without food or water as a form of prayer and sacrifice.

To be named *Akicita* is a lifelong commitment to service—to be willing to die for the people. Rattler certainly lived this commit- ment, as he was one of the water protectors who risked their lives in a high speed chase to stand down the DAPL security officer who tried to infiltrate the camp with an AR-15 in October.

The trials and tribulations the water protectors faced were psychological, spiritual and physical.

Many water protectors who traveled to the camps at Standing Rock reported contracting a condition they refer to as the DAPL cough. In many cases, it wouldn't go away even after being treated with antibiotics. It could have been due to the harsh winter conditions, or possibly chemicals sprayed by low-flying crop-dusting planes at night.

In the early days and months, the numbers of protesters fluctuated from the hundreds to the low thousands, but after some of the more visible trigger events, the numbers surged to as high as ten thousand.

The tribe was not initially prepared to handle the infrastructure challenges of trash removal and sanitation for so many people, and the financial toll was high. There were also serious safety concerns due to the fact that North Dakota winters are truly a survival experience. Those who had lived and grown up there were ready to deal with the challenges, but many of the supporters who came with good intentions were not prepared.

One of the remarkable aspects of the camp was that all was provided to those in need. Everyone was expected to work and do their part, but those who came unprepared could get winter clothes, food or just about whatever they needed. Dinners were a beautiful communal experience. Elders were served first. There was always hot coffee, tea or cocoa by the sacred fire, which burned 24/7.

Under modern industrial capitalism, our elders are not venerated and honored, but discarded and forgotten. Why does our society cast aside elderly and unhoused people? Because in that worldview, our value as humans is not inherent, but limited to what labor we can contribute to production.

After I learned about the constant surveillance from the plane circling above, I picked up an extra ski coat to wear to direct actions.

Someone who was a suspected infiltrator befriended me aggressively my first day at camp. The *#BankExit* campaign was making big waves right out of the gate.

The nights were frigid, unlike any cold I'd ever known. At 3 a.m. there would be a cold snap that would sweep over the camp and chill to the bone.

Every morning, a call to action was broadcast over a squeaky speaker:

"Wake up, my relatives. Greet the morning sun. We have come to protect the water, so get up! You are not on vacation here!"

A small prop plane was flying in a wide circle overhead at all times. This had been contracted by ETP to run surveillance on the water protectors. There were three camps in close proximity: Oceti Sakowin, Rosebud, and Sacred Stone.

Despite all of this, the Standing Rock Sioux and their accomplices remained peaceful and prayerful in the face of violence, psychological torture, public defamation, environmental racism and genocide. They displayed the true essence of what Christianity is supposed to be. Imagine thousands of people being brutalized every day, Indigenous elders ripped from ceremonies, being put in kennels like dogs, maced, shot with rubber bullets and worse, and all the time maintaining an attitude of forgiveness and non-violence. It was astonishing to witness.

Leftist causes and ideologies often have an atheistic bent to them, or perhaps it is just the absence of any spiritual notions. And yet, many of the greatest leaders throughout history have defined themselves by their connection to a Higher Power.

Standing Rock was a moment in which many participants from the progressive movement underwent a profound alchemy under the leadership of the Indigenous people, for whom ceremony and prayer are an integral part of their way of life. We attended sweat lodges that offered deep healing and experiences that can only be called spiritual.

Speaking for myself, those "red road" ways healed me, and helped me prepare and fortify myself for the battles to come.

The Battle of Backwater Bridge

On November 2nd, President Obama went on the internet media platform NowThis to do an interview about his position on Standing Rock. For months, millions of people had been watching the brutality perpetrated by the corporate state, against unarmed Indigenous people on their own land, to protect the interests of a private oil company. Despite the promises he had made to the people of Standing Rock and their children, he had done nothing to stop the violence or to uphold justice. Being Commander-in-Chief of the US Armed Forces means that the Army Corps of Engineers fell under his jurisdiction. The mandate for an environmental impact statement would have immediately halted production and upheld the law.

His response was, "We're gonna let it play out for several more weeks."

Six years and four days prior, Obama had released this statement:

"As we celebrate the contributions and heritage of Native Americans during this month, we also recommit to supporting tribal self-determination, security, and prosperity for all Native Americans. While we cannot erase the scourges or broken promises of our past, we will move ahead together in writing a new, brighter chapter in our joint history."

What bullshit.

In Obama's *NowThis* interview he said nothing about the brutality perpetrated by the Morton County Sheriff's Office and the private mercenaries. He didn't acknowledge the commitment to non-violence maintained by the water protectors. What he was really saying was that he was in bed with the fossil fuel industry. He claimed to be a climate leader and a champion of civil rights, but in truth, he cared more about corporate special interests. I wonder if he has ever felt any shame for this, or for the failures of Flint, Michigan, or the innocent lives destroyed by the wars he has waged.

Meanwhile America, the country Obama was president of, waged war on its own citizens. Water protectors made a line in the frigid water. Black-clad police in balaclavas stood in a line above them on the banks of the river. They calmly sprayed the defenseless water protectors below with industrial canisters of mace and tear gas.

Erin Schrode, an independent journalist working with Josh Fox, was shot in the leg with a rubber bullet. In the aftermath, two of the police turned in their badges, demonstrating that they had some conscience left.

There were always direct actions to agitate. Targets included the bridge on Highway 1801, and the drill pad on top of the hill at "Turtle Island" on the other side of the Missouri River that separated camp from the drill site.

November 20 was a night that would live in infamy, known as the Battle of the Backwater Bridge. Water protectors mobilized at the bridge and a stand-off took place almost until dawn.

The police sprayed demonstrators with water cannons in freezing temperatures. Three hundred people were injured and twenty-six were hospitalized for injuries ranging from hypothermia to seizures, loss of consciousness and impaired vision from the impact of rubber bullets. My friend Sioux Z. Desbah was shot in the eye point blank with a tear gas canister by Morton County sheriffs. Sioux Z. was yelling at them from about thirty feet away and one of the fascists shot her in the head.

Many complained that "the water burned their eyes," leading us to believe that there was mace or some other chemical irritant put in the water.

A nineteen-year-old water protector named Sophia Wilansky suffered a devastating injury from a concussion grenade that exploded and shattered her arm, exposing bone, blood and tissue through the tufts of down lining her winter parka.

Not since the American Indian Movement's stand at Wounded Knee in 1973 had government hostility toward Indigenous people been so overt, and so violent.

All told, Energy Transfer Partners spent over $25 million to push propaganda. The Morton County Sheriff's Office aided in the campaign to spread false narratives in the local media. This was textbook cultural hegemony at work. Leaders like Myron Dewey, Tara Houska (also one of Bernie's Avengers), Dallas Goldtooth, and others combated these lies through independent media and by live streaming events as they happened.

Thanksgiving was four days later. This is considered a day of mourning by many Native Americans.

The water protectors mounted an impressive resistance, finally crossing the river with a makeshift bridge we all walked across made of plywood. Hundreds crossed the spot where only weeks before they had been brutalized while standing in the frigid waters trying to shield themselves with plastic tarps from the onslaught of rubber bullets, tear gas and mace.

Crossing the river was an important symbolic victory. We were just about 150 feet from the drill pad.

We stood at the foot of the hill facing armed men with live weapons pointed at us, ready and willing to scale to the top of the drill pad. They had shotguns and sniper rifles. Imagine acts of violence perpetrated against Native Americans on Thanksgiving of all days. It might have just smashed the foul illusion of the story America tells itself, that this was a day of gratitude for the Indigenous people who saved the Pilgrims. In truth, Thanksgiving was enacted as a tactic to bolster support for the Union Army during the Civil War, while Lincoln and his soldiers committed genocide against the Indigenous people of the land they'd stolen.

This fourth Thursday of November, 2016, the tension in the air was heavy.

It looked like a battle scene from an Akira Kurosawa film. The mercenaries and sheriffs in balaclavas at the top of the hill shouted over bullhorns, somehow framing the water protectors below as the aggressors even though they were only armed with burning sage and "Water is Life" and "Protect the Sacred" banners. I sat and meditated at the foot of the hill, the sacred burial ground of the Standing Rock Sioux for over a thousand years, awaiting orders. Meditation is an invaluable tool to find calm in any situation, no matter how perilous. Clear thinking was crucial at this moment as we could see the sniper rifles they had pointed at us at the top of the hill.

But there would be no celebration on the drill pad that day.

We were held back at the last moment on orders from the headsmen, for fear someone might be killed. We knew the risks after what had happened to Sioux Z. and Sophia only days before, and we were prepared. We knew the risks and were willing to suffer whatever the consequences were.

Then, for reasons known only to those who made the call, we relinquished our advantage and stood down. Perhaps because they did not want to sacrifice more human life upon the altar of the Big Oil death cult.

Afterward we went to Fort Yates for a Thanksgiving feast. It was five years after our Thanksgiving at Occupy Los Angeles. Jane Fonda had volunteered to serve the water protectors in the chow line. We were all pretty exhausted mentally and emotionally, but we shared a fellowship of the spirit. I broke bread with some of my favorite LA Berniecrats, who had come to join the fight. People like Keith Sikora, Carlos Marroquin and Hsingii Teng Bird were true-blue political revolutionaries. We sat around eating, all of us battleworn in our winter gear. Our faces were drawn and hardened, and it was difficult to find joy after the previous year of fighting the corporate state tooth and nail.

It was a small comfort to see so many of Bernie's Avengers at camp and at the casino. It would bring me back to all we had experienced together. The Clooney Counter-Party. Bernie's Coffee Shop. *#ShowMeTheBallots* and the California primary. All of the rallies. The Democratic Convention.

Who would have thought, when Shailene first brought the cause of Standing Rock to the Climate Revolution Is Up To Us rally in Philly and to our WhatsApp thread, that four months later we would have ended up in what was basically a war zone? A great number of the Up To Us caravan participants had come to Standing Rock, fulfilling the intention of the project to continue the political revolution.

Shailene was usually in the middle of the action with Malia Hulleman. Ezra Miller, aka The Flash from *Justice League*, was also part of her crew. Ezra got their *Justice League* co-stars Ben Affleck, Jason Momoa, Gal Gadot, and Ray Fisher to join them in making a video for social media to uplift the cause.

Shailene had enrolled just about all of Bernie's Avengers, not just to support from afar but to join the fight. Frances Fisher was on the front lines during the heat of the Battle of Backwater Bridge.

Sameera Khan and YahNé were often together. Anthony Rogers-Wright was present. Josh Fox, Jordan Chariton and Nomiki were all covering events for TYT. I spent quite a bit of time with Jordan, who let us crash for a couple nights at the casino in his hotel room—it was always a greatly appreciated luxury to not have to sleep in a tent in the bone-chilling cold at camp for a night.

Desiree Kane had been embedded in the communications tent since the summertime. We ran into Max Carver, Kendrick and Connor Paolo on occasion. Seven McDonald came to support Wes Clark, Jr. and the Veterans Respond mobilization—Desiree, Seven and I often found ourselves in meetings in the comms yurt or the casino working on press releases or other media-related projects.

Tara Houska was one of the central spokespeople for Standing Rock, and often appeared on national interviews to offer her legal expertise as a lawyer and activist. Not everyone got along with one another all the time; several Avengers had serious fallings-out. Revolution is messy work, and it is hard to not be triggered when we are being forced to endure constant trauma. But at the end of the day, we were all there to put our hearts and bodies on the line for the cause—for the water, for the people, and to stop the climate apocalypse.

Bernie's surrogates were instrumental in elevating the cause to national attention. Jesse Jackson, Dr. Cornel West, and Mark Ruffalo's trips to camp brought considerable attention. Mark wasn't just a celebrity face, there for a photo op. He had been in the trenches as an activist for a long time, since the beginning of the anti-fracking movement. He was the realest of the real—a true mensch who cared deeply. He was one of us.

We had fought the corporate media hacks, the Democratic Party, the consultants, David Brock's troll farms, and the party loyalists for more than a year, and after the debacle of the convention we were now standing against an oil company, militarized police, paid mercs, and the brutal North Dakota winter.

It was an important thing that was happening, though, for the Bernie movement. The learning curve during the primaries for many Sanders supporters had been steep, but this was an education of an entirely different sort for thousands of political revolutionaries. This was like a war zone, the front line of a class war.

I continued to lobby anyone who would listen to me about the *#BankExit* divestment strategy, but Jane Fonda's visit set into motion a new chain of events. I got a call from Chris Kantrowitz that he and Alex Ebert had been in touch with Kevin Vilkin from the GivePower Foundation. They wanted to meet to discuss organizing a direct action with Jane Fonda, who was planning to publicly take her money out of the bank on her birthday only a few weeks away. Chase Iron Eyes and Alex joined us at the Feast of the Rock to open the discussion of what was to be a life-changing day, but we will get to that soon enough.

First, we had to contend with the veterans coming.

Veterans Respond

Wesley Clark, Jr. was the son of former presidential candidate General Wesley Clark. He had two thousand veterans prepared to storm Standing Rock, to act as human shields. The Standing Rock Sioux had been given an eviction notice that would become effective as of December 5th. People had been watching across the country. American flags were being flown upside-down by the water protectors as a sign of distress. This was a big organizing call-to-action nationwide.

Evan and I drove to meet Wesley in a hotel in Bismarck. Wes was trying to connect with Tulsi Gabbard and was having difficulty getting through, which is where I came in. Tulsi was one of Bernie's Avengers, though she never participated in the discussions.

I tried reaching out directly, but wasn't able to get through to her at first. As fortune would have it, Rania Batrice, Bernie's former director of surrogates, had taken a job with Tulsi as an advisor. She was the one I'd had to clear my speech with before the Bernie San Diego rally. It was a stroke of luck that I was able to get Rania on the phone just as she was boarding a plane overseas, as if by divine intervention. It has been my experience that, over time, when you do the right thing by showing up for others in solidarity, as we had for Bernie, mighty forces will come to your aid at just the right time.

Most days and nights, Evan Duke and I were inseparable. His status as a military veteran and long-time frontline activist earned him respect and access to the Native veterans' groups. Evan was the one who had brought me in to work with Wes's crew on the Veterans Respond mobilization. We often disagreed ideologically about the necessity for an inside-outside electoral strategy, but I knew I could trust him with my life. One time, I asked Dr. Cornel West what it took to build successful movements for justice and he said to me, "We need spiritual exemplars who are so committed to each other that we are willing to die for one another, as many of us were during the fight for civil rights."

Big actions like Standing Rock will often attract movement heavies and serious organizers. I met Lisa Fithian at camp as well, who was also a veteran of the WTO protests and an Occupier. I didn't know this at the time, but in the 1980s she had successfully occupied the CIA in protest of Washington's dirty wars in Central America.

Evan and I were constantly in the mix at camp or at the casino, where we sometimes went to escape the bitter cold of camp, have a bite to eat, use the internet, and charge our devices. When we got pulled over on the road back to Mandan (which was no accident), Duke had nothing but contempt for the cops. When the final raid came down on Oceti, he was one of the last people standing.

The Feast of the Rock buffet at Prairie Knights Casino was perhaps the worst buffet anywhere in America. After a few days it felt like a lead brick in your stomach. Still, after weeks in a tent in −15 degree cold it was worth it to get into a real structure with heat and running water, sheltered from the bitter winds.

There was a rare night of celebration when Jason Mraz, Bonnie Raitt and Jackson Browne came to the Prairie Knights casino for a free concert to boost morale.

The blizzards came. Great gales of wind and snow. If I stepped outside, within five minutes my beard would be frozen with a layer of ice. If you took your gloves off, within thirty seconds your hands would freeze over, like the sharp sting of thousands of needles at once. I heard that the cornea of one medic's eyeball froze from exposure.

The Prairie Knights casino became a refugee camp. Water protectors everywhere—all battleworn and rough around the edges. Tired, wet, and traumatized, but happy to be out of the cold and violence and to get a few creature comforts, like bad mozzarella sticks from the Feast of the Rock, or a charged cell phone and a little contact with the outside world. There were even Sami water protectors, indigenous people from Scandinavia, sprawled out in the hallways trying to stay warm.

There were meetings of members of the Tribal Council, the headsmen, the Native vets and the Akicita.

Because of #*BankExit*, working with Wesley and the Vets, and helping to coordinate Tulsi's visit, I was brought into some very serious meetings with the Tribal Council, the headsmen and Native veterans leadership. Leonard Crow Dog sometimes attended the secret meetings. He was a legend, a medicine man and a spiritual leader of the American Indian Movement.

In 1975, 185 FBI officers, federal marshals, and SWAT teams showed up at Crow Dog's looking for Leonard Peltier, who was a suspect in the murders of two FBI agents at the Pine Ridge Reservation. Two years prior, Crow Dog and Peltier had been veterans of the armed occupation of Wounded Knee by AIM, which had led to a seventy-one-day, armed bloody standoff with the Feds. Leonard Weinglass, the former lawyer for the Chicago 7, represented the AIM warriors in court after the standoff.

His younger brother, Steven Weinglass, was my best friend and one of the people with me the night the cops had raided Occupy LA. He used to tell me stories from all these cases, and suddenly this history was alive now, with Leonard sitting before me in an organizing meeting. Steven gave me a hand-drawn sign that Leonard kept on his desk for decades, that read, Illigitamus non carborundum, the Latinate of "don't let the bastards grind you down."

Back in '75, Jane Fonda, Marlon Brando, and Johnny Cash had used their celebrity to generate public sympathy for the AIM warriors facing charges.

They'd arrested Crow Dog and held him in a maximum-security unit at Leavenworth. He'd served two years in prison as a political prisoner before his sentence was commuted following an outpouring of public support.

"Standing on the hill where so many people were buried in a common grave, standing there in that cold darkness under the stars, I felt tears running down my face. I can't describe what I felt. I heard the voices of the long-dead ghost dancers crying out to us," said Crow Dog.

He sat in the meetings in his wheelchair, like a mountain. The lines in his face told the story of a lifetime of struggle, and the wisdom that comes with it.

Wes was a madman. He had a bit of a Messiah complex, but you couldn't argue with the results. What was astonishing was that the military unit he'd served in was the 7th Cavalry, the same regiment that had fought at the Battle of the Little Bighorn and committed the atrocities at Wounded Knee in 1890.

We walked through the casino one night with Sameera Khan, with his core team pointing out the people he thought were infiltrators. The last time I had seen Sameera, she was on top of a twelve-foot police barricade wearing a Democracy Spring headband and Gucci sunglasses, about to be hauled off by riot police at the Democratic Convention. Wes's people were ex-spooks. One of the guys that they pointed out was the same guy who had sought me out and befriended me on my very first day at camp.

Of all the leaders that emerged out of Oceti Sakowin, there were two matriarchs that to me were matchless. Phyllis Young was Standing Rock's spokeswoman, and tough as nails. She was an elder but had long, straight black hair. She wore large sunglasses just like you might have seen Robert Evans wearing in the 70s. Phyllis Young was the one who'd asked Clark if he could use his connections with veterans to raise awareness of the struggle at Oceti Sakowin.

I also got to spend time with a brilliant elder called Faith Spotted Eagle. One of the faithless electors of the electoral college, she'd actually cast her vote for her instead of Donald Trump following the 2016 election. I remember one night in a hotel room at the casino sitting and listening to her have an intersectional dialogue with Black Lives Matter activists about the complicated history between blacks and Natives. Many members of BLM showed up in solidarity. Activists had come from as far away as Palestine to join the struggle. They could certainly relate to having land usurped and having to face military police violence.

Tensions reached a fever pitch as the veterans' mobilization approached.

Seven McDonald, from Bernie's Arts and Culture team, had been hired by Wes to support with public relations for Veterans Respond, so she, Desiree and I got to work together in the comms yurt where Des had been stationed for almost six months.

It also occurred to me that it was entirely possible that more would respond to the big organizing call to action. Wes's Veterans Respond GoFundMe campaign had raised $1 million from over twenty-four thousand donors. The camp was already past capacity to provide critical services like sanitation for ten thousand water protectors in sub-zero temperatures.

I brought this to Phyllis.

"How many veterans are we expecting?"

"Two thousand," she replied stoically in her Lakota North Dakota accent.

"What if twice that many show up?"

A far-away look came over her. She blinked three times, took a deep breath and then walked away without saying a word to me. The tribe was barely prepared to handle the projected number that was coming. One of the benefits of meditation is that it quiets the chaos and noise of the mind, creating space for new ideas and intuition to arise.

The final number that showed up was close to four thousand. Phyllis was able to make arrangements with several large facilities in Fort Yates to accommodate a potential overflow surge in support. After Standing Rock, Phyllis would always call me "Numbers Man" because of this.

I was tasked with producing an orientation video, to support the vets with lifesaving guidelines and cultural protocols to keep them from creating unintended harm. Well-intentioned white people very often simply assume that they know what is best and will act with impunity regardless of the wishes of the frontline communities they parachute in to serve. The video was meant to let them know that there would be no violence permitted, and that "this isn't *Dances With Wolves*, and you are not Kevin Costner." This was a serious place, where every day the stakes were life and death and there was too much that could go wrong with four thousand potential cowboys coming, and the Standing Rock Sioux were fiercely committed to non-violence.

Tulsi eventually arrived as the cavalcade of cars showed up. The media had all but completely ignored the pipeline fight until they arrived. Then they all appeared, with trucks and camera crews in the blistering winds and snows.

There was a muster with Tulsi and the vets in Fort Yates—a great army of unarmed nonviolent warriors assembled and prepared to mobilize. There was a ton of press … finally. The press had been totally non-existent, despite some of the worst police brutality against American citizens since MLK's Selma to Montgomery marches in 1965.

Later that day, the veterans marched in the snow toward the charred remains of the truck and blockade on the bridge blocking the path to the drilling site. Almost four thousand. Tulsi came to the barracks of our Occupy/Veterans for Peace camp to hang out with the crew that night, huddled around the pot bellied stove.

Luckily the show of force and the potential PR nightmare that the mobilization presented was enough. Between the veterans and the national press, the next day we received word that Obama had finally commanded the Army Corps of Engineers to do their job to halt the permit for the pipeline one day before the eviction was to take place and a potential confrontation between militarized police and four thousand veterans was averted. He could have done this at any time and prevented some unspeakable acts of violence against unarmed civilians.

Chief Arvol Looking Horse gave a profound speech to the crowd that was tightly packed in around the main area near the sacred fire. Arvol was the keeper of the White Buffalo Calf sacred pipe; a lineage that had been unbroken for nineteen generations. According to legend, this was the first sacred pipe given by a mysterious divine being named White Buffalo Calf Medicine Woman, who gave the Lakota People seven sacred ceremonies.

This was a big deal.

After Chief Arvol finished his speech, the camp erupted into cheers and tears of joy. A chorus of "Lee-lee-lee-lee-lee-lee-lee-lee-lee" ululations rose from the crowd and shouts of "Water is life!"

I happened to be with Phyllis on Media Hill when we heard the news over the PA. We both broke down in tears and held each other, choking with emotion.

Shailene said some inspirational words with Malia by her side, remembering how only fifty people had gathered in DC in July when the youth runners arrived after traveling two thousand miles on foot to deliver the petition to President Obama. It was amazing to see the progression of how Shai and her Up To Us tour cohorts were continuing to live the values of their mission on the front-lines. Most had started as wide-eyed hippies, and were now battle-tested warriors. Phyllis announced that the next day, the Sioux would make peace with the US Military.

It was a beautiful moment. Many of us would echo Indige-nous poet and direct action trainer Mark Tilsen's phrase—"No celebrating until we are smoking cigars on the drill pad." But for the moment, it was a win we all needed. Badly.

Of all of the events that transpired at Standing Rock, perhaps the most powerful was the Forgiveness Ceremony. It was the day after we'd expected the militarized police to descend on the camp to evict the thousands of inhabitants of Oceti Sakowin. Wesley gathered a few hundred vets in the theater of the casino. They prostrated themselves before Leonard Crow Dog sitting in his wheelchair. Wes was clad in full 7th Cavalry regalia. He even had the traditional black cowboy hat with gold tassels and crossed swords insignia.

On bended knee, he made this heartfelt plea to Leonard and some of the other elders:

"Many of us, me particularly, are from the units that have hurt you over the many years. We came. We fought you. We took your land. We signed treaties that we broke. We stole minerals from your sacred hills. We blasted the faces of our presidents onto your sacred moun-tain. Then we took still more land and then we took your children and then we tried to eliminate your language that God gave you, and the Creator gave you. We didn't respect you, we polluted your Earth, we've hurt you in so many ways but we've come to say that we are sorry. We are at your service and we beg for your forgiveness."

As Wesley bent in supplication, Leonard Crow Dog placed his hand on his head in absolution. Humility and forgiveness is the way of the Lakota.

"We do not own the land, the land owns us," said Crow Dog, offering forgiveness.

What are the odds that a ranking officer of the 7th Cavalry, the same regiment that fought the Battle of the Little Bighorn and perpetrated the massacre at Wounded Knee, would beg the forgiveness of the spiritual leader of the American Indian Movement, who was also a survivor of the siege of Wounded Knee in '73?

You couldn't make this up if you tried!

The two matriarchs, Phyllis and Faith Spotted Eagle, gave rousing speeches recognizing the PTSD of the veterans and the water protectors, and the healing that was taking place. Ceremonial sage smoke was given to the veterans with an eagle's wing. Natives and veterans shook hands in friendship. The veterans were all given an eagle feather as part of a sacred ceremony.

It is important to remember that this is only one person's story. There were over ten thousand water protectors who stood bravely, and each one has their own story. There are countless peaceful warriors whose contributions deserve to be mentioned. I could only mention a few here, with feeble words to attempt to recount their sacrifice and courage, and I no doubt have failed to convey what it was truly like.

Jane Fonda's #BankExit

There are few names that immediately evoke images of political resistance more than Jane Fonda's. She has spent most of her career using her celebrity status to uplift the voices and causes of those who have been persecuted by the corporate state and the war machine.

On December 10, 2016, the phone rang. The voice on the other end was unmistakable, from classic films I had grown up with like *Barbarella* and *9 to 5*. Steven Weinglass had also told me stories of Jane being a friend and supporter of Abbie Hoffman and the Chicago 7.

Jane told me it was her birthday the following week and she wanted to take her money out of Wells Fargo. She asked me if I could help her do it in a way that would bring attention to what was happening at Standing Rock.

Luckily, I was anticipating the call. Chris Kantrowitz had been the one to connect the dots at camp. He introduced me to Kevin Vilkin, from the GivePower Foundation, who was working with Jane on this. GivePower was the non-profit arm of SolarCity, a subsidiary of Tesla. They went on to work with the tribe to develop their first utility-scale solar project, a 300KW solar farm in Cannonball, ND, which would provide power and funds to the tribal community.

I had barely had a week back from Standing Rock. My nerves were absolutely shot and I was already exhausted, but this was too important not to dig deep for, despite not having had a moment to process the trauma.

Jane invited her friends Lily Tomlin, Catherine Keener, Elliot Page, and civil rights icon Dolores Huerta to participate. Cesar Chavez is often given all of the credit for the United Farm Workers success, but Dolores was really the engine behind those campaigns and was largely written out of history, like so many great women. Obama even got his "Yes we can!" slogan from her "Si se puede!" battle cry.

Our first call was to local Lakota activist George Funmaker from Red Earth Defense. I had originally gotten the idea for *#BankExit* from his speech, so Brother George deserved the honor of leading the action. For non-native accomplices, it's important to decenter as much as possible by deferring to the native organizers when participating in Indigenous-led actions. I also called Lydia Ponce to be the point person for AIM SoCal. She brought in the local Tongva tribal elder, Gloria Arellanes.

The plan was to get George and three other Indigenous singers with a large ceremonial drum into the bank to sing Lakota prayers for the water. Jane would follow and read a letter addressed to the CEO of Wells Fargo listing all of the grievances over the Dakota Access Pipeline and other fossil fuel catastrophes. We went over the game plan several times on organizing calls. Jane was very impressive—clear, direct, and concise. She gave me the latitude to handle the ops, outline the strategy and logistics, and asked good questions. I sent her the talking points for the letter and the media. Once we had the basics worked out, it was time to expand the circle.

I reached out to Bernie's Avengers' Mikki Willis, to capture footage, and Taylor Gill and Cary Harrison to cover the event. I contacted Dawna Shuman to wrangle the press. I put the word out to other Bernie supporters who had been supporting Standing Rock. Most people were understandably pretty burnt out after a very tough year, so it was surprisingly difficult to get enough support to pull off the caper. We needed bodies and press for this action to have the desired impact, and we had no time.

I put together a Signal (an encrypted instant message app) chat thread with everyone I thought I could trust that had the capacity and skill sets to help. Organizing an event or an action is like moving a piano. It can't be done alone, and the more capable people with their hands on it, the better. After an agonizing two days of not having enough support, I had to try something new. I had thought initially that the action was high-profile enough to attract the help we needed, and based on my previous successes, that people would be more inclined to get involved.

They were not, and the piano was way too big to move on my own.

I remembered David Braun's impassioned plea to the Clinton delegates at the platform committee. He spoke from his heart, and got vulnerable with the entire committee about the need for us to listen to nature, that it was telling us we were on the way to ending our civilization.

Vulnerability? I figured it was worth a try.

In our culture, or at least the culture I grew up in, men are not supposed to be vulnerable. We are not supposed to need help. We are supposed to suffer quietly and stoically. There is a reason that suicide rates are much higher for men than for women.

I was at a point where I didn't have much choice.

Either I got vulnerable and asked for help, or the action would fall flat. Trump was president now, so the reality was that the easement for the pipeline would be granted, and divestment was the only real weapon left. There was also the business of our industrial nation's addiction to fossil fuels, and the coming climate apocalypse. It was dubious whether or not there would be an opportunity in the near future to make a statement this high-profile.

Jack Eidt and SoCal 350.org answered the call. They put the word out to their list about the action and were able to wrangle marshalls for the march, and much-needed volunteers.

Lydia, Dawna, and I went to the Hollywood branch of Wells Fargo on Vine St. to do some reconnaissance. We looked for locations to do press, checked their security detail, and checked points of entry. We had a rallying point where people would gather and march to the bank. Kevin Vilkin would fly in and bring

Tokata Iron Eyes to speak. Bernie Avenger Alex Ebert would fly in as well. Emiliano Meno Martinez with AIM SoCal would provide sound.

Plan A was to have the marchers rally at Hollywood and Vine, and march a few blocks down to the Wells Fargo. We would have a presser in the W Hotel behind the bank, or somewhere outside in the courtyard next to Trader Joe's, and then meet everyone marching down Vine outside the bank. We would station one or more of our people inside the bank. If security tried to block the door to keep us out, we could bum rush the door when our people were escorted out, or possibly enter through the back door leading to the garage.

If not, then Plan B.

It's always good to have a back up plan. (And two back up plans are better than one!)

George, Dawna, Mikki, Chris Kantrowitz, Frances, Lily Tomlin, and Jane met in the lobby of the W Hotel in Hollywood. Dawna was able to convince the owner of Bubbles Dry Cleaners behind Trader Joe's to let us use his establishment for the press conference. At first he was definitely not on board, but Dawna was relentlessly persuasive. It was a frenzy. Bubbles was packed with press and photographers. We were interviewed by CNN, *People* magazine, local news, and several other outlets. We sang Happy Birthday to Jane in front of the media and presented her with a cake that had an image of her as Barbarella on it, designed by Kii Arens to say "Bankerella." Brett Banditelli live streamed all of the events for the People for Bernie audience of over 1.5 million people.

When I got word the marchers had arrived, we emerged and headed towards the bank with purpose. Gray Wolf, the director of AIM SoCal, led the charge side by side with Jane, Frances, Lily, and Catherine, brandishing the American Indian Movement flag.

Grandmother Gloria, the Tongva elder from AIM SoCal, was inside the bank. When five hundred people arrived outside the street entrance, security shut down the entire bank with Gloria inside. They would not let Jane or anyone else in. It was a terrible affront to the Indigenous elder, but we seized the opportunity to inform the press and the crowd that they wouldn't let Jane in to read her letter, or let Gloria out.

Jane read her letter to the press. Dolores Huerta spoke powerfully as the people and press crowded around us. Lydia from AIM SoCal also spoke. Lydia was later centered on the cover of *Time* magazine, along with the local Poor People's Campaign organizer, Pastor Eddie Anderson.

It was predictable that we wouldn't get into the bank. That was fine. The bank shutting us out—and Gloria in—was great optics for us. It drove home the fact that Wells Fargo wasn't interested in listening to the needs and wants of the people—especially Indigenous people. They wouldn't even listen to some of their wealthiest and most high-profile clients when it came to their fossil fuel investments.

After a few speeches, it was on to Plan B. We left Wells Fargo and made our way towards Sunset, to the Chase branch, which was also a much better area to hold our rally. All of our publicity had targeted Wells Fargo. They had been ready for us. Chase, however, had no idea we were coming. Chris Kantrowitz and George Funmaker were the only ones that knew ahead of time. Chris was going to divest a considerable sum of money from Chase as a surprise addition to the happenings of the day. George and I agreed that the prime directive, beyond Jane reading her letter, was to get the drum and singers into a bank at all costs. His intention was very clear—he was getting inside a bank with the drum—one way or another.

Just as the Los Angeles water protectors rounded the corner with their banners, George and the singers entered the bank carrying and beating the big sacred drum, chanting as they walked together. The door was unguarded.

Cheyenne Phoenix, a young Native activist, followed with them wearing her brightly colored ceremonial clothes, which included a shawl with long tassels that looked like wings. As she spun around performing traditional fancy dancing, her arms spread wide, the bright greens, pinks, and blues whirled in prayer. Chase Bank even had a large mural of an Indigenous man wearing a ceremonial war bonnet of eagle feathers in the background as the singers chanted loudly and the dancer danced. The policeman on duty stood in shock with his palms turned up in disbelief at the scene inside the bank. George and his crew were victorious. Alex Ebert and The Young Turks camera crew followed them, livestreaming the display while the crowd gathered outside.

Meno quickly set up the sound system on the steps of the Chase bank. Tokata Iron Eyes made a rousing speech to the crowd assembled below. There were a number of speeches that followed, from Gray Wolf and local Indigenous organizers, Jack Eidt, and the 350.org activists. Michael Mowgli Vincze played one of his inspiring songs with an acoustic guitar that we had played together at the Bernie Rally in San Diego. The owner of Bubbles Dry Cleaners even ordered ten large pizzas and had them delivered to us. It didn't take long for Chase Bank to follow Wells Fargo's example and lock its doors to the public for the rest of the day. Two banks shut down is better than one.

Now for Plan C.

We had discussed moving the crowd into the highly trafficked intersection of Sunset and Vine and doing a round dance.

Here is Pow-wow.org's description of the history and significance of this dance:

Be The Revolution

"The Round Dance was in earlier times known as The Dance of the Slain. Women were the main performers of this dance, which allowed them to show their pride and mourning at the same time. Because the Round Dance is a circular chain dance, it is also referred to as a circle dance because the dancers are connected in a circular chain. Various connections are possible; among these are hand-to-hand, hands-on-shoulders, and paired couples. Today, the Round Dance has evolved into a dance of friendship and is performed by all ages and is easily taught to tourists. Everyone is encouraged to dance by forming a circle and dancing in a clockwise [direction]. Dance outfits are not necessary."

Just as the energy of the rally was starting to wane, George and I locked hands and began walking toward the intersection. One by one, the members of the crowd followed. Jane, Lily, the members of AIM SoCal, Frances, the singers, and everyone else began moving into the street in a long chain, bouncing up and down in a rhythm, not unlike the four-beat gait of a horse's trot, until we'd closed the circle. Jane joined the round dance even though she had a bad hip and was in a lot of pain. She is a truly remarkable woman. We all went out to celebrate the success of the action and her birthday dinner.

We'd badly needed a win. I've learned that in the rough and tumble world of organizing, I've not been as connected to the feelings of others at times as I should have been. My number one intention has always been to have the team succeed at what we had set out to accomplish, and to have our message spread far and wide. I've learned since then that it's equally important to be extra aware of how we speak to others, and how they're receiving what's being communicated. The reason I've put results as the number one priority is because the work of political revolutionaries can be agonizing at times! At the time, even though the

Army Corps of Engineers had temporarily halted construction on the pipeline, we knew that with Trump in the White House it was only a matter of time before the Black Snake would cross the river.

Standing Rock is Everywhere

Despite tens of thousands of water protectors putting their bodies on the line with the Standing Rock Sioux Tribe to stop the Dakota Access Pipeline, and millions supporting them in solidarity, Donald Trump pushed through the project as one of his first executive orders on his second day in office as president. This endangered over 18 million people, and would create pollution equivalent to millions of new cars on the road. Trump is personally invested in this project, which is made possible by lines of credit from financial institutions like Wells Fargo, Bank of America, Chase, and others.

Oceti Sakowin was eventually raided on February 22, 2017. I watched Evan Duke and other comrades being arrested via livestream as the cops descended upon the camp. The water protectors burned all the structures in ceremony just prior to the eviction. It was with a heavy heart that we watched the fires burn against the stark North Dakota sky.

In March of 2017 we staged another action, taking over the stage at a Los Angeles Fashion Week runway event with a giant Divest banner. Bernie Avenger Connor Paolo and Cheyenne Phoenix gave impassioned speeches as we marched before an unsuspecting crowd who gave us a standing ovation.

Water protectors Red Fawn (who was set up by her FBI informant boyfriend) and Rattler were brought up on bullshit charges, convicted, and remained political prisoners for years. Other akicita like Michael Giron (aka Little Feather), Brennon Nastacio (aka Bravo), Jimmy White (aka Angry Bird) and Dion Ortiz all faced federal prison time for the crime of standing up to an oil company and corrupt government.

But they would not let the corporate state kill their warrior spirit.

"I'll include Judge Hovland in my prayers," Rattler said. "I already do. We all live on this Earth together. They segregate us because we have a different color skin, but we're all red underneath. I'll also be praying for the people at other pipeline struggles: the Mountain Valley Pipeline in West Virginia, Bayou Bridge in Louisiana, Line 3 in northern Minnesota, KXL in Montana and South Dakota, and those standing in opposition to mining the Black Hills. They may lock me up but thousands will take my place," he said.

"I am praying that they have the strength to keep up the fight and to get more people out there," he says. "Standing Rock was a training ground. It was started by children, by the youth. Those are the generations that we're thinking about. What are we going to leave them—birds, animals, rivers? What kind of legacy do you want to leave your children? For rich people, it's a big bank account. For me it's Mni Wiconi—water is life."

After the initial actions of *#BankExit*, the divestment movement continued to grow and evolve with groups like Mazaska Talks in Seattle, who won fights for cities to pull billions of tax dollars out of the banks funding pipelines and the climate crisis. The climate movement galvanized the strategy with an international campaign called *Stop The Money Pipeline*, railing against the same toxic financial institutions we fought during Occupy Wall Street. They targeted trillions of dollars managed by investment banks like JP Morgan Chase, university endowment funds, and pensions.

According to the S.T.M.P. website, "by 2022, more than *$40 trillion* worth of investment capital had committed to some form of divestment from the fossil fuel industry" due to the ongoing collective efforts of committed activists.

Standing Rock water protectors would continue to stand with other frontline communities and elevate important issues like MMIW, or "missing and murdered Indigenous women." This crisis was elevated by screenwriter Taylor Sheridan with his critically acclaimed film *Wind River*, which dramatized the issue of fossil fuel worker "man camps," where transient oil laborers who are isolated for months at a time at extraction sites rape and murder Native women.

Also tragically, many water protectors suffered physical, mental and emotional issues following the stand at Oceti. Greg Gallup, my friend who convinced me to come to camp when the buffalo ran, died in 2019. He ended his own life by drinking a bottle of bleach after a drug relapse. He live streamed his final hours. I have had many friends perish, but this one hit me hard. It was a powerful reminder of how important it is to do the inner work and deal with our traumas.

Myron Dewey was also tragically killed in a car accident on September 26, 2021. He had co-directed a beautiful film with Josh Fox in 2017 called *Awake, A Dream from Standing Rock*. He and Greg left behind enduring legacies. Indigenous people have continued to stand against other pipelines, creating frontline resistance camps against Line 3, Bayou Bridge and other fossil fuel projects.

Many of us struggled after 2016. Struggle and trauma can also be a doorway to liberation. Those red road Native ceremonies put me back together after all the trauma. I attended regular sweat lodges with George Funmaker and his father John, and with Wolf and Lisa Wahpepah. Those warm glowing red stones that they call "grandfathers" brought healing medicine and visions. I would not have written this book without them, nor had the strength to go on. I am forever grateful for all who have kept those ceremonies alive, in spite of it being a federal crime to practice them until the 1978 American Indian Religious Freedom Act was passed, and to all of those who continued to fight for the land, the water, and the people.

This ended the first chapter in the saga of our burgeoning movement. But the seeds planted during Occupy Wall Street, Ferguson and the Bernie Sanders Campaign would continue to sprout. The seedlings continued to grow, cracking through the concrete sidewalks of the corporate state, and inspiring the next generation of activists who would continue the struggle.

Chapter 9

Divest LA: Farewells Fargo

You are an Acceptable Level of Threat and if
You Weren't You Would Know It.
-Banksy

For millions of Americans, November 8, 2016 was a day that will forever remain emblazoned in the halls of infamy. There was a creeping horror that set in as the final state vote tallies were displayed on screens across the country. Mouths gaped, unable to choose between expressions of horror and disbelief.

It had been a foregone conclusion that Hillary would win, and in doing so break the glass ceiling as the first woman POTUS. Instead, America had elected a billionaire celebrity reality television star who had zero experience in governance and who had once been featured on WWE Wrestling.

When the result was made official, mobilizations erupted in every major city in America.

Downtown Los Angeles quickly descended into chaos. I stood on an offramp of the 101 Freeway as thousands of protesters formed a blockade, illuminated by the bright magenta glow of road flares as police armed with shotguns attempted to contain the uprising. This was a paradigm change unlike anything we had seen in US electoral politics.

The cops lost control of the area near City Hall. I witnessed a black SWAT vehicle with about twenty riot police inside fleeing the scene, while demonstrators stood on top of a luxury car that was abandoned in the middle of the street with its doors wide open. It looked like a scene out of *Grand Theft Auto*. Sound systems blasted the YG & Nipsey Hussle track *"FDT (Fuck Donald Trump)"* at maximum decibels.

Liberals went into a full-scale meltdown. The neoliberal corporate media went into overdrive, blaming Russia, third-party voters, Bernie supporters, and even Susan Sarandon. These hacks seemed to conveniently forget that they were the ones who had catapulted Trump into dominating the national spotlight, giving him billions of dollars in free publicity.

Ride-or-die Democrats lost their minds—shuttling back and forth through the five stages of grief—but mostly between anger and denial. They were manically obsessed over the possibility of impeachment, even though there was never a scenario where the Republicans would vote to convict and remove Forty-Five from office.

But for a group of mostly millennials meeting in a coffee shop in Los Angeles, Trump's election was both a wake-up call and an opportunity to start a revolution, to challenge the old financial system and usher in a new one. A system that was of, by and for the people.

The Divestment Revolution Continues

Hashtag BankExit certainly was not the first effort to promote divestment from fossil fuels, but no previous campaign had been able to generate so many impressions and so much energy so quickly. It was a big organizing call to action. When we'd launched the #BankExit campaign I could never have anticipated how the divestment movement would continue to escalate and evolve. The campaign solidified, targeting bank branches to draw the connection between capital and fossil fuels as a tactic.

The difference between a movement and a simple campaign is that the momentum continues beyond those that have ignited the spark. For it to be considered a movement, there must be a shared sense of ownership that it is up to everyone, if the vision of change is to be realized. A movement is like a wave that may begin as a ripple and end as a tsunami that breaks with such force that it alters the landscape forever.

After Jane Fonda's *#BankExit* birthday divestment action, I stepped back for the better part of six months to recover from exhaustion and to get the heat off. Little did I know that, in a coffee shop in Los Angeles in February 2017, a small group of citizens with no prior experience in activism were planning to pick up the torch and burn down the hold that the big banks had over our city's tax dollars.

Trinity Tran, Phoenix Goodman and Ben Hauck were the central organizers of one of my all-time favorite affinity groups, called Divest LA. In the beginning they had simply been a group of people who were inspired by Occupy Wall Street, Bernie Sanders and Standing Rock. They didn't have any previous organizing experience, and had first started meeting in 2017 in coffee shops as Revolution LA, discussing how they might make a difference. The election of Donald Trump was a wake up call for millions of Americans from all walks of life.

Adam Elfers from the Up To Us tour, Caleb Buchbinder, and I had merged the *#BankExit* campaign and DefundDAPL efforts, and divestment actions were getting visibility nationwide. Indigenous activists would enter a bank and set up a full-sized teepee. It was amazing to watch. I'd started *#BankExit* with only the consumer strategy in mind, to target individual customers.

An Indigenous activist in Seattle named Matt Remle, with a group called Mazaska (Money) Talks, took the movement to a whole new level by forming a coalition to lobby his city council to divest from Wells Fargo. That meant billions of dollars of the city's tax funds. All at once.

Mazaska enlisted the support of Kshama Sawant, a former Occupy organizer who was the first socialist to be elected to Seattle's City Council. When the motion passed, Sawant made this statement:

"As far as I know, Seattle is the first city to have divested from Wells Fargo. The example that we have set today can be a beacon of hope to activists all around the country, looking to change the economic calculus of corporations who think that investing in the Dakota Access Pipeline will be good for their bottom line.

"We're making it bad for their bottom line.

"The real power of this ordinance is that it can be used as a tool by movements to put real financial pressure on Big Business by first putting pressure on politicians. And I really agree with those of you who said we need to use this momentum not only against the pipeline—put that pipeline to rest once and for all, and will be critical in our fight against climate change, and fight for indigenous rights—but we should also use this to build our fight for Seattle's rights to a public bank.

"Some of you have personally traveled to Standing Rock to join the protests. Others have demonstrated solidarity here, through our NoDAPL Seattle movement, and together we are building the power of regular people to fight to take our world back from Trump, the billionaires, and the oil lobby."

The Seattle divestment was like Roger Bannister running the four-minute mile in 1954. In recorded history no one had ever accomplished the feat, but once the barrier was crossed, fourteen others followed in the next ten years. Since then, the four-minute barrier has been broken by over fourteen hundred athletes. The same is true for visionary ideas; like the four-minute mile, people just need to release the mental barriers they have allowed to be built against them. One person or group, standing out on the skinny branches on the bold frontier of change, can give permission to everyone else to do the thing they thought couldn't be done.

Soon after the Seattle resolution passed, Revolution LA started their Divest LA campaign. I eventually joined this group in the final stretch of their campaign to pressure the Los Angeles City Hall to divest billions of dollars and close their accounts with Wells Fargo.

During a celebration party after the direct actions and public announcement of victory, we sat down to recall what had transpired over the previous nine months.

Many people want to get involved in activism but don't know where to begin. Here we shall examine some best practices, using Divest LA as a case study in good organizing.

Beating Wells Fargo

Divest LA knew that Trump's presidency would make change at the federal level nearly impossible, as the regime had control of both the House and Senate, but that some of the most important policy changes could happen on a local level.

According to Trinity, "We were inspired by the Occupy movement in 2011 and to bring the discourse of the 99 versus the 1 Percent to the common masses. What we wanted to do was figure out a way to tackle some of the problems that arose out of the Occupy movement. We felt that in order to attack these banks, a logical approach would be divestment. As opposed to investing, where you put money into an institution, with divestment you take money out. So we are leveraging our power to dismantle these financial corporations."

Trinity was one of the most effective natural organizers I have ever met. Even with no prior experience, she was like a heat-seeking missile. She possessed such an unwavering determination that one got the sense that there would be nothing that would stop her from achieving whatever she set her mind to.

Phoenix, her partner at the time, was the most cerebral of the crew. He was well read, and versed in the history of revolutionary movements. His face would light up as he spoke for hours about his theories concerning life, the universe and everything.

Prior to this campaign, Goodman said, "We were not professional organizers nor high-level activists. We were simply passionate individuals coming together from humble beginnings, literally meeting in coffee shops, and doing screenings in church basements."

The church where they held their community gatherings in Koreatown had been used during World War II to shelter Japanese Americans from the internment campaigns, like the Underground Railroad or those who hid Jews from the Nazis.

Phoenix also introduced the group to the idea of public banking, which would become the next stage in Divest LA's efforts, but we will come to that eventually.

Inspired by Seattle and Standing Rock

"For us," Trinity recalled, "we had heard rumblings of divestment coming up, but what we started was primarily inspired by what Kshama Sawant did in Seattle. She worked with grassroots activists on the ground as well as Indigenous leaders that came out of Standing Rock."

"It was so inspiring to see activism bridge that path between just protesting on the periphery of city government and entering through its corridors. Working with legislation and working with policy. Understanding the system to create real systemic change."

Phoenix shared in an interview that they were originally considering pushing for a more consumer-based divestment strategy, like #*BankExit*, but that "the penny dropped when Kshama Sawant did what she did. We realized you could leverage enormous power through the government, because with the stroke of a pen billions of dollars could be moved."

Along with Trinity and Phoenix, there was Ben Hauck, who was the most soft-spoken central organizer of the group, but he was steady as a rock. Ben did not have a rough edge on him. He was in his 30s, but worked as an executive in a telescope company. He usually wore a button-down short-sleeved shirt, dark glasses, a baseball cap and close-cropped facial hair that hugged his jaw line, more than a scruffy five o'clock shadow but not quite a full beard. The intelligence shone through his eyes, which belied his simple disposition, indicating he was much brighter than his humble nature let on. He could always be counted on to be a sympathetic and patient ear, especially when I would get frustrated with Trinity, who sometimes struggled to strike a balance between getting results and being mindful of the needs and feelings of others.

Ben was a Bernie supporter who, like many of us, had traveled to Oceti Sakowin to experience a profound awakening. Like Ben, some of our members had returned from Standing Rock in 2016 and realized that they needed to find a way to take effective action on a local level.

Madeline Merritt, Victor Casas, Trew Love, OG Occupy LA organizer Carlos Marroquin and local Indigenous organizer Irene Montantes were also dedicated members of Divest LA. With every new fight our movement family grows, with the old heads and young bloods coming together to meet the next moment.

"When you look at the fossil fuel industry and building out fossil fuel infrastructure, it requires a huge amount of capital. And when the banks are looking at risk and reward for building fossil fuel infrastructure, anything we can do to increase the level of risk or decrease the level of reward can have a severe impact on the fossil fuel industry's ability to build out this infrastructure. There was a lot of discussion about divestment at Standing Rock," said Ben, recalling his inspiration for joining the Divest LA efforts.

Build Your Team

In the following sections we will examine the strategies, tactics, and organizing fundamentals that Divest LA employed in the quest to transform our broken financial system. This case study is primarily focused on divestment, but the principles can be applied to mobilizing policy change around any issue.

It can be overwhelming thinking about how to make a difference. There are so many problems to face in our society. How do you get started?

Everyone who has ever changed the world had to start somewhere. Everyone.

The easiest thing to do is to think of all the issues that stress you out and search the internet for the organizations near you that are addressing those issues.

Another option is to start an affinity group, like Divest LA did.

The upside of starting an affinity group is that it's easy—unless you are a terrible person and no one likes you.

Even if you have no friends, you can still create an affinity group! For whatever idea you have, there are people on the internet that will get behind it. All you have to do is put it out there. Plus, when you tell them that you are starting an affinity group, you can feel cool—because they probably won't know what you are talking about, but it will sound impressive.

First things first, though: it's probably a good idea if you learn what an affinity group is. So here goes.

Affinity Groups in Social Movements

The affinity group organizing strategy came out of the Spanish Revolution, when anarchists referred to their cohorts as "grupos de afinidades."

Technically an affinity group is any collection of individuals who share an affinity for each other, or a common cause. Typically, the minimum number of people required to form an affinity group is four.

One of the advantages of affinity groups is their size: they don't involve any of the red tape or weighted-down bureaucracy that can make nonprofits so slow and hidebound. They are nimble, easy to form, and relatively easy to organize.

Divest LA's organizing philosophy was to recruit the right people for the right positions, and to get to know all of the skillsets of those who showed up to volunteer.

They had volunteers phonebanking to demonstrate public support, but discovered quickly that this alone wasn't going to be enough.

There were four main strategic areas the campaign was broken down into—Policy, Protest, Partnerships, and Community Outreach.

From the very outset, their theory of change was based on an inside-outside strategy that focused on writing and lobbying City Council for policy change, and on direct action to put the heat on elected officials. They also incorporated relational organizing to build a coalition with influential leaders, and to create deep roots in the community.

At the end of the day it's about building power. Wells Fargo might have had hundreds of billions of dollars, an army of consultants and lobbyists, and hundreds of thousands of employees, but with the right strategy and execution, a small group of committed citizens can defeat Goliath. Ultimately the 99 Percent is the real Goliath when we build big broad coalitions. Even though the affinity group was unknown in city politics when they first started out in 2017 they were able to build support by bringing on board over ten neighborhood councils.

In the beginning, as soon as they represented a coalition of all of those powerful groups, the city council members listened to them. So building up those initial partnerships and coalitions was critical to their success.

Neighborhood councils represent on average forty thousand Angelenos, and they created Community Impact Statements. This is also a great strategy when running for office. Even though the group was new and unknown, having the support of so many constituents from each of the councilpersons' districts meant that they were taken seriously right away.

They power mapped the members of the council. Power mapping is a dynamic tool to identify allies and opposition, to decide who to approach to enroll in the cause and who is most likely to require public pressure—in other words, who gets the carrot and who needs the stick. It's also worth noting that the stick should only be used as a last resort, and if it is used it should be effective.

In the beginning, as soon as we represented a coalition of all of those powerful groups, the city council members listened to us, and they listened to us right away. Building up that initial partnership and coalition was absolutely critical to our early success.

Divest LA filled the council chambers with supporters holding signs on days when the issue was being discussed. These supporters also made public comments to demonstrate massive public pressure to all the council members who were reviewing the case.

In the general council chambers they had between fifty and sixty people nearly every week for three to four months. In the budget and finance committee they packed the room to capacity—a hundred people.

That points to how important it is to do your homework: find other organizations that already are out there doing something that's similar to what you are doing, so that you can network, reach out to them, send an email to the organizers and tell them what you want—and then tell them that you want a coalition to form between you, so you can get everyone on board.

Another superpower of the Divest LA crew was due diligence. So often activist groups are content with prefigurative actions that don't have any real impact on the machine they are raging against. To be fair, most people are barely surviving late-stage capitalism, but realizing the advanced, egalitarian and just society we want to live in is outside of our comfort zone. Divest LA realized that one of the challenges of pushing the City of Los Angeles to divest from Wells Fargo was that the tax dollars collected totaled over $8 billion and were held in over eight hundred accounts.

This was a problem, because only the five biggest banks could handle that much business. So even if the city withdrew all of the funds from Wells Fargo, the money would just go to another giant parasitic bank investing our tax dollars in destructive industries.

Trinity, Ben, Phoenix and the rest of the crew spent months strategizing, mobilizing community members, and lobbying elected officials. They read through thousands of pages of banking contracts and motions.

Trinity said, "An important aspect to consider from a practical standpoint is that people have different strengths. Some people may have knowledge that the core team might not. Recruiting the right people for the right thing is really important. Somebody that's really good at organizing protests might not have a good grasp of how to read through motions or banking contracts.

"The people that can read through those might not be good at organizing protests. So having those different legs is important. Also, through the networking aspect of things, especially through the team building, as we recruited, some people came on that had already had history in City Hall. None of us did. They provided excellent consulting, helping to navigate the process."

According to Trinity, the first step is to have someone contact the city treasurer's office, the Office of Finance. If you are going to divest, you need to know at least what you are divesting from and what the numbers are.

They also discovered that making assumptions was a liability. The council members themselves didn't know much about the city's finances. It turns out that Los Angeles paid $100 million a year in fees alone for Wells Fargo to manage the city's money.

Make Your Presence Known, but Know When to Scale Back

Divest LA made noise from the very start. They burst onto the City Hall scene with a vengeance. Some council members thought that they were aggressive, because in addition to creating public pressure in televised sessions, they were also organizing regular phonebanking.

Meanwhile, they made sure to send information about their campaign to all the council offices. The point is not to just make noise, but to start a dialogue about real policies.

Getting to Know Your Council

Having discovered that phonebanking alone without any kind of direct relationships with council members produced little if any results, they found that networking with city officials was critical to success. It is important to realize that some of them do have good intentions and care about good governance. The key is to create a first name basis, either with the council members or their staff, because when they know you by name, they'll take your calls.

They knew that in order to get this motion passed and supported, they'd have to get the legislative coordinator for each council member, so the initial first step was alliance building. In this process, maintaining a professional tone is advantageous. Ultimately, access is crucial to developing an effective inside-outside strategy.

Be Authentic, Sincere and Transparent

They were going head-to-head with Wells Fargo, who stood to lose $8 billion in business.

It was no secret to any of the council members that one side came from real passion and the other side was basically just paid to be there and lobby. As cynical as some people are about their elected officials, these people are human beings and some of them are very sincere.

One of the lessons they learned was, when approaching elected officials, it is more effective to demonstrate a basic level of respect and professionalism, even if you don't think they deserve it. This is where power mapping can be particularly useful, so that you know which officials are open to being allies or who will be in active opposition.

If you encounter something you don't know, don't pretend that you do. As an alternative to saying "I don't know," you can tell them, "I don't have that information yet, but we will get back to you on that."

It is better to lead with the carrot than use the stick. Many times, groups who embody prefiguratism are satisfied with performative actions that shout at stakeholders, as opposed to progressing with any sort of strategy in mind that will make lasting change. It is better to try to leverage those in power into giving you what you want based on the number of constituents you can mobilize, rather than to make an enemy that does not take you seriously. It is also important to carry a metaphorical stick, so that you can back up your words with a credible threat of disruption, or perhaps a primary challenge.

If you do choose to engage in direct actions, here are a few tips to consider and questions to ask yourselves:

1. Who is the target?
2. Do they have the power to affect the outcome you are fighting for?
3. Do you know specifically the outcome you hope to create in terms of policy?
4. How will your action pressure the stakeholders to act, or refrain from acting?
5. What kind of press and optics will the action generate?
6. What is your message and who will deliver it?
7. How will your message be received? Are you speaking in jargon that only preaches to the choir, or will the optics of your action change the hearts and minds of the larger community and society?

8. Will it inspire others or make them cringe? Test-market your idea to people outside of your group to get their reactions, and spend a good amount of time brainstorming with your most creative and media-savvy comrades. Don't be afraid to use a tactic from the past. When we threw the money at Clinton's motorcade, that tactic had been used before by Abbie Hoffman in the 1960s and by activists targeting FIFA officials.

Understanding the Process

Understanding the legislative process is crucial to achieving results. With respect to Los Angeles, in order for the divestment to occur:

1. A motion had to be introduced, which means you have to have a champion within the city council to introduce it.
2. Ideally, you will have multiple co-authors on the motion.
3. Get the support of additional council members who will second the motion, which will demonstrate that you have a lot of support behind that initial motion.
4. The motion has to go to a committee. In this instance, it was the Budget and Finance Committee.
5. It has to pass there, so you have to rally your troops to get it through that committee.
6. Then it goes to a full city council for a vote.

Find a Champion

It took a couple of months for Divest LA to find sponsors and really build those relationships. (This will take time, so be patient and diligent.) They were surprised to discover that some of our allies on the council were in favor of divestment from Wells Fargo and truly wanted to work with us.

They were extremely encouraged that we were approaching them in this fashion to get this done. If they were to garner the support of the full council, it would be critical to know who was on the council, and who was on the committee so that they could encourage them to vote yes on the motion.

At the end of the day, though, it is about *people power*. Elected Republicans fear the NRA because they have four million committed members who can donate and be mobilized. In truth, Republicans and most elected Democrats don't really believe in anything except keeping their seats. It's better when you can influence officials because of the value you can bring to the table in moving votes, dollars and public support, but real power also means being able to bring fear to their cold hearts. It's important to remember, though, that this is the last measure after all other options have been exhausted. If an elected official is a potential ally, don't lead with the stick. Some activists will go in guns blazing, calling people out, badgering staff. This is a great way to never be taken seriously or build real power. If you have done the groundwork and power mapping to form effective coalitions and partners, it should be relatively easy to set up a meeting.

Power Mapping

Power mapping is one of the most useful exercises in strategic organizing. It is a matrix to determine the degree to which stakeholders are sympathetic to or oppose your cause, and how much power they might have politically. It is one way to make sure you are not operating out of a mindset of prefiguratism (which focuses on emotional or symbolic outcomes instead of strategic ones).

Construct a square graph with four quadrants. The horizontal axis is how progressive they are toward your cause. The vertical axis is how much influence they have in City Hall. This will create a visual matrix of which council members to approach.

The most desirable category (upper right) are those members who are the most sympathetic to the cause. These are our potential champions. They are probably the ones that will push this motion through.

The next category (lower right) are those members who, perhaps if you offer the right argument, or leverage the right way, will sign on board.

Then there is the category of council members who are most likely going to oppose it, unless there's extraordinary circumstances. This creates a visual map of whom to court and whom to strategize against and neutralize.

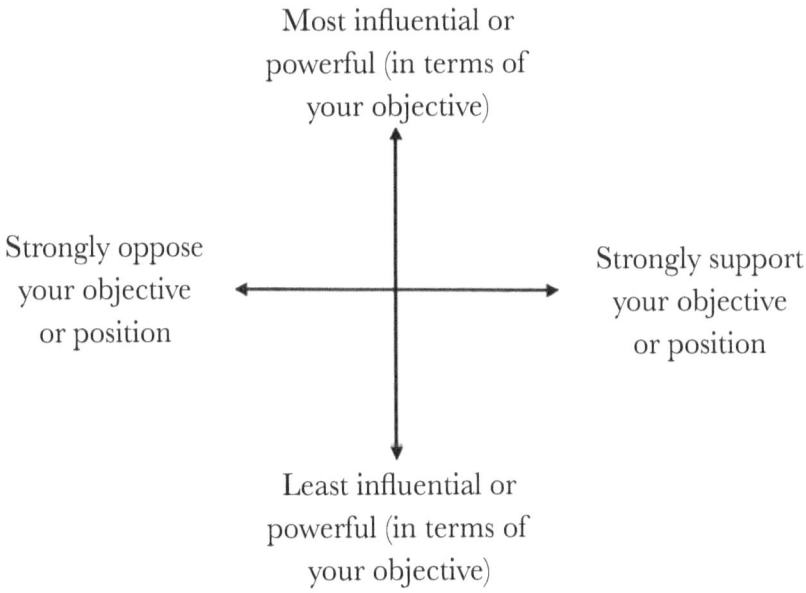

Divest LA created a coalition with environmental, Indigenous, and social justice groups within the city, which are very visible and very well known in City Hall. When they had built to the point where they could claim to represent these powerful groups, the city council members immediately took them seriously.

If you are thinking of organizing your own local civic divestment campaign, do your due diligence to figure out which council members are going to be your allies, and which will be your opponents. If you have opponents, make inquiries as to who might be most likely to influence them or who they are partnered with. Are they partnered with labor unions or are they partnered with various other organizations? Who are the power players for them?

If they don't go for the carrot, there is always the stick.

Always Center Indigenous and Frontline Community Leaders

When launching a divestment campaign, it is critical to align with Indigenous leaders and frontline communities. An important part of this process is to familiarize yourself with the cultural protocols that govern each tribe. I recommend bringing an offering of tobacco as a show of respect when first meeting with an Indigenous leader.

Divest LA learned this lesson the hard way.

It may be uncomfortable work, but it will pay off in the long run to center Indigenous leadership, who are traditionally the tip of the spear when it comes to organizing against fossil fuel companies. The Indigenous communities and Indigenous leadership in LA were integral to the divestment campaign. They showed up time and time again at City Hall to put pressure on the council, and led rallies and marches.

One risk of not having input and alliances with the frontline communities is that they will not support your efforts. They will quickly see through your lack of consultation with them or lack of working alongside them. This is called parachuting.

It's also important to avoid tokenism, by approaching these relationships with a genuine commitment to center their concerns and leadership, making sure that this is reflected in the legislation directly. For members of Divest LA like Ben and me, our experiences at Standing Rock solidified our commitment. We had stood shoulder to shoulder with Indigenous people who had been fighting for their community and for future generations facing climate extinction.

Indigenous leaders always spoke at the Divest LA press conferences and led with an opening prayer. Inside the meetings they occupied, the Indigenous leaders submitted public comments. We also worked side by side very closely with frontline communities, including ACCE and the Community for Better Banks, who lobbied side by side until the very end.

They knew it had to be an inside-outside game from the very start.

The Opposition

Everybody knew going into the campaign that there would be opposition. Wells Fargo was one of the biggest, most powerful banks in the world and had enough money to apply lobbyist pressure on City Hall every single day—which they did. After all, there was $8 billion at stake. Wells Fargo made $100 million annually in fees managing the city's funds.

They had a relationship with council staffers, whom they had been lobbying heavily prior to each of the divestment votes. This did not deter Ben, Trinity and Phoenix from their own direct lobbying efforts. They were going to see this through to the end, and beyond. They had a vision not only to win, but to transform the system itself.

Be In It To Win It

Very often in organizing, mindset alone can be the difference between success and failure. *Assume that success is possible and always look for the pathway to victory, no matter what the obstacles.* Be determined: victory is going to happen. It is yours. Be fearless. Have confidence that you and your team can win, and if there is a gap in your knowledge, or a skill set you don't have, you can always find someone with the right experience and expertise, or you can research and learn.

Always remember that you are doing something heroic. It will change history. Let yourself be fueled by that sentiment, and keep your eyes on the prize. Think big, be daring, and always stay humble.

FareWells Fargo Action

They don't like it when you fuck with their money.

I came on board the Divest LA campaign in the final couple of months. After returning from Standing Rock I was all but destroyed. Perhaps annihilated is a better word. It comes from the Latin word meaning *to be reduced to nothing.* In 2016, I'd traveled twelve thousand miles across the country. By New Year's Day 2017, I had traveled for seven months non-stop, fighting DAPL, the banks and the Democratic establishment.

I got back from the beautiful horror show that was Standing Rock to be hurled into a seven-day crucible to organize the Jane Fonda *#BankExit* action. When the adrenaline finally wore off, I discovered that I was not okay.

My nerves were shot. I was completely exhausted, to the point where I could not get out of bed for weeks. It was as if I had been running on adrenaline for an entire year, and when it faded I was incapacitated. On top of that, I decided to lie low because there had been a fair amount of heat from the opposition. I'd decided to take a much needed sabbatical. It had been a hard year of travel, organizing, direct actions and a fair amount of heartbreak. It's important to take time off sometimes. Self care is one of the most needed and least adopted practices in activism.

It was just before Christmas, and I had returned home to my parents' place for the holidays. It was the day that I was met with the harsh reality of the feeling that comes when you are no longer just one of many in a movement, but you are specifically singled out. It was only a few days after Jane Fonda's birthday *#BankExit* direct action and I was out at the mall doing some last-minute shopping with my father.

We were having lunch in some shitty corporate chain restaurant when I noticed a man at the bar. There was a dark aura about him and he was not staring directly, but it was very apparent to me that he was watching us. If you have ever worked with veterans or have known veterans who have worked in special forces or seen heavy action, some have a different energy about them—a steely thousand-yard stare. He had dead black eyes and definitely stuck out.

I told my father not to react, but that he was watching us. My dad dismissed this quickly as paranoia. Until after lunch, when we found ourselves in a clothing store at the other end of the mall. "Hey, Pop, check it out," I said. There he was again. Not really browsing, just milling about. My father's expression changed. We went to a department store at the other end of the mall. Same thing again. My father, who'd also served in the military, was visibly nervous this time.

After all, over lunch I had been recounting stories of how we had just put the big banks and the oil companies on blast in the national press with one of the country's most iconic and beloved icons. Susan Sarandon had been doing interviews on mainstream programs like *Chelsea Handler*, talking about the campaign.

Sarah Silverman also did a personal call-to-action video in support of *#BankExit* on *NowThis*. It meant a lot that she was using her platform to support the cause, especially after her harsh words at the Democratic Convention. At the end of the day, she was a progressive who cared about the people and the planet over shitty psychopathic corporations. Meanwhile, Native American groups began organizing local direct actions at banks all over the country to keep the heat on and help people to understand that their money was funding the climate apocalypse and Indigenous genocide.

But here's the thing—it turns out that when your campaigns threaten their bottom line and public image, they don't like it. This wasn't the first time I had been aware that I was directly under surveillance. There had been times at the convention when I was followed or there were people clearly eavesdropping on our conversations. Once I was at a meeting with an environmental leader outside a coffee shop, when a car pulled up abruptly. A man who'd been crouched down in the passenger seat popped up quickly with a camera, took some pictures and then sped off.

We were the only ones outside.

However, this was the first time that I was authentically scared. The dude in the mall had been like something out of one of those Jason Bourne movies.

My father and I made our way quickly to the car and we went home without incident. For the next year and a half or so, as the divestment movement gained momentum, the surveillance would continue to be more overt. On calls with my future wife, there were frequent loud noises that sounded like a death metal singer on the other end of the phone.

So I decided to step back for a while and lie low.

There are great people like Dolores Huerta, Bill McKibben, Linda Sarsour, Ilhan Omar, AOC, or Joye Braun who carry on when they get this type of pressure—or outright death threats—but I'm not a great person. Also, I was dealing with PTSD after a year of operating past my capacity and pretty constant trauma. I think that to a greater or lesser degree, this was true for just about every water protector and everyone who'd fought for the Bernie movement in 2016.

I resurfaced in the fall as the Los Angeles divestment campaign was really escalating. It was just remarkable to watch how the idea had spread, evolved and taken on a life of its own. It was truly a feeling beyond description.

Trinity called me to let me know that they had won the vote and that after nine months of exhaustive organizing, the City Council was going to not only divest from Wells Fargo, but had agreed to unbundle eight hundred bank accounts. That meant that multiple smaller banks could bid to manage the city's funds. Divest LA, working directly with the city officials, was able to change the application process to create the highest standards in the country to qualify. There was a point system to disqualify banks that were invested in fossil fuels. This was a big deal.

We decided that the narrative would be better if we organized some direct actions to generate media attention. Otherwise this historic vote would most likely come and go without anyone ever knowing about it. Also, with a big direct action, it would look like the people rising up was what finally pressured them to make the decision. It would create the opportunity for everyone in the coalition to share in the moment of victory.

Just as we were about to mobilize the community for the action, disaster struck.

I was driving back from an Indigenous sweat lodge ceremony in Ventura, when I noticed an orange glow set against the black night skyline. I made the critical mistake of driving closer to catch a glimpse of the blaze. I was low on gas, but I figured I would find a station along the way. I got very close to the spot where the blaze had begun.

It was terrifying and beautiful.

Human beings have always had the hubris to try to dominate the natural world, but in the end Mother Nature always humbles us into insignificance. This was to be one of the worst climate catastrophes to date. The problem was that the fire caused power outages for nearly a fifty-mile radius. I was lucky to get out, and to this day I have no idea how I made it home. The needle was buried on empty for what seemed like twenty miles of steep uphill driving on the 101 Freeway. Every gas station for miles was dark due to the power outage.

This was ultimately why we were fighting. The climate emergency was no longer an abstraction. The Thomas Fire destroyed over one thousand structures and caused over $2.2 billion in damage. The sky was gray with smoke. It rained ash. The Skirball Fire turned the stretch of the 405 Freeway near Mulholland Drive into a nightmarish hellscape of orange-and-black burning hillsides.

The wildfires dominated the news cycles, which presented us with a problem in getting any media attention for our direct action.

We decided to call it #FareWellsFargo.

Cause fuck Wells Fargo. They had to go.

And … what was happening was important. A group of mostly Millennials, with no money and very little resources, had gone toe to toe with one of the top five biggest private commercial banks in the world—and had won. This deserved to be known. Progressives and leftists so often focus only on what's wrong, and we forget to celebrate when we win a fight. This is perhaps because our culture isn't about winning. We define ourselves by the fight, and because of this, we end up fighting everyone—especially each other.

We formed a coalition of our local friends and allies, like the Alliance of Californians for Community Empowerment (ACCE), SoCal 350, and the SoCal chapter of the American Indian Movement. Even though Trinity, Ben and Phoenix led a great deal of the lobbying efforts, there was a general sense that we wanted to share the victory with the community.

A young filmmaker named Blair Avery, who had also been to Standing Rock, had the idea to serve Wells Fargo with a giant eviction notice stenciled on a giant white sheet. The plan was to spell out "FareWellsFargo" with people in Grant Park next to City Hall to take an aerial photo, and then proceed to the south steps for a rally. My friend Robert Kennedy, Jr. agreed to speak on the day. Robert had been an environmental lawyer for decades, and a champion of Indigenous Rights. We'd met years before, when I'd brought Ohio Congressman Tim Ryan to meet him at his Malibu ranch. I'll never forget him asking us if we wanted to meet his pet emu. We paused, turned to look at each other for a moment, and said, "Yes, Bobby, we'd love to come and feed some blueberries to your emu."

We reconnected during the NoDAPL movement to support some water protectors who were still battling legal cases. He would eventually take some unfortunate Covid-19 vaccine conspiracy positions in 2020 but, at the time, he seemed like a great addition to the lineup. His steadfast advocacy of environmental causes was more prominent than his support for fringe vaccine conspiracy theories.

When we organized the *#FareWellsFargo* action, neither I nor any of the core organizers had told anyone that we planned to march the rally down to Wells Fargo about a mile and a half away from City Hall.

They were waiting for us as if prepared for a standing army. The bank was already shut down, and there were six black-suited guards with ear pieces behind barricades. Only a handful of people knew that we were going to march from City Hall to the bank, so we have no idea how they could have known. To be honest I took it as a compliment.

Comedic actor Justin Long came down to join us and support the action. We'd met when he'd shown up to join the many influencers that had offered their time and platforms to our Bernie PSAs in 2016. Justin was a surrogate for Bernie, and continued living his values by driving across town from the westside to downtown during peak traffic. Angelenos will understand that this is an act of love.

Because of the fire, it was nearly impossible to get any significant press to show up, except for The Young Turks, who always sent a crew down to cover the actions I was involved in. Jimmy Dore and TYT were great assets to uplift our campaigns and stunts. Unfortunately, this unified support would not last forever.

It sucks to pour your heart into doing something that is high risk, incredibly hard, thankless work, and to have no one have any idea that it even happened. What is the point of disrupting and challenging the system if it never gets past the choir of those involved? I didn't go through the pain and heartbreak to simply feel good for a minute that I was doing something. This is nothing more than prefiguratism. The point of the work is to make the biggest impact on the most people possible, by putting the greatest amount of pressure on the defenders of the status quo.

During the process of the divestment campaign, Phoenix had brought the idea of public banking to the group after reading Ellen Brown's book on the subject. What Divest LA realized was that even if Wells Fargo lost the vote, they would never stop lobbying to win back those billions of dollars. Public banking offered an elegant solution: instead of the private banks managing the billions of dollars in city tax funds, Los Angeles would simply create its own bank. The City of LA had spent $100 million a year in fees and commissions to manage those funds. The State of North Dakota had had a public bank since 1919 and had weathered every financial crisis better than any other private lending institution.

Right around this time, Divest LA started to pivot to form a sister affinity group called Public Bank LA. If the resolution had passed and there was no more vision or strategy, the mission would have been over. One of the reasons I loved this group is that they were committed to a lasting vision of changing the system. They reached out to David Jette, who had expertise in tech finance and startups, real estate, securities and cryptocurrency, to support the technical aspects of creating a public bank. He was a part of the Los Angeles DSA's research committee, whom they were petitioning for support.

The *#FareWellsFargo* action was a big success, even if it didn't garner the media attention we had hoped. The news still made waves in national activist circles and helped fuel ongoing divestment efforts. These wins are so important because so many people believe that the system is beyond repair and that our elected officials are completely corrupt, and therefore there is no point in trying to change things. Not only winning, but celebrating these wins, gives others permission to challenge the system and the status quo. They hopefully lead people to ask questions about how exactly this group achieved their objectives without giant bags of money from George Soros. (... Just to be clear, this is a joke. None of us get Soros money. We often wonder, how do we get our hands on it? Is it a meeting in a parking garage in trench coats at midnight to get a briefcase situation?)

The Young Turks had agreed to cover the *#FareWellsFargo* action, which created a great opportunity to pivot in the messaging to public banking. Only when the video came out, TYT had turned the footage of our direct action into a commercial for Aspiration Bank. Granted, Aspiration was a bank committed to 100 percent clean money, but it was still disappointing that our efforts were co-opted and turned into an advertisement. Basically everything Phoenix had said about public banks in his soundbyte had been turned into a testimonial for a private bank.

Of course, right on cue, a few leftists in Los Angeles were in an uproar over this and immediately called out TYT, arguing for them to be canceled. I told our people to *be like little Fonzis* and chill out for a minute so that I could reach out and see what was happening. It was good that people had raised the issue as a problem, but so often we jump immediately to "call-outs" when we should first consider a "call-in." This is one of the reasons that leftist and progressive efforts fail—we constantly waste time with public infighting instead of having conversations with each other.

This is a phenomenon I call "the bucket of crabs."

When fishermen catch crabs, they place the live crustaceans in a bucket or a simple hole they dig in the sand. Do they bother to cover the hole or the bucket?

Nope.

As each crab attempts to crawl out of their prison to freedom the other crabs pull them down, trying to climb on top of one another while the fisherman goes about their day.

The bucket of crabs is thus perhaps the perfect metaphor for the greatest obstacle most efforts for peace and social justice face—sabotage from within. In this case, the fisherman represents the bad actors of the corporate state who happily sit back and watch leftist causes self-destruct.

Nothing can derail a movement or campaign more effectively than its members fighting amongst one another. This happens for a variety of reasons. Some see the opportunity a campaign or movement offers to advance their position, and reason that to do so they need to eliminate those whom they perceive to be competition. They may feel threatened by other organizers who are achieving results or gaining notoriety. Gossip, character assassination, and petty backbiting are usually signs of immature and inexperienced activists.

They may be more experienced organizers who lack the imagination, leadership and skill sets to achieve results, and feel jealousy towards emerging leaders. Maybe these up and comers are employing new methods or ideas that challenge the old ways of doing things. There are most definitely old paradigms within the progressive movements that are difficult to change.

Make no mistake, gossip and character assassination are a cancer that will inevitably devour the heart and soul of a movement or a campaign. Inevitably this will lead to hurt feelings, censure, infighting, and the dying of the love that binds comrades together through a common struggle. The light and connection fostered between activists will dim. People will retreat into silos. They will wage campaigns against each other, telling all who might listen about the wrongs of the other in an attempt to control the narrative and protect their own reputation.

This is called perpetrating from the victim position. They will try to force others to choose sides. They will be passionate in their pursuit, driven by an indomitable self-righteousness. This may even escalate to social media platforms or the press, depending on the profiles of those involved.

This notion seems absurd at first glance. Isn't everyone supposed to be on the same side? Isn't everyone supposed to be working together to focus on overcoming the innumerable and daunting obstacles put forth by the opposition?

Gossip, public shaming, and infighting are some of the prime manifestations of horizontal oppression, where members of marginalized groups continue to perpetrate systems of oppression by targeting each other. This is one of the more insidious mechanisms of colonization, patriarchy, racism, class warfare, and so on.

The corporate state employs consultants to infiltrate organizations and activist groups, both to gather intelligence and to derail progress by manufacturing dissent amongst the members. This is such an effective tactic for agents provocateurs because this paradigm is so prevalent on the left.

This does not mean stepping over bad behavior or abuses happening in movement spaces. Having strong agreements and operating principles defining our organizing culture is crucial to our success, along with processes for working out our disputes.

Kurt Cobain once said, *"Everyone seems to be striving for Utopia, but there are so many different factions. I mean if you can't get a fuckin' underground movement to band together and stop bickering about unnecessary little things that they don't agree on, then how the fuck do you expect to have an effect on a mass level?"*

With this in mind I did something radical, and called Cenk directly to ask him why this had happened. As it turned out, he'd had no idea it was happening. The whole thing had been spear-headed by the ad department. Of course this was still a bad look, but he immediately agreed to pull the ad and do a long-form thirty minute interview with Trinity and Phoenix on the main

TYT program on public banking. This was one of the first major long-form interviews on the subject.

Not long after this, Alexandria Ocasio-Cortez began publicly supporting public banking. Public Bank LA, led by Trinity and LA Berner Carlos Marroquin, organized a town hall with AOC on the subject—thus demonstrating that a small group of committed citizens, even with no money or resources, can defeat behemoth corporations, change laws and raise a fringe issue to national attention. Public Bank LA would go on to help form the California Public Banking Alliance coalition to pass several bills in the state legislature. This coalition included former Bay Area Occupy Wall Street activists like Susan Harman, who also had been working on organizing around public banking since OWS, and who saw it as an ongoing policy legacy of our movement.

As much as these efforts represented some historic victories and showed what was possible, we were a long way from the type of systemic change that we all so badly wanted to create. It was clear to me that the road ahead would require a bigger vision and strategy for poor working people from various movements to rise together to stand for a world that works for everyone, not just the few.

Chapter 10

Building a Movement:
The Poor People's Campaign

*Those who love peace must learn to organize
as effectively as those who love war.*
-Dr. Martin Luther King, Jr.

I t was 8:46 a.m. on a Friday when the first plane struck the tower. My friend lived down the hall in our apartment building and told us to come right away. I walked in to see a thick plume of black smoke from 1 World Trade Center on the television. I didn't own a TV at the time (and haven't since). At first, we thought it was just an accident, but then another plane struck the south tower. Just when it didn't seem it could get any worse, they collapsed an hour later.

I spent days in a fugue state. Bewildered. I had to do something with myself. So I decided to organize a benefit concert for 9/11 victims. I was playing in a hard rock power trio at the time in

Northampton, Massachusetts, and many of the hometown bands had struggled to get gigs after a real estate developer had bought up the major music venues and cut out the local scene. Western Mass. had once had a vibrant music scene in the early nineties and was home to seminal bands like Sonic Youth, the Pixies and Dinosaur Jr.

What does 9/11 have to do with building social movements? We'll get there soon enough.

Not only did organizing take my mind off of the traumatic images of people jumping out of the towers to avoid burning to death, but it was a game-changer for my own band. We were really good, but we struggled to build a following.

The show injected life into the local scene. I started a musicians' co-op called JP Diddy Productions. We took over a Fraternal Order of Eagles Club and a bowling alley and started throwing punk rock shows. Our music scene had been officially declared dead at the time of our benefit show by the local press.

Previously, each band would play to the same fifteen friends every weekend, but we would ask both bands to work together to promote the show. Playing a show to thirty people is much cooler, especially if there are fifteen new potential fans. Then we would bring in an out-of-town band from Boston or New York City to play in the middle slot. Everyone worked together to tell their fans how cool the other bands on the bill were so that they would show up early and stay late. We gave all of the door money to the bands and made a cut of the bar and we would give the out-of-town bands a place to crash. We would throw a killer party afterwards, which was only for the people who came to the show.

We had bands of all different genres, but the operation was pure DIY punk rock.

Within six months our shows were packed and the scene was hopping. Within a year my band was selling out venues, and had been signed to a major agency and brought out to Los Angeles by the A&R rep for the Rolling Stones. Despite just being poor musicians, my partner and I at the age of twenty-four were voted by the press as being in the top ten most influential people in Western Mass., and we were sometimes getting national acts, over the real estate mogul's corporate venues. I made lots of mistakes, most of them due to excessive ego fueled by immaturity, alcohol and bad choices, but they were also some of the best times of my life.

I continued to organize for various projects and causes. As I became more involved in grassroots activism, the notion always stayed with me that the problem our movements faced was the same as those bands in our struggling music scene—we were too siloed (segregated), too divided. The more I learned about the issues, the more it became clear that the problems we faced were interdependent, and therefore so were the solutions. What if leaders across various movements and other causes worked together in solidarity?

Ultimately we cannot separate these issues. Fossil fuel extraction sites very often are located in poor Black and brown communities, who lack the resources to fight. These citizens suffer the adverse effects of living near these sites, and yet have little to no access to healthcare. Therefore the movements for racial justice, climate justice, economic justice, and health justice are inextricably interdependent.

The principle that the music scene operated on was simple—that everyone is on the same team, and everyone helps everyone. The energy in the community was electrifying. There was a feeling of connection, purpose and solidarity. It has always stayed with me.

I later discovered that this was one of the principles of John Nash's famous Nash Equilibrium in game theory.

Nash's postulate, which was made famous in the film *A Beautiful Mind*, theorized that in competition, everyone wins when individual ambition serves the common good—in other words, when they do what is best for themselves and for the group. This has been the cornerstone of every organizing effort I have been a part of. Solidarity means not only acting out of self-interest, but sharing resources to amplify. Oil companies have used this principle very effectively to coordinate their price gouging of consumers.

What if we leveraged our collective power, rooted in the knowledge that we all shared the same struggle? I founded an organization in 2011 to organize training sessions for leaders called Peacelink, with the hopes of kickstarting this vision. We were part of the executive committee for the UN's International Day of Peace, and we produced an annual broadcast, but I was never able to get the organization to run sustainably. In 2014 I facilitated a leadership training that Dr. Jill Stein participated in after her first presidential run with the Green Party, but was never able to get much traction with the bigger vision. I still had a lot to learn about leadership, movement theory and history. But my belief in fusion coalitions never wavered.

The concepts we will examine in this and subsequent chapters are crucial to realizing the world we want to live in, as well as to understand why our movements have so often been sabotaged from within—and that the solution is solidarity!

The Poor People's Movement

In 2017, when I heard Reverend Dr. William Barber II and Reverend Dr. Liz Theoharis had reignited Dr. Martin Luther King's Poor People's Movement, I was all in.

Since 2012, the Koch brothers' network had launched co-ordinated campaigns to win conservative majorities in over twenty state legislatures. They had also passed "Equalize Voter Rights," a bill that would revoke the tax credit given to parents if their dependent college student registered to vote at their college address, thus suppressing the youth vote. Their minions passed legislation in the North Carolina state house that would require voters to present government-issued photo identification. This was a classic rightwing voter suppression tactic that most adversely impacted Democrat-leaning poor voters of color.

Reverend Barber launched a multi-religious, multiracial initiative called Moral Mondays, that mobilized coalitions to do acts of nonviolent civil disobedience, occupying state capitol buildings in North Carolina, Georgia, South Carolina, Illinois and New Mexico.

On the 50th anniversary of the Poor People's Campaign, Reverend Barber and his coalition would seek to build a nation-wide fusion movement to unite various causes, to stand together and risk arrest to end systemic racism, ecological devastation, income inequality, voter suppression and an immoral national narrative.

It was beautiful. The launch of the campaign featured activist hubs in thirty-five states, meeting together simultaneously on a Zoom webinar.

There was an electric feeling knowing that we were carrying on the legacy of Dr. Martin Luther King, Jr. and all of the other civil rights activists who had died and risked their lives to end the apartheid cruelty of Jim Crow oppression.

The late civil rights organizer and Georgia Congressman John Lewis once said, "Without storytelling, the Civil Rights Movement would have been like a bird without wings." The history of the original Poor People's Campaign is not widely known and is worth examining for context.

Dr. King announced the first Poor People's Campaign at a staff retreat for the Southern Christian Leadership Conference (SCLC) in November of 1967. This was a strong strategic move, as it is beneficial to get the buy-in of core leaders before launching any campaign. What was different about this campaign was that it expanded the distinctions of the Civil Rights movement by centering the immorality of poverty and the Vietnam War. This was a particularly dangerous idea as the Anti-War movement was beginning to reach its height. On October 21, 1967, a hundred thousand protesters gathered at the Lincoln Memorial, and thirty thousand marched on the Pentagon in hopes of putting their bodies on the gears of the war machine.

The original vision was to mobilize thousands of people to descend on DC to demand an Economic Bill of Rights for poor people.

Along with the outside organizing, there was an inside strategy where impacted people from the northern and southern states would lobby government officials to demand unemployment, education, a living wage and an end to the Vietnam War.

An inside-outside strategy is necessary to create a dialogue with policy makers, and then leverage the power of thousands of people to disrupt the status quo. If there is no direct dialogue with specific policy makers to make specific policy demands, and if those making the demands do not have a credible threat of making life uncomfortable for those lawmakers, there will be no reason for them to offer concessions.

When thousands of people create bad optics for these so-called leaders in the court of public opinion, it shines a light on their failed leadership. This said, leftists and progressives must understand that calling people and problems out on the internet alone is not a viable theory of change. Social media can be used as a leveraging tactic, but only when matched by strategic on-the-ground organizing, focused on hard goals.

The Poor People's Campaign established a three-thousand-person protest camp to occupy the Washington Mall in the spring of 1968, where they stayed for six weeks. Politicians care about one thing only—getting re-elected. Therefore, a movement must strategically mobilize enough people to take action in order to challenge the perception that life is better because of the leadership of those in power, and enough people to potentially vote out the incumbent. Dr. King and other civil rights organizers had employed this theory of change.

The Civil Rights Movement was considered a serious threat to the stakeholders in power, as was the Anti-War Movement. These two movements becoming one, centering class consciousness and racial equity, was potentially an existential threat to the ruling class and the military industrial complex.

Like the Rainbow Coalition Fred Hampton would create on the one-year anniversary of Dr. King's assassination—April 4th, 1969—both movements sought to build a multiracial coalition to elevate the lives of poor people. Leaders from the American Indian Movement, the Brown Berets and the Students for a Democratic Society (SDS) pledged their support.

Both visionaries were assassinated for these efforts, which had challenged the paradigms of white supremacy, capitalism, colonialism and imperialism. Hampton was drugged with fentanyl by a police informant and then executed by law enforcement, who perpetrated a pre-dawn no-knock incursion. They shot him as he lay asleep in his bed. He was only twenty-one years old. Hampton was a true savant as an organizer. There's no telling what he might have achieved if he had lived.

After King's assassination, his wife Coretta Scott King led a second wave of thousands of women on Mother's Day as part of the Poor People's Campaign. This was a very symbolic day for these actions. Julia Ward Howe worked to establish a "Mother's Day" of peace as a call to action for men to lay down their arms and to abolish war. Here is her proclamation to women everywhere, made in 1870:

"Arise, then, women of this day!

Arise, all women who have hearts, Whether our baptism be of water or of tears!

Say firmly: 'We will not have great questions decided by irrelevant agencies; our husbands will not come to us, reeking with carnage, for caresses and applause. Our sons shall not be taken from us to unlearn All that we have been able to teach them of charity, mercy and patience. We, the women of one country, will be too tender of those of another country to allow our sons to be trained to injure theirs.'

From the bosom of the devastated Earth a voice goes up with our own. It says: 'Disarm! Disarm! The sword of murder is not the balance of justice.' Blood does not wipe out dishonor, nor violence indicates possession. As men have often forsaken the plough and the anvil at the summons of war, Let women now leave all that may be left of home for a great and earnest day of counsel.

Let them meet first, as women, to bewail and commemorate the dead. Let them solemnly take counsel with each other as to the means Whereby the great human family can live in peace, Each bearing after his own time the sacred impress, not of Caesar, But of God.

In the name of womanhood and humanity, I earnestly ask That a general congress of women without limit of nationality May be appointed and held at someplace deemed most convenient And at the earliest period consistent with its objects, To promote the alliance of the different nationalities, The amicable settlement of international questions,

The great and general interests of peace."

The organizers of the Poor People's Campaign pressed on, even in the wake of MLK's murder. Robert Kennedy, the antiwar candidate for president, was also assassinated two months later. They were political revolutionaries who truly threatened the dominant paradigm, and they paid the ultimate price.

The Poor People's Campaign occupied the National Mall in D.C. for three months. The encampment, called Resurrection City, consisted of rows of triangular wooden houses stretching across the commons that looked like a mobile military barracks.

The Rev. Jesse Jackson was elected mayor of Resurrection City. He was a member of the Greenville 8, who had been arrested in a 1960 direct action for using a whites-only library in South Carolina. In 1966, the SCLC selected Jackson to be head of the Chicago chapter of its Operation Breadbasket, whose mission was to organize boycotts as a means to pressure white businesses to hire blacks and purchase goods and services from black contractors.

Boycotts and divestments work!

Later, in 1984 and 1988, Jackson would run for president in an attempt to transform the Democratic Party into a multiracial, class-conscious "Rainbow Coalition." He did not succeed.

Richard Nixon, while campaigning for the 1968 presidential election, asked Congress not to give in to the campaign's demands. The FBI and military intelligence conducted heavy surveillance and infiltration operations to gather information on participants, routes, finances, and supplies. They paid informants and posed as journalists. It is important to know the opposition and their tactics.

Very often, our social movements face highly organized, strategic, and very well-resourced opponents. This creates a need for better systems across a range of areas, including training, communications, strategy, and the sharing of history and knowledge.

Nixon had twenty thousand soldiers activated, who were prepared for a military occupation of the capitol. The thousands of PPC occupiers were evicted when a thousand riot police stormed Resurrection City with tear gas and engaged in acts of brutality.

Exactly fifty years later, the movement was reborn under the banner of the Poor People's Campaign: A National Call for Moral Revival. The notion of carrying on this legacy was very exciting, like picking up a once-great torch with only a few smoldering embers remaining. Everyone grows up hearing about Dr. King and the Civil Rights Movement, but how can one experience any meaningful connection to that great wave that rose and fell?

In 2018 the US was waging war in seven countries without so much as a whimper of domestic resistance. Reverend Barber and Reverend Theoharis's goal was forty days of coordinated action in the spring of 2018 at state houses across the country. A fusion coalition of organizations—representing gender justice, racial justice, climate justice, health justice, housing justice, and an end to the war machine and the distorted moral narrative in America—would simultaneously occupy the capitol buildings, risking arrest. Each week for six weeks we would highlight a different set of issues and center the stories of impacted people.

This was the dream I'd had for many years for our social movements. It was the fullest manifestation of the idea that had found me organizing bands in my hometown seventeen years prior.

There were state and local Poor People's Campaign groups organizing actions.

According to Reverend Barber, "Four diseases, all connected, now threaten the nation's social and moral health: racism, poverty, environmental devastation, and the war economy—sanctified by the heresy of Christian nationalism."

I joined the California Poor People's Campaign as the strategist for the direct actions centering around the climate crisis and ecological devastation.

The campaign was to be strictly non-partisan. No elected officials or candidates from any political party would be allowed to speak at events or be part of the organizing committees.

Reverend Barber and Reverend Theoharis believed that a moral revival was necessary to save the heart and soul of our democracy. We all had to attend non-violent civil disobedience training and sign an agreement stating that we would remain committed to non-violence at all times. Only people who had attended the training sessions and who had registered with the National Lawyers Guild volunteer legal team could risk arrest during direct actions. I also acted as a training facilitator.

In my opinion it is crucial for direct action trainers to model the type of opposition that one might face risking arrest so that we can truly prepare non-violent warriors to stand their ground, even when threatened by vile racism, sexism or homophobia.

The campaign was committed to lifting up and developing the leadership of frontline people to organize on a state level, where many of the most regressive policies were passed.

We stood for the vision of transforming the "War Economy" into a "Peace Economy" that values all humanity, and believed that people should not live in or die from poverty in the richest nation ever to have existed.

The campaign was a bottom-up movement rooted in the understanding that poverty and economic inequality cannot be understood apart from a society built on white supremacy, and a distorted moral narrative of religious nationalism that blames poor and oppressed people for their own poverty and oppression.

The theory of change in this next iteration of the Poor People's Campaign was to organize at the state and local level, since many of the most regressive policies were being passed at the state level.

It all sounded great.

There was a tremendous amount of work that went into organizing the coalitions and coordinating the actions. People were trained as theo-musicologists, to lead the group in protest songs. We would start meetings with these chants:

Everybody's got a right to live

Everybody's got a right to live

And before this campaign fails

We'll all go down to jail

Everybody's got a right to live!

I think this is an area the left needs to work on. So often, marches and rallies feature the same single lyric that drones on endlessly. It can be an invigorating experience for those participating, but outside observers should feel invited to join the movement. To them, it can come off as tired and unimaginative.

Leftists and progressives droning on for hours chanting, "*WE ARE THE 99 PERCENT!*" or, "*BERNIE! BERNIE! BERNIE! BERNIE!*" gets old really fast, especially for anyone who is not already a hard-core supporter.

The Poor People's Campaign was one of the best movements I have seen in this area, because they had a team focused on music.

There was so much heart. These were some of the finest, bravest, most loving people I had ever known.

Around this time our Divest LA group had begun to shift its focus to public banking. I went up to Sacramento for a lobby day set up by an old mentor of mine, Reverend Bill McDonald, who was a decorated veteran and an advocate for veterans' issues. The citizen's lobby is one of the most underrated and little-known tools available to political revolutionaries. Any citizen can simply go down to their local city hall, state or federal policy maker's office and lobby staff or legislators directly. Ben Hauck, Phoenix Goodman and I did some power mapping to identify the most progressive-leaning state legislators likely to support public banking, and simply went door-to-door to their offices. David Jette helped me get into the weeds on the wonky particulars of the policy so I could field difficult questions.

I was also doing reconnaissance on the building for the purpose of planning the PPC direct actions in Sacramento.

At the time I was experiencing what I would describe as heavy surveillance. That day in Sacramento I had a full phone battery that drained to nothing in almost no time. This had been common at Standing Rock, where security forces had deployed "StingRay" technology that hijacked our cell signals and drained our batteries.

The people who joined the campaign were extraordinary. Yet, like all organizing efforts, there were some inherent challenges. The campaign and organizational model were old school. There are a lot of advantages to Ella Baker-style structural organizing. This is a powerful way to build deep relationships and solidarity. Unfortunately for this type of organizing, when used alone, it is (in my opinion) an outdated model.

The Poor People's Campaign was way too structured and top-down in its approach, even though it claimed to be a bottom-up organization. Everything moved very slowly, and by approval. The goals themselves were also vague. There were no specific policy demands, only a general demand. There were very few young people involved. There is always great wisdom to be gained from our elders, but if you look around the room in an organizing meeting and there's barely a single person under thirty, your campaign will most likely fail to connect, catch fire and be relevant.

Also the local groups had no autonomy and had to serve whatever their particular State committee decided.

We put together an Indigenous-led statewide coalition of activists for climate actions. A few of Bernie's Avengers and some Standing Rock all-stars joined in. I got to work again in person with Caleb Buchbinder—one of the co-founders of DefundDapl. org—which was a blessing.

Our coalition's actions would be taking place on the fourth week of the forty days of civil disobedience, so if we were going to have the element of surprise, we were going to need to get creative. My original plan was to smuggle a teepee in to cover the Christopher Columbus statue in the rotunda of the Capitol building in Sacramento. Christopher Columbus is viewed as a genocidal maniac, like some version of Hitler, by Native People, and is an enduring symbol of colonialism.

The teepee would have required negotiating too many Native protocols, as every tribe has different customs. It is always important to approach organizing with Indigenous people with humility and respect for their culture and traditions. Also getting the teepee poles in would have presented logistical challenges. Desiree Kane came up with the plan to make a giant medicine wheel out of a parachute. The colors red, black, yellow and white represent the peoples of the earth and the four directions, which would be perfect symbolism to cover the Columbus statue and perform a traditional round dance around. Once the plans were in place I asked Desiree, who was from the Miwok tribe, to take my place leading the action. How could we have an Indigenous-led action led in turn by yours truly?

I stepped back.

There were plenty of very capable direct-action organizers from southern and northern California. I didn't feel the need to get another "direct action badge" and I felt I would be more useful working in comms to generate press. The campaign was committed to developing the leadership of impacted people, but one of the challenges is that there is a learning curve to disciplines like public relations. I have always focused on recruiting people with specific skill sets and networks that can elevate the message to the masses in the most compelling way.

One of the campaign's stated goals was to shift the distorted moral narrative in the country. More than two thousand people were arrested nationwide during the forty days of civil disobedience, in thirty-five states. An incalculable number of hours had gone into coordinating the campaign. We barely made a ripple in the national narrative. If you asked a hundred people on the street about the Poor People's Campaign, you would be hard-pressed to find one that had so much as heard of it.

This is salty but true.

At the end of it all, why didn't the Poor People's Campaign achieve its stated goals?

I mean, this was the dream: movements for racial, health, climate, economic, and LGBTQIA+ justice standing together in solidarity across the country to put their bodies on the gears of the machine, carrying on the legacies of Dr. Martin Luther King, Jr. and Fred Hampton's Rainbow Coalition. I believe that any time people come together to stand for justice it is a good thing (perhaps with the exception of QAnon and *#SaveTheChildren*, but we will get to that later). Why didn't we achieve all that was possible?

The one bright spot was that our actions, and the continued lobbying by Indigenous people, pressured the State Government to remove the Columbus statue from the rotunda. It was a small victory, but it would still warm my heart to see the empty space that it used to inhabit.

Big Organizing

As we have previously stated, paradigms resist change. This is true in all walks of life, and the left is far from immune. The problem is that the world is constantly changing and evolving. There has been an exponential growth in technology. The internet and social media have fundamentally transformed the fabric of our society. And yet the theory of change and the organizing models many progressive campaigns operate out of haven't changed since the 1960s.

Mark and Paul Engler in their book *This Is an Uprising* examine the tension between what is known as structure-based organizing and mass mobilization. This is an important concept to unpack for political revolutionaries who would undertake the complex work of movement building.

In *Poor People's Movements*, Frances Fox Piven and Richard Cloward were two of the first movement theoreticians to examine the distinctions between mass mobilizations and structure-based organizations.

The Engler brothers expanded on their work by proposing that "mass mobilizations alter the terms of political debate and create new possibilities for progress." "Structure-based organizing helps take advantage of this potential and protects against efforts to roll back advances; and countercultural communities preserve progressive values, nurturing dissidents who go on to initiate the next wave of revolts."

The movement to end the war in Vietnam, the Arab Spring, Occupy Wall Street, Ferguson, Standing Rock, and the Yellow Vest uprising were all examples of mass mobilizations. The Engler brothers liken this to a whirlwind insurrection of citizens rising up en masse to challenge the established order and shift the political weather around an issue.

Where mass mobilization differs from structure-based organization is that these movements are largely decentralized. They often begin with trigger events that spark various segments of the population to rally in public displays of civil disobedience. Veteran organizers (who have not become too disillusioned) seize these flashpoint moments in the hopes of shifting the course of history, to sail it in the direction of their vision for change. Organizing during status quo periods of social stability can be demoralizing. When there is a paradigm-changing event, most longtime organizers will jump on the opportunity to connect with the fresh energy and new blood attracted to these happenings, sometimes within a matter of only a few weeks or months.

You can trace a through-line to see how these whirlwind mobilizations have built off one another, shifting the cultural landscape and creating important opportunities for activists to be radicalized and gain real experience in the trenches. We can see how veterans of the 1999 WTO Battle for Seattle helped plant the seeds for Occupy Wall Street, which in turn influenced Black Lives Matter, the Bernie Sanders Movement, Standing Rock and so on.

For all the opportunities mass mobilizations represent, there are also many vulnerabilities. The thing about whirlwinds is that they can pass as quickly as they appear. With so many new people they are also susceptible to infiltration by agents provocateurs.

Structure-based organizing is an entirely different approach to social change. The theory of change is incremental because it involves building the capacity of people from the bottom up, through relationships and mentorship. The civil rights movement is synonymous with names like Dr. Martin Luther King, Jr., Malcolm X, and Medgar Evers, and too often overlooks the work of Ella Baker, whose name has become synonymous with structure-based community organizing.

According to Mark Engler, "Her organizing was about building relationships—about forming deep ties with people who had not necessarily considered themselves part of a political movement before. She instilled in people a belief in their self-worth and ability to lead, and she cultivated their capacities for independent action. This is what Baker called the 'spadework' of movement-building, less glamorous than giving a speech to a crowd of thousands or participating in headline-grabbing protests, but just as critical to generating social change, if not more so."

Reverend Barber's Poor People's Campaign: A National Call for Moral Revival was deeply rooted in structure-based organizing. The problem with this was that the forty days of civil disobedience plan was a mass mobilization. The world had changed since the 1960s and yet we were operating out of the same organizing principles. Structure-based organizations move slowly. A call to action to mobilize thousands of people risking arrest in thirty-five states is not slow work. Mass mobilization requires a certain degree of decentralization. You cannot control a whirlwind. They are not meant to be controlled, but they can be incubated.

The Sunrise Movement

On November 13, 2018, 250 people stormed Capitol Hill to stage a peaceful sit-in at Nancy Pelosi's office with a freshman congresswoman named Alexandria Ocasio-Cortez. Before this, no one had ever heard of the Sunrise Movement or the Green New Deal.

In an interview with Ezra Klein, Sunrise co-founder Varshini Prakash said that five thousand articles were written about climate change and a Green New Deal within forty-eight hours of the AOC action. In a span of three weeks, they went from having twenty-five to over one hundred "hubs" or local organizing chapters.

Sunrise sought to create a new political alignment. According to Sunrise co-founder Varshini Prakash, "A political alignment is a grouping of social, economic, and political forces that are able to define a shared agenda for society. We've basically had two major dominant alignments in the US in the last eighty years. The first was the New Deal alignment of FDR that lasted through the sixties and seventies. It was defined by an active government passing massive social policies that helped elevate and support working Americans. The second was the Reagan alignment, which was a new set of values that focused on government as the problem and the market as solving our problems."

The founders of the Sunrise Movement developed their organizing model and strategies in a training institute called Momentum. Momentum was an incubator and training institute whose mission was to give organizers the tools and frameworks to build massive, decentralized social movements.

Momentum founder Max Berger was an OWS activist who understood the strengths and weaknesses of both mass mobilizations and structure-based movements. He had witnessed the power of the whirlwind in Zuccotti Park, and its lack of sustainability.

Momentum's theory of change did not advocate for one or the other, suggesting a hybrid of the two modalities.

Sunrise incorporated both structure-based and mass protest strategies in its organizing model.

Berger and Momentum also helped found IfNotNow, a Jewish progressive group that is opposed to the Israeli occupation of Palestine.

The model is worthy of serious examination as a theory of change for those who are serious about movement building. Most people think that Occupy failed, when in truth it never ended.

Sometimes It Takes a Pirate

In 2008, after the corrupt financial institutions crashed economies around the world, one country did something about it.

Rick Falkvinge, the founder of Sweden's Pirate Party, had ideas. Big ideas.

He'd developed his swarm theory of change based on his time working in IT, where work is often approached in a decentralized way. There may be managers overseeing teams, but the workload can be distributed amongst individual programmers who might be anywhere in the world, working together on a project.

> *"A swarm organization is a decentralized, collaborative effort of volunteers that looks like a hierarchical, traditional organization from the outside. It is built by a small core of people that construct a scaffolding of go-to people, enabling a large number of volunteers to cooperate on a common goal in quantities not possible before the Net was available."*

The internet has fundamentally transformed the organizing principles of our society, and yet so many institutions have resisted evolving in order to rise and meet the new world.

Swarm organizing shares many of the principles of Marshall Ganz's snowflake model, but necessitates the decentralized call to action of what Becky Bond called "big organizing" as we discussed in Chapter Three.

One classic example of this was when the mothers of Greenham made a call to action to ask for sixteen thousand women to join them in 1981 to encircle the Royal Air Force Base, which sheltered nuclear arms at the height of the Cold War. Over thirty-five thousand answered the call virtually overnight to put their bodies on the gears of the war machine.

Iceland's economy was hit hard by the fallout from the crash in 2008. A man named Hörður Torfason staged a one-man protest every week and invited people to come up on the microphone and speak their mind. By January the protests swelled to thousands of outraged citizens demanding accountability for the corruption.

This was reminiscent of another courageous individual who, in August 2018, at the age of fifteen, started spending her school days outside the Swedish Parliament to call for stronger action on the climate crisis. She sat on the ground with a sign reading *Skolstrejk för klimatet* (School strike for climate) and ignited the Fridays for the Future global youth climate strike movement. Greta Thunberg's historic stand earned her a Nobel Peace Prize nomination and she was honored as the youngest person to ever be made *Time* magazine's Person of the Year, proving once again that one person can change the world.

Political revolutionaries must always strive to evolve our ideas and our strategies, to adapt to a world that is constantly changing. You cannot transform the dominant paradigm while clinging to old ideas. The curve of technology's evolution is parabolic— meaning that it is advancing exponentially. Moore's law states that the number of transistors in microprocessors doubles about every two years. That means every two years, the same amount of money will allow you to buy a computer that's twice as fast and half the size.

These advancements in technology have led to irrevocable changes in our society. Various factions of the corporate state will use all available resources to take advantage of technological advances, in order to control the masses and to thwart grassroots organizers. We saw this at Standing Rock with weaponized technology like the StingRays. We witnessed Steve Bannon and Cambridge Analytica using technology to revolutionize voter microtargeting for Trump in 2016.

Activists must make use of new platforms and technology; just as the availability of drones enabled water protectors at Standing Rock to run counter-surveillance operations, we must always endeavor to innovate in order to make the best use of our greatest weapon—people power.

We can build the people power to transcend the hegemony of the corporate state when we:

> build rainbow fusion coalitions uniting movements for racial, climate, health, and economic justice.

> have inside-outside strategies that harness the power of mass-mobilization, to give our legislative advocates the leverage to pass people-centered policies.

> rally our cultural influencers and media platforms to support our big organizing calls to action, with messaging that inspires the masses to action.

> empower others, especially young people, to step into leadership instead of trying to control everything with centralized top-down organizing.

> ⟩ use tools like power mapping and make well-thought-out plans instead of simply reacting with performative prefigurative actions.

> ⟩ do the uncomfortable inner work of healing trauma and transforming the subtle assumptions of white supremacy, patriarchy, classism and colonialism that live within us.

Unfortunately, we do not do all of these things, nor do we always learn from our history, as we will examine in our post mortem examination of the Sanders 2020 campaign.

Chapter 11

Not Me. Us

Some rise by sin, and some by virtue fall.
-William Shakespeare

The term "hot wash" comes from the old Army practice of soldiers using extremely hot water to remove grit from their field rifles after firing them. I once heard an infantry soldier describe it as something "quick and dirty" that saves time down the road. This has become shorthand for doing an assessment of a team's strengths and weaknesses after an event to extract the important lessons and to improve its effectiveness. Just like the Democratic political establishment after they lost the White House to a reality TV show host, the Sanders campaign and political revolution also never performed a proper post-election autopsy.

If we had, history might have turned out differently. People may not like all of what is reported in this chapter, or some of the conclusions it suggests, but as Maya Angelou once said, "History, despite its wrenching pain, cannot be unlived, but if faced with courage, need not be lived again." The next generation of political revolutionaries do not have the luxury of spending a decade learning these painful lessons.

Leading up to 2020, there was a powerful sense of optimism. Bernie was the clear frontrunner. He had become one of the most famous and powerful men in the world. The Sanders movement had inspired groups like Brand New Congress and Justice Democrats to lead successful primary challenges against establishment incumbent Democrats. The 2018 midterm elections had witnessed a critical mass moment, when a twenty-eight-year-old Berniecrat bartender from the Bronx named Alexandria Ocasio-Cortez had unseated the fourth-ranking elected member of the Democratic Party.

Ocasio-Cortez—or AOC as she became known—was a self-avowed Democratic Socialist who had been inspired by Occupy and Standing Rock to take on the structures of power. Many of us had reached a similar conclusion after watching the Occupy encampments get dismantled by riot police. To truly challenge the power of the corporate state, it is necessary to have allies who are elected officials inside the system working together with grassroots coalitions committed to outside strategies, including direct action. Progressive and leftist movements have rarely achieved a cohesive and sustained inside-outside strategy.

I sat down with Jake DeGroot, who joined in supporting AOC's congressional bid early on. He was part of the Occupy Wall Street tech ops team with Charles Lenchner from the People for Bernie, Harry Waisbren and the crew for Act.tv. After the occupation at Zuccotti Park ended, Jake had gone back to doing freelance lighting design for the theater. When Trump was elected, DeGroot decided it was time to get back in the game and looked for a candidate to support.

He eventually decided to back the twenty-eight-year-old Democratic Socialist. The campaign would send her to subway stops to talk to potential working class voters, but Jake noticed that they weren't converting those conversations into useful voter data and contact information for follow up. According to Jake, the AOC campaign was experiencing challenges with traditional canvassing, as New York apartment complexes make going door-knocking difficult.

Jake went to Saikat Chakrabarti, the former Director of Organizing Technology for the Bernie Campaign, with an idea for a peer-to-peer canvassing application that would allow volunteers to record the info they'd collected from those valuable subway stump speeches and other events and convert it into voter files. The app supposedly accounted for 10 percent of the voters who helped Ocasio-Cortez unseat one of the most powerful incumbents in the Democratic Party leadership, sending shockwaves throughout the country and the political establishment.

AOC was joined by two powerful young Muslim women in Congress, Rashida Tlaib and Ilhan Omar, both Bernie supporters, and African American Ayanna Pressley. The emergence of four progressive women of color onto the national scene—soon dubbed collectively as "the Squad"—precipitated conservatives and the Democratic establishment to lose their fucking minds.

Around the same time, membership in Democratic Socialists of America began to skyrocket, growing from five thousand members by the end of 2016 to nearly forty thousand. As of 2021, after Bernie's second presidential run, the membership had reached over ninety-two thousand.

Justice Democrats was founded shortly after Trump's inaugu-
ration in 2017 by progressive YouTube politicos Kyle Kulinski of
Secular Talk and Cenk Uygur of The Young Turks. Saikat
Chakrabarti and Zack Exley, two of the architects of the 2016
Sanders campaign's barnstorm distributed-organizing strategy,
were also credited as co-founders. Justice Dems was dedicated to
electing grassroots candidates committed to rejecting corporate
Super PAC money and supporting the progressive policy agenda.
Alex Rojas was also a founding member but would come on board
to replace Saikat as Executive Director in 2018.

In 2018, Cenk was forced to resign for misogynistic blog posts
unearthed from two decades earlier, and Kulinsky left the organization in protest. The #*MeToo* movement was a seismic paradigm
change in the American patriarchal landscape following revelations
of Harvey Weinstein's pervasive rape and sexual abuse. The
Women's March mobilization in cities across America following
Trump's election was a powerful statement to signify that Donald's
blatant misogyny would not be normalized—at least not without a
fight. It started as a national organizing call to action by a woman
named Bob Bland, who put up a Facebook event that spread
like wildfire. Linda Sarsour and Winnie Wong also helped lead
the organizing effort.

Organizers reported that around 673 marches took place on
seven continents. There was even a Women's March event in
Antarctica, which meant that even in the most remote corners of
the earth, in subzero weather, women came out in solidarity to say
"fuck Donald Trump."

As we supported the mobilization I remembered the words of
Rose McGowan, who once said to me sometime in 2015 with steel
in her eyes and voice, that she "would one day bring the whole
rotten system down." At the time, I nodded with widened eyes and

slowly backed away. She was super intense. But it turns out that with enough intention and resolve, she was right—all things are possible. Little did I know, at that moment, I represented the majority of men who were blind to just how pervasive the problem of sexual assault is. Rose sent shockwaves through Hollywood after being one of the first to publicly accuse Harvey Weinstein of raping her, and then Amazon executives of covering it up. What followed was an outpouring of women coming forward in solidarity to publicly talk about their personal experiences of sexual assault.

She was right—I just couldn't hear it at the time. I guess this was always the problem to begin with.

The *#MeToo* campaign was first used to raise awareness about sexual assault by Black organizer Tarana Burke in 2006. After Alyssa Milano appropriated it without crediting Burke, the interwebs came to the rescue and Tarana got acknowledgement for her work.

#MeToo was an important piece of the political picture going into the 2020 election. Liberals had spent the better part of two years in a mania over allegations of Russian collusion with the Trump campaign, but other issues were beginning to push their way back into Democratic politics—led by the progressives' push to organize and prepare for a second Sanders campaign.

Our Revolution

The 2016 Sanders campaign was very different in many ways because it was purely an insurgent crusade.

Many organizers had run their own local canvassing operations to knock on doors. This was necessary, because in 2016 Sanders could neither afford, nor had access to, top Washington political consultants and operatives. Election professionals were terrified of incurring the wrath of the Clintons, leaving Bernie effectively blackballed. This turned out to have been a blessing, because it forced the campaign to embrace to a great degree the decentralized power of the grassroots movement that had powered his success. The 2016 campaign was more open to innovative models like the distributed organizing of the barnstorms.

The 2020 climate was very different. To the horror of the Washington establishment, Bernie began as the presumptive front-runner. Over the past four years he had built a fundraising avalanche and one of the most sought-after email lists in the world. Bernie had smashed all campaign fundraising records and was backed by a million dedicated volunteers.

The Sanders 2020 campaign did not have the shadow of Clinton retribution looming over it, as was the case in 2016. This meant the campaign had greater access to the professional consul-tant class. Unfortunately, this time around, it would not be so much of an advantage. Occupiers like Winnie Wong and Melissa Byrne also got jobs as high paid campaign consultants.

By 2019, the Sanders network had also built a great deal more infrastructure. Bernie, his family and his former campaign staff launched the Sanders Institute and a national political action organization called Our Revolution. The board consisted of Bernie heroes like Ben Jealous, James Zogby, Jane Kleeb, and our own Avenger Shailene Woodley.

Despite the persistent attempts of corporate media hacks to paint the broader Sanders movement as made up predominantly of young disaffected misogynistic males, the movement had grown incredibly diverse, a fact reflected in Our Revolution's surrogates: Indigenous leader Deborah Parker, former Nevada Assembly-woman Lucy Flores, and Catalina Velasquez, an immigration, reproductive justice and Trans Queer Liberation activist.

Still, the paradigm of patriarchy is in the fabric of every facet of our society, and despite all of the conscious efforts to uplift women leadership some senior staffers reported that there was a *boys' club* operating in some of the highest leadership positions within the campaign. For all of the positive efforts toward equity there were still endemic issues that would make the 2020 offensive a bumpy ride.

Over twenty-five hundred people hosted house parties across the country to watch Bernie announcing the launch of Our Revolution via livestream. When Bernie did a national livestream to barnstorm events, people would gather together amid a palpable feeling that we were watching our father or grandfather stand up to the establishment for our future.

The launch was far from smooth sailing, however. A number of staff immediately resigned when Jeff Weaver was named the Our Revolution president, citing his deficits in leadership.

When Claire Sandberg was asked by Amy Goodman during a *Democracy Now!* interview why she and other staff had quit, she said, "Jeff's leadership and advice as a legal adviser … hamstrung Our Revolution before it even launched, specifically [his] decision to constitute the organization as a 501(c)(4), which prevented us from doing effective down-ballot organizing for candidates…. He wanted to form a 501(c)(4) for the express purpose of accepting billionaire money, which of course flies in the face of what all of our supporters were so excited about, that we were taking a country back from the billionaire class without the use of billionaire money, $27 at a time."

A year after the launch of Our Revolution, Weaver stepped down and Nina Turner became the president of the organization.

In addition to this, former member of Bernie's Avengers Ann Kleinhenz reported that she and Shailene made efforts to help the 2020 staff learn from some of the mistakes of Bernie's previous run, but their concerns fell on deaf ears. They displayed little interest listening to the anxiety of two of Bernie's most dedicated and effective political revolutionaries. Consequently they, like many others who were disregarded, would remain on the sidelines during the most important political race of our lifetimes.

Mic Check at the Cuomo Fundraiser

The lead-up to the 2020 Democratic primaries also witnessed a very different field of candidates. All of the issues Bernie had run on in 2016 had become Democratic litmus tests for candidates four years later. Sanders and the grassroots movement behind him had fundamentally shifted the Overton Window on issues that had so recently been belittled as "too radical."

I believe that it is a principle in life that if you are about to reach another level, you must be prepared to face a bigger devil. And there would be no shortage of opponents that the Bernie Movement would have to face.

Beyond Senator Sanders's growing infrastructure of organizations, the Bernie Movement network had also continued to grow. It was natural that there was some attrition after the heartbreak of the 2016 campaign, but there was also an influx of new young people. Many who had been fans of Bernie but were too young to vote had since come of age. In the years leading up to 2020, some of us were thinking ahead and organizing. California Berniecrats were cutting canvassing turf years before the campaign even existed.

One day in November 2017, I got an urgent call from Nomiki. Bernie had not expressed any intention to run in 2020, but we understood that "if we built it, the Bern would come." There was a potentially big problem, though, in that Andrew Cuomo, the Governor of New York, had apparently amassed a $25 million war chest and the word on the street was that he was going to throw his hat in the ring for the Democratic primaries.

This was a problem.

He was a centrist, but potentially could position himself as a formidable opponent to Trump, and the liberals loved him. They loved him mostly because they didn't know that behind closed doors he was enabling a band of corporate Democrats in the New York state legislature called the Independent Democratic Conference (IDC), who had formed a coalition in the New York State Senate to give Republicans a majority in the chamber. New York progressives had been haunting the Governor about the issue.

The call from Nomiki was to let me know that Cuomo was going to be in Beverly Hills for a fundraiser, hosted by the nation's top media executives at the home of NBC Universal chairman Jeff Shell.

It cost $50,000 to be on the host committee. Minimum price for a ticket to get access to Governor Shithead was $5,000.

Who could afford that? His braintrust included Bob Iger, chairman and CEO of The Walt Disney Company; Leslie Roy Moonves, CEO of CBS Corporation and Co-President of Viacom; Kevin Tsujihara, CEO of Warner Bros. Entertainment; Bob Bakish, CEO of Viacom (now Paramount Global) since 1997; Jim Gianopulos, then-CEO of Paramount Pictures; Jeffrey Katzenberg, co-founder and CEO of DreamWorks; and Stacey Snider, then-Chairman and CEO of 20th Century Fox.

Basically a James Bond league of supervillain media moguls.

This would not stand. Not in our town, motherfuckers.

We worked with Leah Garland from SoCal 350 to get a crew together to go stand outside Jeff Shell's mansion as the guests arrived. When these media titans arrived I approached each guest and said, "Excuse me, I forgot my wallet, could I borrow $5,000 so I can go ask Governor Cuomo why he is enabling the IDC and not joining the other governors meeting at the Climate Convergence in Bonn, Germany?"

We then did an Occupy-style mic check outside the fundraiser for about two hours straight. It was loud, relentless and impossible to ignore.

That was the last we heard of Cuomo making any overtures toward running for president.

Less than a year later, Leslie Moonves was forced to resign as CEO of CBS when twelve women came forward with allegations of sexual harrassment and sexual assault.

A few months later Cynthia Nixon, star of the classic show *Sex in the City*, unsuccessfully challenged Cuomo in the gubernatorial race. Moumita Ahmed from the People for Bernie group and many New York Berniecrats passionately supported her race and the platform it represented.

She lost, but Cuomo later resigned in disgrace after multiple allegations of sexual misconduct.

One predator politician down. Many more to go.

Bernie 2.0

In 2016, people generally assumed that if Bernie were to win, it would require every individual taking the initiative and doing anything and everything they could. Leading up to 2020, the tone shifted from the ingenuity and leadership of individuals, to a general sentiment that Sanders's organization was leading the charge. He was no longer the long shot outsider. The fear of Clinton retribution no longer loomed over the campaign talent pool. Bernie was one of the most famous and powerful politicians in the world, had an enormous people-powered war chest and in many ways was the clear front runner.

Money is like blood in the water, and where there is blood in the water you can be sure that the sharks will begin to circle.

To the public, Bernie and his movement were gaining momentum. The decentralized organizing among the grassroots again powered Sanders's success, but 2020 was a much more top-down campaign than 2016. Here it is important to recognize that there was the Sanders Campaign, and then there was the Bernie movement or Political Revolution.

These were not the same.

But the main difference this time was that Sanders wasn't trying to build the airplane while it was trying to take off. Now there was infrastructure.

I think many of us had given so much of ourselves in 2016 that we were more than willing to believe for a time that we could trust that Bernie's team knew what they were doing.

Chris Kantrowitz reached out to me and said the campaign was interested in getting the 2016 band back together, so to speak. Bernie's stepson had proposed that the campaign work directly with Bernie supporters in Hollywood to make content for the campaign, instead of hiring out-of-touch Washington political ad agencies.

Thus Bernie's Wizards was born. It was an homage to Luis Calderin, Sanders's former Arts, Culture, and Youth Vote Director whom you might remember was the lead point of contact with the campaign for our Bernie's Avengers team in 2016. He used to call us wizards.

My first call was to Jamie McGurk, one of my favorite class traitors from the 1 Percent. Her husband Chris had once served as the president of Walt Disney Studios and as a top executive at Universal and MGM. Together they were a very media-savvy couple. We met at their house in the Hollywood Hills. It was like our Sanctum Sanctorum.

We put together an impressive crew of creatives to workshop content for the campaign. Some leftists and progressives draw hard lines in the sand, but I personally believe that anyone who is willing to stand and offer support to the 99 Percent is a welcome comrade. It's true that class privilege can result in blind spots, but in my experience it's possible to shift consciousness by holding conversations and building relationships. A class traitor from the 1 Percent can be a powerful ally—revolutions since time immemorial have been supported by rogue members of the ruling class.

At the end of the day though wealthy people and celebrities are still members of the 1 Percent so it is unrealistic to expect that they will remain dauntless comrades in the class war for the future. Don't be heartbroken if at some point they turn out to be just another rich asshole parachuting in to cosplay revolutionary for a hot minute, only to retreat back to the safety of their luxurious and comfortable lifestyles when the going gets hard. Even if they grew up poor working class, at some point they would have inevitably forgotten what it is like to struggle to survive. They may make empty promises, but take everything with a grain of salt. As a rule, expectations will always lead to let-downs.

There are outliers like Danny Glover, Mark Ruffalo, and Jane Fonda that are ride-or-die lifelong activists, but as a rule it's best not to have expectations of influencers (or of anyone for that matter).

Regardless of what happens, it is best to try to keep good relations and be grateful when anyone is willing to join in the fight. The only thing you can control is to keep your own side of the street clean.

The Wizards met regularly with the national campaign staff to discuss events, the wrangling of surrogates, and content creation. It was a great idea, except that six months into our regular meetings and organizing it became clear that the campaign had no intention of funding or using our content ideas. As my friend Susie Shannon put it, the campaign "kept us sharpening pencils" while we enjoyed the illusion of contributing. But in truth we were just being kept busy, like children. Susie was the California political director for the campaign but was one of us. She was a part of the PDA Musician's Union event for Bernie in 2015 but had been fighting for the poor and unhoused Angelenos for over fifteen years.

The honeymoon finally ended for me when Charles Lenchner from the People for Bernie group called me in August 2019. He was deeply concerned that the campaign was operating off some bad assumptions and had abandoned traditional relational organizing. He knew I had the ear of the national staff because I was one of Bernie's top surrogate wranglers, and was distressed because it seemed that the campaign was operating under the belief that the path to victory lay solely in targeting and mobilizing the enormous swath of disillusioned voters who had never participated in the political process.

At first I challenged his assertion because it seemed that the campaign was really engaged with us and with the grassroots, but the more I looked, the more I saw the truth behind what he was imploring me to understand—we were not on a course that would bring us to victory.

It would be reductive to suggest that this was the only strategic and tactical approach of the campaign, but as time went by it did become evident that this was the driving theory of change.

This became more clear as Elizabeth Warren's campaign generated momentum and began to absorb supporters that otherwise would naturally have backed Bernie. I warned the national staff that Bernie was going to lose the Working Families Party endorsement to Warren. Her campaign, unlike Sanders's, had embraced relational organizing of grassroots leaders and recognized its value with influential groups like Black Womxn For, a group of two hundred black women organizers that had created an influential coalition. Senator Warren was actually sitting down with these organizers and courting their support, which was an approach that Bernie 2020 resisted. The campaign leadership did not seem to want anyone outside of their direct network to build power.

The campaign did attempt this through their "Victory Captain" program, which sought to engage super volunteers, but it did not have the scalable impact that the 2016 barnstorms did, because those who signed up were never allowed to build any real power or agency to lead. Victory captains never had a meaningful role in the campaign. There was a Bernie app that would allow vols (volunteers) to collect the data from their peers, but the user experience and design were clunky. There were functionality issues, including the fact that there was no ability to push text users to take GOTV actions. The digital and field programs were often at odds with one another. This was a far cry from the approach that AOC's campaign had taken—where all resources were deployed to work in synergy to exploit any edge possible when it came to relational organizing, new technology, and a scrappy field program that worked to empower volunteers, not bring them to heel.

The Bernie 2020 Campaign, having drunk its own Kool-Aid, also largely rejected the traditional old school politicking that has run elections since time immemorial. We loved Bernie for his uncompromising nature, but this also meant he wouldn't promise cabinet positions for endorsements, and down the stretch this would prove to be a fatal liability that the establishment would exploit.

Not-So-Radical Rulers

There was often talk amongst campaign staff that the theory of change was still distributed organizing, but really the distributed model of the 2016 campaign had all but been abandoned. The new "big idea" was consultant-driven, neo-Alinsky, top-down organizing.

Most political consultants adhered to the same traditional models of political organizing. There is a sense of the *way things are done.*

All paradigms by nature are resistant to change.

Since the 1950s, Saul Alinsky's organizing philosophy has been the gold standard in grassroots power building. Alinsky, who was called "the father of community organizing," developed his style of organizing in the 1930s, working with the most oppressed and exploited people to build power in their own communities and therefore giving them agency over their own destinies.

The Alinsky method relied heavily on relationships, knocking on doors and having many one-on-one conversations. As Alinsky led communities to victory he eventually began to raise large sums of money. Though he personally rejected the idea of top-down hierarchical organizing, the paradigm driving campaigns and non-profits that arose out of his philosophies were very much this way structurally.

Alinsky's landmark primer *Rules for Radicals* expressed a moral relativism that one could argue defined the political philosophy of one of his most famous acolytes—Hillary Clinton.

"In war," Alinsky said, "the end justifies almost any means." He also said that "The judgment of the ethics of means is dependent upon the political position of those sitting in judgment."

Hillary Clinton wrote her senior thesis at Wellesley College about the Alinsky model of organization and once personally interviewed him. His influence dominated grassroots political organizing for decades, eventually becoming the paradigm for big, well-funded and well-staffed hierarchical organizations.

In 2016, while Steve Bannon was reinventing modern politics with psychographic microtargeting of voters on social media, the Democratic establishment was doing the same things they had always done. This paradigm of neo-Alinskyism is rooted in a structure that empowers a class of professional consultants running heavily-staffed organizations that stifle innovation and often try to suppress more transformational forms of working-class mobilization.

In Los Angeles grassroots organizers persisted in GOTV efforts, but many were stonewalled by professional consultants who worked to maintain their control over the volunteer base. I know this because one of my favorite LA activists, Susie Shannon, told me.

She had been part of the initial PDA efforts to recruit Bernie in 2015, and was even made the California Political Director for a time, until she was finally run out of the position in a very toxic, knife-in-the-back, Macchiavellian fashion. The worst part about it was that she was undergoing surgery for cancer at the time. She called me, in tears, immediately after the incident took place but swore me to secrecy because she didn't want it to get out and potentially hurt Bernie's run. Susie and Levi Sanders (Bernie's son) shared a great many insights into what was happening in the inner circle of the campaign.

Bernie was largely insulated from these political machinations. Carlos Marroquin—one of the most ride-or-die Bernie activists, who had organized bus trips of volunteers to canvas in different states, had helped organize the Rose Bowl parade action. Who was responsible for this shift in organizing philosophy? Who had hired these people? One name kept coming up: Chuck Rocha.

Who the fuck was Chuck Rocha?

Rocha, it turned out, was a former labor consultant brought on by Jeff Weaver as a strategist, mostly because he claimed he could deliver the Latino vote in Texas.

Rocha had pleaded guilty in 2013 to one felony count of union embezzlement for stealing funds from the United Steelworkers Union in 2008 and 2009, when he was its political director. According to federal Office of Labor-Management Standards records listing criminal convictions of union officials:

> *On July 30, 2013, in the United States District Court for the Western District of Pennsylvania, Charles E. Rocha, former Political Director for the Steelworkers International Union (located in Pittsburgh, Pa.), was sentenced to two years of probation and was ordered to pay a fine of $2,000. Rocha had previously made restitution in the amount of $12,449.*

This raised the question for many of us: why was Rocha being protected by the campaign? Darius Khalil Gordon, a highly respected Black organizer from The Center for Popular Democracy, was fired for tweets that he'd made over ten years ago, when he was barely out of high school.

In both cases there was bad press, but why was Rocha beyond censure, while Darius was immediately cast out? As a director for the Center for Popular Democracy, Darius had deep roots in grassroots community organizing. Rocha, by contrast, was an inside operative. It also raised the question: why wasn't the press doing deep dives into the tweet archives of staffers working for Biden, Buttigieg, Klobuchar, Kamala, Beto, or Bloomberg?

These questions point to an underlying truth about American politics: If you are challenging the system, then you and everyone in your employ have to be spotless. But if you are from the establishment, the attitude is simply, "Boys will be boys."

I learned in 2019 that Rocha and Weaver had plans to launch their own super PACS to fundraise off of the progressive base. Rocha would go on to form the Nuestro PAC, and Weaver would launch America's Progressive Promise.

The names of these organizations are misnomers, in my opinion.

Weaver initially called his political action committee, "Future to Believe In," co-opting Sanders' 2016 campaign slogan. According to a report in *Vice*, the Senator was "pissed" about the fact that Weaver had created a super PAC, the political entity that he had been railing against for five consecutive years. This super PAC's chief goal? You guessed it: to raise money for Joe Biden.

What followed was an ideological and strategic rift, driven by campaign staff looking to join the establishment and capitalize off of the bacchanalian feeding frenzy of consultant money that accompanies US presidential elections. Since Rocha and Weaver were mostly in charge of the hiring process, their influence had a huge impact on the leadership tone of the campaign, which as far as we could see was anything but "change from the bottom-up," as Bernie had evangelized.

Union organizing is highly regimented and hierarchical. American Labor Unions have built enormous political power due to the fact that they are structured like a standing army with a chain of command. Union leaders are able to leverage the large numbers of their membership. They have inside strategies working with allies in the political establishment, and outside strategies to strike and do direct actions.

We must confront the reality that, though they are critical to protect workers, they have also failed to innovate over the last four decades. The modern world changes radically on a yearly basis, but unions have largely failed to evolve. Just as there has been a civil war within the Democratic Party between the neoliberals and the progressives for control, there has been a growing tension between the union leadership and the rank and file who, around the time of Occupy, began to realize that they should have power over their own destinies.

Prior to Occupy Wall Street, union membership and approval ratings were at an all time low. Union leaders had sold out workers with years of bad contracts and concessions to the corporate bosses.

It was no secret that Bernie was a ride or die union ally. In 1979 Sanders made a spoken-word documentary about his hero, the legendary union leader and founder of the International Workers of the World, Eugene Debs.

But the philosophical incompatibility between the top-down approach of the labor leaders hired to advise the campaign, and the bottom-up ethos of the message of the political revolution, created an incoherence and friction that would prevent 2020 efforts from realizing their full power and potential to harness the whirlwind of the Bernie Movement.

It makes perfect sense that Bernie would support having union leaders like Chuck Rocha in key positions, but it is also clear that there was a gap in understanding with respect to how the organizing philosophy of those leaders would clash with the movement behind him. Senator Sanders always evangelized that "real change comes from the bottom up"—unfortunately some of his top lieutenants created a paradigm in direct opposition to this principle. According to confidential sources, they would seek to prevent grassroots leaders from building power in the context of the 2020 campaign.

In their defense, it is important that political campaigns be disciplined. Progressives and leftists historically are the most anarchic and thus the hardest to organize into a highly regimented standing army. A populist grassroots movement is also largely made up of poor working people, which means there will be greater challenges in terms of the historical trauma, internalized classism, racism, and patriarchy that volunteers will bring to their efforts. This will inevitably result in obstacles with respect to infighting and personality conflicts. These factors also make insurgent campaigns more susceptible to paid infiltrators, creating fracture points and internal drama that can derail efforts.

Having said that, there is a virtually limitless supply of potential talent in the grassroots. The most successful areas utilized and developed the talent in their communities, though in many cases this was in opposition to senior national staff members who often put forth mandates to neutralize some of the most influential local leaders.

Another dirty secret when it comes to campaigns is that political consultants run some of the most successful rackets in the world— taking a percentage of funds raised, media buys, printed literature, and even snacks for volunteers.

In total the Sanders 2020 campaign shelled out more than $200 million, at least half of which went to political consultants. Sanders's campaigns for instance have paid Rocha's Solidarity Strategies $12 million since 2015. Tim Tagaris' Aisle 518 Strategies Firm made over $16 million.

This becomes a problem when a consultant negotiates a contract for all of the campaign literature, for which they take a large commission off of every piece and control all the vendors used. Instead of areas being able to print lit as needed, using local shops, they would have to have it shipped from across the country. Many field organizers were forced to hoard literature. It becomes a problem when those at the top use the hiring process to bring in their own boys' networks, enriching themselves and preventing local leaders from building any power independently of their direct control.

The truth is that there is a whole consultant class that exists only to make money off of the backs of working people, who donate what little they have to the few candidates they believe will actually represent their interests. The truth is that they will get theirs regardless of the outcome of the election. Democratic consultants paid themselves over $1 billion to lose against a reality television star in 2016.

It's a grift of truly epic proportions.

This doesn't necessarily mean that all political consultants are bad people with bad motives, it just means that over time, the money and power available can be more seductive than solidarity with the working class.

The Neoliberal Empire Strikes Back

In the run-up to the California primary, Jamie McGurk and I continued to put the word out to our network of Los Angeles creatives to expand the Bernie's Wizards team. My first call was of course to Kii Arens and a few other Avengers alums. Ron Placone, a frequent guest on the Jimmy Dore show, became a regular. We helped organize meet and greets for LA influencers and the campaign surrogate team. Jimmy Dore, though he had been a part of Bernie's Avengers in 2016, didn't come into the fold. He expressed deep hurt and frustration that the Sanders 2020 staff wouldn't grant him an interview with the Senator.

We also were experiencing growing frustration because the campaign had asked us to bring together creatives to make content for Bernie, but then seemed to just be jerking us around—with the exception of onboarding our network of celebrities to which they were very responsive. Despite the frustrations, The Wizards carried on regardless with various projects to support the political revolution.

Meanwhile, Leftbook—the anarcho hivemind that exists in leftist social media spaces—collectively aligned on a strategy to target Bernie's opponents one by one. First on the list was Beto O'Rourke, an Irish-American state senator from Texas with a fake Spanish name who had become a national sensation running against America's most hated Zodiac killer look-alike, Ted Cruz. Beto grossly misinterpreted the enthusiasm and underestimated the extent to which progressives would take him to task over his filthy Texas oil money donations.

It was heartbreaking to learn that Bernie 2016 heroes Becky Bond and Zack Malitz had worked on Beto's Texas campaign—and then stayed on for his 2020 presidential bid—instead of coming back to Sanders. The flow of campaign money can be seductive even for progressive consultants, which is why leaders and progressive political operatives must maintain solidarity through relational organizing. There is no victory without solidarity, and no solidarity without relationships.

Then there was former prosecutor and senator from California Kamala Harris, the heir apparent to the Clinton network of wealthy donors. Her greatest hits included not prosecuting future Trump Treasury Secretary and architect of his tax scam, "California foreclosure king" Steve Mnuchin. Earlier, Mnuchin had defrauded the public with his banker-ponzi scheme. He was a big donor. She had also prosecuted poor working parents of color for allowing their kids to skip school.

In many progressives' eyes, Elizabeth Warren presented the biggest impediment to the success of the Bernie campaign and movement. This was a hard fact to accept. The truth is that we all would have followed Warren into the fires of Mordor in 2015 if she had answered Occupy's call to run for president.

There had been a great ideological divide between Bernie and Hillary in 2016 and no other serious challenger. In contrast, 2020 featured a wider field of candidates. There was a moment when it looked like Warren would seize the momentum. Her campaign was a well-oiled machine, and had garnered the Working Families Party endorsement—which most had assumed would go to Bernie—and Black Womxn For, a coalition of influential grass-roots leaders. Her campaign had embraced relational organizing.

The velocity of her campaign had a few hiccups when it was revealed that she had gone to law school by applying as an Indigenous Cherokee woman despite having zero Native American DNA. She did, however, run a very well-organized campaign. It's a shame that there was no capacity for real solidarity with the 99 Percent and the robust movement that had been continuing unabated under the Bernie moniker.

I warned the national staff that Bernie was going to lose the Working Families Party endorsement to Warren because her campaign, unlike Sanders's, had embraced relational organizing and recognized its value with influential groups like Black Womxn For. Warren actually sat down with these organizers and courted their support, which was an approach that Bernie 2020 resisted. The campaign leadership did not seem to want anyone outside of their direct network to build power. It didn't matter; just as Lenchner had predicted, they seemed to be drunk on the kool-aid that they were marching inevitably toward victory, even if fate had other ideas.

It is my hope that, one day, revolutionary progressives begin to organize our own coalition primaries with blockchain voting, early enough for the 99 Percent to align behind a single candidate before the race begins. One of the reasons we lose is because we split the vote and self-segregate, rather than focus on building bigger coalitions and deepening solidarity across the ranks.

Bernie also had significant challenges farther to the right of the neoliberal spectrum. An unknown young gay mayor of South Bend, Indiana named Pete Buttigieg had entered the race. He ticked all of the liberal technocratic identity candidate boxes. He was a Harvard and Oxford grad, a Rhodes Scholar, a member of the LGBTQIA+ community and even a veteran.

Upon graduating from Oxford, Buttigieg chose the McKinsey & Company management consulting firm.

Who exactly is McKinsey & Company? Imagine the ominous James Bond villain organization SPECTRE, who pride themselves on developing a cult-like relationship with their so-called elite employees. They are basically corporate mercenary consultants for the world's most unethical corporations and authoritarian governments. They allegedly offered their expertise to Purdue

Pharma on how to "turbocharge" OxyContin sales and keep users hooked on the product, thus fueling the opioid crisis.

How do you know you live in an oligarchy? The Sackler family made billions of dollars killing five hundred thousand Americans, knowingly creating the opioid epidemic. Even after fines they are still billionaires and not a single one was ever prosecuted, and neither were any of their executives. The oligarchs are not subject to laws or the standards of basic human decency.

And Mayor Pete was on the team that helped them.

The *New York Times* reported that McKinsey also did more than $20 million in consulting work for ICE, helping the agency figure out how to execute Trump's xenophobic doctrine against undocumented Americans. McKinsey proposed spending cuts on food, medical care and supervision for detainees … because they are garbage people with no conscience or connection to humanity.

Mayor Pete ran on the brand of being a vanilla centrist alternative to the more "radical" progressives. It was no surprise that Buttigieg quickly became the favorite candidate of Wall Street, garnering more campaign donations from the financial, insurance and real estate sectors than any other White House hopeful, according to the Center for Responsive Politics.

He was endorsed by Matt Kaczmarek, vice president of BlackRock, the world's largest investment manager, controlling a fund worth nearly $7 trillion. It was reported in December 2018 that BlackRock was the world's largest investor in coal plant developers, holding shares worth $11 billion among fifty-six coal plant developers. BlackRock owns more oil, gas, and thermal coal reserves than any other investor, with total reserves amounting to 9.5 gigatonnes of CO^2 emissions—or 30 percent of total energy-related emissions for planet Earth.

Amazon Watch called them the "world's largest investor in deforestation."

Pete was also endorsed by Karen Mathiasen, former acting executive US director at the World Bank, the neocolonial institution that uses debt to seize the natural resources of developing nations.

Billionaires hosted wine cave fundraisers for him in Napa Valley.

As excited as the Wall Street fat cats were about Buttigieg, he generated the most enthusiastic support from the military and intelligence communities. His campaign released a list of over two hundred endorsements from members of the CIA, NSA, and DoD and other "foreign policy and national security professionals."

This included endorsements from David S. Cohen, the deputy director of the CIA from 2015 to 2017; Charlie Gilbert, former deputy director of the National Clandestine Service, one of the highest leadership positions at the CIA; and Robert Stasio, the former chief of operations at the NSA Cyber Center.

Based on his consultant contracting and military escapades in Afghanistan and Iraq, there was speculation that Pete himself may have been a Central Intelligence spook, when *#CIAPete* began circulating. Then this tweet surfaced in response to Trump's joint press conference with Putin:

On July 16th, 2018, Pete tweeted, "Today, friends of mine are risking their lives to serve the US Intelligence Community, as I once did. For the US president to say they are no more credible than the hostile foreign dictator standing next to him is a national security disaster. He must resign."

Memes of Mayor Pete bearing a striking resemblance both to Evil Morty (from the show Rick and Morty) and the poster child of the Evil Empire from the Rage Against the Machine album of the same name were quickly disseminated online. The best description I heard on Twitter was, "Mayor Pete looks like Howdy Doody, if he was a fucking narc."

He was confronted by Black Lives Matter activists from his home city. Henry Davis, Jr. said about Mayor Pete, "As a Council-man in *#SouthBend*, I know why @PeteButtigieg looked like a deer in headlights last night when talking about systemic racism in the South Bend Police. He tolerated it, he perpetuated it, and last night he lied to millions of Americans about it."

Wendell Potter, former public relations VP of Cigna Health, and a self-described reformed insurance propagandist, was once called the "Daniel Ellsberg of corporate America" by Michael Moore. Potter became a whistleblower after the death of seventeen-year-old leukemia patient Nataline Mary Sarkisyan, when the insurance company he worked for denied her claim for a life-saving liver transplant. Potter had recommended the company approve the payment for her surgery. They reversed the decision after protesters raised awareness of Nataline's case outside of Cigna's offices, which generated media attention, causing her mother to jump for joy, hugging demonstrators on live television at the news. Nataline died just a few hours later.

Potter had this to say about Mayor Pete's refusal to acknowledge his role in McKinsey's consulting for the health insurance industry in a series of tweets:

> *"Why is this relevant to 2020? I'll leave analysis of @petebuttigieg's transparency, or his potential role in rate hikes and layoffs, to political experts. What I can speak to is how this experience might lead him to defend and protect health insurance companies now.*
>
> *"Pete is fighting to preserve the role & profits of health insurance companies, spending huge sums on ads slamming plans to rein them in. I'll be watching to see if my former insurance colleagues send him big campaign checks. He's probably one of their favorite candidates.*

"As I know firsthand, insurers intentionally deny coverage to Americans, to hoard their profits. The result is people dying and millions in medical bankruptcy. Pete's plan protects and preserves this very system. Now we may know why."

For political revolutionaries, stopping these candidates and electing allies is one of the most important fronts in the class war for the soul of America. Shills like Mayor Pete are the tip of the spear for the corporate state and military industrial complex, who support people like him because they understand well that they are but empty vessels for their interests. Anyone that comes from the consultant class has no business in elected office.

The biggest threat to the success of the Sanders campaign and our movement, however, was former Vice President Joe Biden. It has been a longstanding American political tradition to assume that vice presidents are "next in line." This was true even if that candidate wrote the 1994 Crime Bill, had been accused of sexual assault, and opposed desegregation.

The fact was, liberals liked Joe. Despite everything in his past, he was Obama's guy—the classic archetype of the jocular, elder white politician, the kind who might get cast as president in a Michael Bay movie.

Despite what conservatives think, leftists are neither liberals, nor Democratic Party loyalists. There remains enormous power to be had in harnessing the collective energy and intelligence of the Internet, if you have enough numbers and a clear outcome. Bannon understood this in 2016, and was able to mobilize the darker corners of the web and to convert them to political power. We were depending on doing something broadly similar from the left.

The Democratic establishment had learned to not take this threat lightly with respect to the massive grassroots army and the reality that he was the clear frontrunner in 2019. David Brock publicly acknowledged wrangling other Democratic operatives (code for shitbag corporate consultants) to intentionally derail Bernie's efforts. Neera Tanden, a well-known player in the neoliberal establishment, played a central role in coordinating the Stop Sanders efforts. Typical in this was a series of dinners hosted by Wall Street CEO Bernard Schwartz that were attended by Nancy Pelosi, Chuck Schumer, and Indiana's favorite former McKinsey hack, Mayor Pete Buttigieg. They collectively referred to themselves as the "Never Bernie" crowd.

The real test of any movement is when the opposition begins to vigorously organize against you, as we experienced when mayors and sheriffs across the country had meetings to plan the demise of Occupy Wall Street and Standing Rock, often under the guidance of consultants hired by private corporations.

The irony is that Bernie had for months remained the obvious frontrunner in the race and was always the candidate with the best chance at defeating Trump. Yet party leaders did exactly what they had accused Bernie of doing in 2016: they sabotaged the Democrats' strongest candidate and best chance at winning back the White House.

Chapter 12

The Bernocalypse

Where there is unity there is always victory.
-Publilius Syrus

In October, tragedy struck when Bernie's daughter-in-law, Rainè Riggs, died at age 46 of cancer, followed by the candidate's own heart attack. The media sharks circled, smelling blood in the water. They would take any opportunity to attack Sanders, and if no opportunities presented themselves, they would invent and orchestrate them. On one occasion, the *Washington Post* fact-checker Glenn Kessler went out of his way to undermine the bulletproof veracity of Bernie's statement that "millions of Americans are forced to work two or three jobs just to survive."

After Bernie's heart attack, the hyenas went in for the kill. Never mind that Biden could barely put together a single coherent sentence, and presented an endless series of racist gaffes and inappropriate gropes. Joe even got a full pass with respect to allegations of sexual assault by a former staffer named Tara Reade. Liberal identity politics is used as a weapon in the court of public opinion against movements for justice, but rarely are the same standards applied to the agents of the establishment.

But as things seemed like they couldn't get any worse, a ray of light burst through the dark clouds. Just when Bernie's campaign was on the precipice of a total meltdown, AOC shocked the world by publicly endorsing the senator that had inspired her to run in 2018. Hers was one of the most sought-after endorsements of the campaign cycle, and unlike the majority of self-interested phonies who pretend to be progressive, AOC showed her quality. Rashida Tlaib and Ilhan Omar subsequently endorsed Sanders, too. That was three-quarters of The Squad.

They kicked off the announcement with a massive forty-thousand-person rally in AOC's home district of Queens, where she famously referred to him as "Tio Bernie." One perk of working with the surrogate team for the campaign was getting the inside track on these happenings, which we often helped organize after getting last-minute calls to wrangle bands and speakers.

The Queens event was epic. In Bernie's speech, he asked everyone listening, "Would you be willing to fight for somebody you didn't know?" This phrase and slogan, "Not Me. Us.", came to define the spirit of the 2020 campaign—meaning that the movement was never about Bernie, it was about every one of us coming together and rising up.

Bernie's Wizards continued recruiting surrogates and developing projects. Orion Solarion brought in Jason Mraz. The last time we had met was backstage at the Prairie Knights Casino at Standing Rock where he was performing a benefit show for the water protectors. Comedians Jeff Ross (the Roast Master General), stand up comic Helen Hong from the hit show *Silicon Valley*, and Ron Placone also came into the fold. Matthew Cooke, who had made PSAs for Bernie and our *#BankExit* demonstration video, also joined the wizard party.

One of the highlights of the year for our squad was being called upon to help wrangle cultural influencers for a clutch (meet and greet) with Bernie and AOC before the big Venice Beach rally. I was able to bring in Willow Smith, daughter of Will and Jada Pinkett Smith, to the campaign, and she was absolutely psyched to come on board.

The Wizards helped fill that entire room in Venice with celebs and got no props whatsoever. We brought a lot of heads to the party, but the campaign staff took all the victory laps. It became apparent that we were putting up results for the campaign consultants who were making five figures a month in salaries off of our work and relationships but giving us zero credit.

On another occasion, The Wizards organized another party at the request of the campaign at McGurk's house in the Hollywood Hills to recruit more entertainment industry influencers. Instead of engaging these new influential with opportunities to support the campaign, we witnessed some of the top national campaign advisors address the crowd and simply talk about themselves for about an hour. It was at that moment I finally realized that Charles Lenchner was right—the campaign was like a runaway train with no real conductor. Our general sense that the campaign had everything under control and knew what it was doing was a terrible assumption. At one point one of the former Occupy comrades working as a senior advisor stood in front of the Bernie's Wizards and told them that they should just be phonebanking instead of pitching the ideas that the campaign had asked us to

curate in the first place; because "*they* were the campaign, not us."
Our crew was dumbfounded.

So much for *not me, us.*

It was a huge psychic blow.

As traumatic as this was, we did our best to brush it off and
carry on with the work. All that mattered was that Sanders was on
track to win the nomination. This was the best chance humanity
had to have a Commander-in-Chief who could help the world
save itself from the climate apocalypse.

Director Adam McKay and Josh Hutcherson had been
passionate supporters in 2016. We were able to help them get back
in the game in the final stretch. I waited for McKay to come out of
the theater he had been speaking at like a stalker, and told him we
were getting the band back together. Josh showed up at GOTV
events to fire up the troops, especially at the colleges where he
would inspire young fans of his work as the character Peeta in the
Hunger Games.

We felt like we were very close to making history when a young
LA progressive and music manager named Ed Ellis, known for his
roster of Korean Pop artists, called me to pitch an idea. Ed also
was able to introduce Ariana Grande and reconnect Miley Cyrus
to the Sanders campaign. As it happened, some of the Wizards
had been workshopping something along similar lines so it all
came together.

David Lynch once said, "We don't create ideas, we just catch
them like fish. No chef takes credit for making the fish, just preparing
[it]." I very much subscribe to this notion. I also believe that many
people might catch the same idea, but what separates us from the
rest is finding those who have the courage and tenacity to act on it.

But just because we catch an idea and act on it, doesn't mean
it always goes according to plan.

Bernfest

One night Ed Ellis called to pitch me on organizing an idea he had to put together: a giant stadium sized for Bernie. Before I'd gotten involved in the Sanders campaigns, I was known for organizing cause-driven events, but a festival of the magnitude suggested by Ellis was above my paygrade. The biggest events I had ever produced had been between two to four thousand people. But Ed was not deterred; he asked what we would need to pull it off. I told him that to do it right we would need someone like Coachella founder and producer Paul Tollett.

A couple of days later, Ed had contacted Tollett's brother and business partner. Kii Arens had worked with him on designing flyers for some of his iconic festivals, so he and Jamie McGurk joined the effort to close the deal and make it happen with the campaign.

We all met at Golden Voice's production suite in Downtown LA. Present was Caleb Wilson, Bernie's National Advance manager, who had submitted our proposal and tried to get Paul onboarded as an official surrogate. It turns out that, along with writing the '94 Crime Bill and fighting to gut Social Security, Biden had waged a war on rave promoters, which is how Paul got his start organizing events. Needless to say, he signed on.

He put a date on hold for the Rose Bowl for Bernfest within days. This was a venue with a capacity of ninety thousand. The line-up we initially discussed would have put even Coachella to shame, and sent shockwaves across the nation. Between Paul Tollett and the Campaign, the sky was the limit. Imagine an all-day rally and music festival featuring Bernie, AOC, Nina Turner, Cardi B, Bon Iver, Jack White, Ariana Grande, Killer Mike, and a number of other top-tier names supporting the Senator. Paul was also planning to put in a call to Rage Against the Machine.

This would have been the biggest election event ever, general or primary, and would have sent a clear message that Bernie was still the frontrunner and it wasn't even close.

Except the event never happened.

Why did the campaign pass on Bernfest? We were told that Faiz Shakir, Bernie's campaign manager, got sticker shock when he saw the upfront costs.

What he didn't realize was that the campaign would have made it back and more. Paul Tollett was arguably the top concert promoter in the world. In my opinion, this would have been a game-changer in the national narrative early in the race. It was also clear that Caleb wanted to micromanage the discussion and flex that he was in charge. It was mind-boggling to me that the campaign didn't just let Paul Tollett and his team, who were the best in the world at organizing events, do their thing.

A few years later, I got a better sense of what happened after sitting for coffee with Winnie Wong and Claire Sandberg in June of 2022. Apparently, Faiz had failed to keep track of the budget and the campaign was running out of money, despite Bernie again breaking all campaign fundraising records by receiving over two hundred million dollars in small-dollar donations. They painted a picture of Faiz, Jeff Weaver, and Chuck Rocha, like three blind mice trying to drive an aircraft carrier. Their egos would not hear the truth from their subordinates—that the campaign was not on solid ground.

According to Claire and Winnie, the campaign had been co-opted into a boys club that existed for one purpose: to build and maintain power for themselves. Bernie was largely insulated from the grim truth of the situation, though in reality, at this stage it is unlikely he could have done anything about it. He had already handed them the keys and, in the home stretch, that would matter.

Pussy Riot Feels the Bern

Kii Arens and I went to a music festival at a lake outside of Riverside, California, to recruit bands. Mark Mothersbaugh from Devo told me that Bernie was the only politician he would open for. I tried but struck out with U-God from the Wu-Tang Clan backstage, whom I had known from our work together on Free and Equal Fest back in 2015, a concert promoting third party candidates being allowed to participate in national presidential debates. We had a hearty reunion but he wasn't into The Bern. On our way home from the backstage area, I saw that Pussy Riot had their own trailer. I suppose it might be considered brash or even rude, but we didn't have much to lose, so I knocked on the door. One of the bandmates popped her head out from behind the doors.

"Sorry to bother you, and I know this is super weird, but I'm helping book bands for Bernie Sanders if you are interested," I said.

Then another head appeared from behind the white door of the portable star trailer. It belonged to Nadya Tolokno, Russian political activist and founding member of the anarchist feminist musical group Pussy Riot. "Bernie?!! I would die for Bernie Sanders!!" she said without missing a beat.

This was great, because Pussy Riot was the epitome of empowered political feminism and they were the ultimate symbols of defiance against the Putin regime. This would be a powerful counter to the centrist narratives and tropes about the Sanders movement being manipulated by Russian propaganda.

Nadya was a badass.

She had been imprisoned for two years for performing a song critical of Vladamir Putin in a Russian cathedral. During her incarceration, she'd gone on a hunger strike to protest conditions.

Most of the relationships with cultural influencers I have developed over the years were made possible by a combination of two factors: unabashed boldness, and being able to clearly, directly, confidently and most of all succinctly communicate the mission I would like others to support. Remember that most social influencers are constantly asked to support an endless number of causes. I try to use a very grounded, matter of fact, direct tone of voice and to convey with confidence that my cause is worthy of their consideration. I try not to use too much pathos in my pitch.

Make your ask and then stop talking. Don't be afraid of the pregnant pause and always look them in the eyes. Don't seem too eager.

One of the advantages of being a poor person is that you have nothing to lose, and no one is going to hand you an opportunity. I met Shepard Fairey for the first time after sneaking into the afterparty of a Radiohead concert in 2016, on the very day I returned from traveling twelve thousand miles in support of the political revolution. A friend of mine went to the venue ahead of time, took a picture of security's sample badge posted outside of the entrance to the building, and then made some fake DIY backstage passes on lanyards at a local print shop.

When you are poor, you learn that no one is coming to save you. Punk rockers in the 70s and 80s knew this. Occupy Wall Street and Bernie Sanders supporters knew this. You've got to make your own luck, and political revolutionaries often have to make do with very little resources. It has also been my experience that many actors, musicians and artists come from humble backgrounds and authentically appreciate having an opportunity to use their platforms to make a difference. This can give you a great deal of confidence in making your ask, which in turn increases your odds of successfully enrolling them in your cause. My suggestion is to be respectful, but don't put them on a pedestal.

One of the coolest things that happened for us that year was Pussy Riot agreeing to play our Bernie's Wizards Holiday Party.

Once Nadya was asked if she could have anyone become a member of Pussy Riot, and she said, "I think Bernie Sanders. We've met a couple of times, but I haven't had a chance to put a balaclava on him."

Bernie was not the only nontraditional populist candidate in the 2020 primaries. Andrew Yang rose to popularity through his signature policy that he called the "Freedom Dividend," a universal basic income of $1,000 a month to every American adult to offset the inevitable loss of jobs due to automation. He drew impressive crowds because of his relatable, straight talk. (Like Beto, the young parvenu would grossly misinterpret the enthusiasm around his campaign and run unsuccessfully for Mayor of New York City.)

Marianne Williamson was another unique candidate. She became a meme legend and was dubbed "the orb mother" by the Internet. This was an interesting development because her Sister Giant conference was where I had first met Bernie Sanders, and it again presented an opportunity to engage the yoga, New Age and mindfulness communities in the political process.

Williamson became a phenomenon after dropping truth bombs in her debate appearances, using a New Age parlance never before heard on the national political stage.

She was not surprisingly lampooned on *SNL* for non-traditional political statements such as her declaration that Trump has been harnessing "dark psychic forces." But in truth, she was the first person to shift the Overton Window on reparations for African Americans on national television.

Yang and Marianne weren't the only outlier candidates. After Donald Trump opened the floodgates for rich celebrities seeking the highest office in the land, Kanye West threw his hat into the presidential ring, as did former Mayor of New York and billionaire Michael Bloomberg, and billionaire climate champion Tom Steyer.

Of all of these, Bloomberg was the biggest problem for Occupy Wall Street veterans, who knew him as the symbol of all we'd stood against. (Remember, the original Occupy encampment had been called "Bloombergville.") He was an independent and was prepared to spend $1 billion of his own money and could have garnered the support of centrists still trying to make the "winning the middle" strategy happen, appealing to the mythical swing voter and to moderate Republicans. Bloomberg basically paid for supporters, but online leftists used their superior meme warfare skills to keep the heat on.

Tulsi Gabbard also entered the fray, and proved a magnificent attack dog against Kamala Harris and Joe Biden during the debates. When Kamala seemed like she was gaining traction, Tulsi obliterated her on national television over her criminal justice record. She was so effective that Hillary Clinton then stepped in to insinuate publicly that Tulsi was a Russian asset.

When it came to Bernie, there was so little ammunition left after five years of attacks that the media was forced to go after his proxies. Susan Sarandon and Nina Turner became regular targets of flying monkeys like Neera Tanden and Sally Albright. (The latter was the one who'd been caught employing sock puppet accounts to amplify her Twitter attacks.)

The most ridiculous direct criticism of Bernie followed his appearance on the Joe Rogan podcast. Rogan has one of the biggest followings in the country, with a strong Trump supporter and libertarian crossover. The hour-long interview generated more than 14 million views. There were thousands of comments, many by conservative-leaning voters who found the conversation persuasive and admitted to shifting their views on Bernie's populist platform.

The brouhaha over this interview was a great example of prefiguratism rearing its counterproductive head. Instead of taking the opportunity to use a thoughtful longform interview platform to win over new supporters, the critics thought Bernie should cede the digital space to the toxic ideas of the alt-lite and alt-right. The left is never going to make necessary gains if it does not figure out how to have conversations with people whose worldview, or past, does not align with rigidly enforced in-group values and ways of being. We must lean in to having uncomfortable conversations with people with whom we do not agree if we are ever to achieve transformative justice on a national scale. Movements for climate, racial, health or trans justice will not succeed by remaining siloed in social media echo chambers. No silo by itself has enough members to achieve the very specific vision or culture it thinks is correct.

Joe Rogan would eventually be outed for a history of egregious racist remarks in 2022. It was appropriate that he was publicly excoriated for saying the N-word on camera in over 22 instances, but in my opinion it was still a mistake for the left to cede this digital real estate to the alt-right, who recognized it as a battleground in the cultural war for ideologically fluid populists. The Joe Rogan Experience Podcast received over 11 million downloads per episode.

Paradigms of prefiguratism prevent us from recognizing the strategic value of having long, nuanced conversations with those who are still ignorant of white supremacy, classism, transphobia, and so on. This does not mean apologizing or accepting toxic behavior or treating active opposition as allies, but it does mean we must recognize that not everyone can be as woke as we are and that enlightenment is a long and uncomfortable process. When we approach these conversations through retributive justice instead of transformative justice we are operating out of the same conditioning that has justified the United States's draconian criminal justice system.

Not everyone was out to get Sanders, though. One of the biggest surprises was Peter Daou, one of Hillary's staunchest supporters and a vicious critic of Sanders in 2016. In 2020, he came to recognize that Bernie and his enormous base was the best chance the Democrats had to depose Trump. Daou was castigated by his establishment cronies for his switch, but was welcomed with open arms into the Sanders movement, where he earned the tongue-in-cheek nickname "Chairman Daou."

What the establishment couldn't understand about the movement's appeal was best captured by Cornel West when he said, "Justice is what love looks like in public."

The Bernie movement was all about the love. But this was a different kind of love; it was the kind of love that would drive one to volunteer hundreds or thousands of hours, and stand shoulder to shoulder with people you would never normally hang out with. To drive twelve thousand miles around the country. It would have your blood pressure skyrocket during primary election result reporting, which you would never have thought in your life was something that would keep you up at night. In a way, Peter Daou joining the Bernie movement provided a jolt of hope just when we needed it.

Peter wasn't the only one.

Jane Fonda also came around to endorsing Bernie's run in 2020. She had previously supported Hillary in the 2016 primary. We'd had an uncomfortable exchange of words over this at her birthday *#BankExit* post action dinner when I brought up my frustration over the treatment that Sanders climate activists had received at the Democratic Platform Committee six months prior. Of course I understood completely that for activists like Jane, who had been on the frontlines of the women's liberation movement for half of a century, Hillary as the first viable woman frontrunner was the symbolic externalization of a lifetime of struggle against the patriarchy. In 2020 however the choice between Bernie and Biden was an easy one, as Sanders was the best chance we would have to lead the world in an unprecedented climate mobilization.

Naomi Klein also went all in for Bernie in 2020. She was a celebrated author and one of the foremost thought leaders on the intersections of eco-feminism, climate, fascism and disaster capitalism. She made it clear that it was the first time in her life she had ever officially endorsed and campaigned for a presidential candidate.

As the 2020 election drew near, the momentum was still with Bernie. Elizabeth Warren dropped a bomb in January by publicly making the desperate claim that in a private meeting Bernie had told Warren he didn't think a woman could win the presidency. This was so ridiculous that not even the corporate media pundits supported the narrative, especially since Bernie had not only campaigned for Hillary Clinton in the general election, but had told Warren that he would step aside if she chose to run in 2016, when Charles Lenchner and friends had tried to draft her.

Katie Halper and Krystal Ball joined the growing army of progressive independent media voices who could bring cogent analysis to the corporate media fuckery.

In many ways, the 2020 campaign lacked some of the wide-eyed purity and innocence of 2016. We were all much more jaded after witnessing our dreams crushed by the political and media establishment. At least for the OWS folks, 2016 wasn't our first rodeo in seeing our aspirations trampled by the boots of the corporate state—we had had some practice.

It was also a strange place psychically, for progressives to be aligned with the front runner. I think one of the greatest challenges of the progressive paradigm is the conundrum of power. We tend to define ourselves as the underdogs, standing outside and against the machine, like children throwing rocks at soldiers and tanks.

How can you take power when you define yourself in a one-down relationship to it? If you hate it? Those who hate power will never truly wield it, nor maintain it; they will, in one way or another, be inclined to attack all allies who acquire even a little bit. I believe that Bernie, on some level, never really wanted to be president. He would have been forced to make decisions about possibly ordering the death of human beings as commander-in-chief. He'd spent his entire life fighting the Man, and it must have been difficult to confront the very real possibility of becoming Him.

This was the essence, I suspect, of why Bernie was so beloved. We could relate. He was one of us.

The election fuckery in 2020 began right out of the gate with the Iowa caucus.

It was chaos.

Much of the confusion arose from the Shadow app used to count the caucus vote. Lee Fang of the *Intercept* uncovered that the DNC was directly involved in its development. Bernie's Avengers alum Jordan Chariton elaborated on this in an article after obtaining an internal transcript from the Iowa State Party. They reported that, "The Shadow app was developed by veterans of Hillary Clinton's 2016 campaign. Buttigieg's campaign used the firm Shadow Inc. as a vendor, paying the developer $42,500 for text messaging software."

Shadow CEO Gerard Niemira had also previously served as the Director of Product for the Clinton Campaign. COO James Hickey worked as Engineering Manager for Hillary for America in 2016. Chief Technology Officer Krista Davis was previously Hillary's backend engineer. The company also worked directly with Greta Carnes, the National Organizing Director for Mayor Pete, who was formerly the Regional Digital Director for Hillary for America.

Shadow was also a client of the Joe Biden campaign.

Do you see the problem with all of this? Is it not obvious?

The DNC had demanded the developers grant them access to the raw data before the results were made public. Following the pandemonium, the DNC denied any involvement with the firm.

Despite the debacle and inconclusive results, Mayor Pete falsely claimed victory. It didn't matter that Bernie won by 6,000 votes—it was really about controlling the media narrative in order to seize the momentum (or "Big Mo"), or at least preventing it from going to Sanders.

We cannot know if there was outright collusion or intentional sabotage. But we can say definitively that high-ranking members of the Democratic establishment, the wealthy donors, and the consultant class conspired to derail the Sanders campaign. We know that the intervention of the DNC in the caucus and the incestuous network of establishment actors created a context that at the very least made it impossible to ensure a fair and equitable democratic process.

Despite this, Bernie went on to win New Hampshire and Nevada and become the first candidate from either party in the history of the United States to win the first three contests of the primaries. It appeared as though our years of sacrifice and toil were going to finally pay off because the Senator from Vermont was about to run away with the primary.

The media response was summed up by Chris Matthews, host of MSNBC's *Hardball*, who compared Sanders's victory in Nevada to Nazi Germany overrunning France in 1940.

"It's too late to stop him. It's over," he said on-air.

In a just and democratic society, Bernie's momentum would have been unstoppable, but that's just not the state of the world as it is today.

Chris Matthews was sacked a week later for allegations of sexual harassment.

Seeing one of the neoliberal corporate media's staunchest hacks getting canned felt like karmic justice and would be one of the small consolations for what was to come.

At various points, many grassroots organizers contemplated talking publicly about some of the deficits we saw in the Sanders campaign, but we didn't want to give any ammunition to the media who would have inevitably run with predictable headlines: "Bernie's army in disarray" or some such flaming bullshit.

For a moment, one impossible, shining moment, it seemed like we were going to win.

Almost.

Biden finished no higher than third in any of the first three contests, but South Carolina proved to be his firewall state. As Charles had correctly noted, the Sanders campaign had almost entirely abandoned traditional relational political organizing. Biden was able to secure a key endorsement in Jim Clyburn, the highest ranking African American Democrat in Congress and a very influential party member in South Carolina. Joe and his team did not abandon the relational organizing of old school politics.

Traditionally, South Carolina is where primary candidates take the gloves off.

Some of Bernie's cabinet members urged him to go on the offensive. When he refused, many of his most dedicated supporters grew exasperated. *Why go through two presidential campaigns if you are not prepared to do what it takes to win?* It was reminiscent of when Bernie gave Hillary the biggest pass of the 2016 primary by letting her off the hook for her "damn emails," especially when the Republicans certainly weren't going to give her a pass for this down the home stretch.

The crowded field of establishment hacks had been an advantage, but only to a point.

In a show of solidarity, Marianne Williamson dropped out of the primary race prior to Iowa to throw her supporters to Bernie. Unfortunately, despite being too far behind to win, Warren and Tulsi did not suspend their campaigns before the decisive Super Tuesday contest. Predictably, they proceeded to split the progressive vote.

I collaborated with Marianne and Bernie's step daughter Heather Shereé on a Hollywood GOTV event on Monday, March 2nd, 2020, the night before fourteen states would hold primaries, (including California). Heather was the founder of the Sedona Yoga festival, so the common thread that united the rally was targeting the transformation, mindfulness and wellness communities.

Meanwhile, Carlos Marroquin, Nomiki Konst, and some of the Public Bank LA comrades were rallying on a busy street corner not more than three blocks away. We had the Ricardo Montalbán Theatre, so I invited the gang to join us and give everyone who was speaking time on stage. This was a perfect metaphor for the progressive movement. If we had better systems of communication, more alignment of vision and solidarity, we could have worked together from the beginning to have a bigger impact. Still, it was a hearty and wholesome evening. Jordan Chariton showed up to cover for the *Status Coup* outlet.

It was the calm before the storm, and the last time we would come together to stand for a legitimate chance at a Sanders presidency. Once again as we took the stage to give our impassioned pleas for a future we could all believe in, little did we know we were basically shouting into the void. The Democratic establishment had spent a year carefully organizing and strategizing to stop Bernie and his movement at all costs. At that moment, on the eve of Super Tuesday, they were about to throw a rainmaker the likes of which the political world had never before seen.

As Super Tuesday approached, the so-called progressive candidates failed to show anything resembling solidarity. The establishment candidates, however, banded together in a way never seen before in electoral politics.

The Democratic Party leadership had learned well from the clown car of the Republican 2016 primaries. It was the "every man and woman for themselves" approach to the early contests that had allowed the GOP to split the vote and had paved the way for Trump's glide path to the nomination. They were not going to let the same thing happen to them, and allow the candidate of the 99 Percent to win the nomination and possibly the presidency. This was an existential threat to the system that they'd created and thrived off of, where they needed only to serve wealthy donors, and could remain unaccountable to everyday people. Bernie and his movement sought to end the influence of money in politics and this they could not let stand. The Never Bernie contingent were some of the most powerful inside operatives, elected officials, highest-paid consultants, and most wealthy donors who had been organizing and strategizing for years to prepare for this contingency.

In this respect, progressives can learn a thing or two from conservatives and neoliberals when it comes to building power. We seem to constantly be playing flag football when the game is really a knife fight and the contest is to the death. Take for instance the GOP's *Operation Chaos* in South Carolina; it was a campaign to encourage Republicans to vote in the primary for the Democratic candidate they viewed as a weaker challenge in the general election. The media reported that conservatives— once enthusiastic about a Sanders-Trump match-up—had switched to voting and rooting for Biden. They knew Trump would have a greater chance of beating Joe than Bernie.

Bloody Tuesday

Bernie was the first candidate in American history from either political party to have won the first three primary races. South Carolina had acted as a firewall for Biden, but it was unclear whether or not it would be enough to turn the tide.

Then it happened.

On the eve of Super Tuesday, Klobuchar and Mayor Pete dropped out of the race and endorsed Biden. Beto had dropped out of the race in November and Kamala only a month later after running out of money. Bloomberg had spent almost $600 million of his own money to fund his campaign (and only had a single victory in American Samoa to show for it) when he bowed out. Once again, Gabbard and Warren stayed in the race and continued to split the progressive vote. Tulsi never really had a chance, and Warren refused to drop out and endorse the best chance in the history of the union for a real progressive to occupy the most powerful office in the world. If this had happened in South Carolina, in all likelihood it would have clinched the nomination for Bernie.

A Sanders presidency would have meant that the sixty thousand people that die every year from lack of health care might have had a fighting chance, as well as a human race who desperately needs to stop putting carbon in the atmosphere. They could rise above their own ambitions to see the bigger picture. At the end of the day, we all know that if the tables were turned and Senator Warren had emerged the frontrunner after the Nevada Caucus, that Bernie would have done the right thing, dropped out and endorsed her, even if there had been bad blood.

In all fairness though, Claire Sandberg's pleading to the top campaign leadership to reach out to Warren's camp to personally make the appeal to join forces with Sanders fell on deaf ears. They allegedly never made the call.

The comedian Chris Rock once said, "They don't want you to vote. If they did, we wouldn't vote on a Tuesday—in November. You ever throw a party on a Tuesday? No. Because nobody would come." And on top of that it is cold in November, which further discourages people from exercising their sacred franchise.

The Democratic primary heavily favors whatever candidates the Democratic establishment selects as their proxies, to rule the electorate in the name of the billionaire class. There has never historically been anything democratic about the Democratic primaries. Until Jimmy Carter, the candidates were mostly selected in smoky rooms in the invisible primaries.

Just like 2016, however, Bernie would not go negative against Joe Biden. At one point, he went as far as to say that, "Joe Biden is my friend," on a late-night talk show.

Hearing those words was like a dagger to the heart. It felt like a betrayal. Bernie's empathy for his fellow humans was one of the qualities that had made the movement fall in love with him. Word on the street was that Biden was genuinely nice to Bernie in Washington, in a place where Sanders had found few friends. The Senator, despite being an effective legislator, was very much an outsider. But again: *what was the point of running for president if you aren't prepared to do what it takes to win?*

In truth, Obama was the only one who could have whipped the other candidates to drop out and fall in line behind Biden. This was truly a desperate Hail Mary, as it was common knowledge that Obama and many Democratic insiders had serious doubts about

Joe's ability to perform in the general election against Trump. One point that is often lost in the white noise of the political football and corporate media circus is that the Democratic Establishment was fine with a second Trump Administration. They got to raise a ton of money fear mongering about Forty-Five and Russia and not making a single promise about policies that would improve the lives of working Americans.

It turns out that they were even more afraid of Bernie and the grassroots ascending to power.

Once again, Super Tuesday was a bloodbath.

It was as Mark Twain once said, "history never repeats itself, but it does often rhyme."

Despite the fundamental disconnect between the campaign and the movement, Sanders won California by a huge margin on Super Tuesday. It is important to note that Bernie won in spite of his own campaign staff, thanks to the strength of grass-roots organizers who never stopped organizing after 2016. This was no secret. And yet, many of the senior staff would absurdly claim credit for the victory.

The End Times

The first reports started coming in from Wuhan, China, in December. A novel coronavirus had been traced to a local animal market and had caused dozens of locals to fall ill.

Before most Americans were paying attention to the news spreading through Europe and Asia of rising infections, I got a text from Alex Ebert on Tuesday, March 8th. He gave us a heads-up from a relative who worked in the government: there were quarantines and lockdowns on the way.

This was the first time in our lives that shelves of the grocery stores were absolutely bare. People fought for basic necessities like water and toilet paper. There were bread lines over an hour long in cities across America. The anti-socialist conservative tropes about people in Venezuela not being able to buy things ended pretty quickly as the free market failed to save us.

When the pandemic hit with full force in March of 2020, many Bernie organizers rose to meet the moment, pivoting from campaigning to community-level mutual aid.

Mutual aid was an anarchist theory of change where people take responsibility for caring for one another to provide people with food, medical care, and other necessities like personal protective equipment (PPE).

With mandatory quarantine measures implemented by state and local governments, unemployment soared to historic levels, leaving millions of people unable to afford food, rent, or other basic necessities. Poor communities of color were three times more susceptible to contracting the virus and twice as likely to die from it.

Bernie immediately displayed presidential leadership by calling on Trump to enact policies to save poor and working people. Biden, meanwhile, was barely heard. When he did make public addresses, they were usually a gish gallop of incoherent rambling. I presented a detailed proposal to the Sanders campaign to convert the ground game local campaigns into mutual aid operations that would not only ask for votes but would demonstrate Bernie's commitment to working people by immediately addressing their needs. I sent this to almost every senior staff member, including Faiz, the campaign manager, but got no response. It became apparent to me that the campaign was just phoning it in.

It was as if they had already conceded.

What do you expect when some of our top advisors have already begun plans to launch political action committees for Joe Biden?

Mutual aid is an important concept that in my mind organizers for justice must operationalize regularly. It is based on deep roots and relationships in communities that build trust, openness, and solidarity, and it could be the greatest strategy to bring frontline communities into our movements. Progressive and leftist issues are often abstract concepts. Meeting people face to face to give them the resources they desperately need is not an abstraction. The Black Panther Party understood this, providing free breakfast programs for school children, and medical and legal services for their communities until they were sabotaged by the US government.

We were in a moment when literally anything could happen. The entire world had just been turned upside down, practically overnight. But even though the new frontrunner, Biden, showed signs of mental decline Bernie refused to fight.

Some leftists accused Bernie of sheep-dogging, or intentionally tanking the election in order to act as controlled opposition for the Democrats. I don't believe this at all. I had many long conversations with his son Levi, who maintained that what was really at stake was the fact that his father didn't want to be seen as another Ralph Nader—a spoiler whose refusal to concede would contribute to a calamity for the United States and the world. Did you know that Al Gore, who lost the election to George W. Bush in Florida by only 537 votes, was calling for radical climate action as early as 1982? We would be living in a very different world right now—a world where the second Iraq War never happened.

As the 2020 pandemic and primary voting continued, there was a divide amongst the staff over whether or not Sanders should have continued the campaign until the convention. According to sources who preferred not to be named, Squad member Rep. Ilhan Omar and Larry Cohen, Bernie's campaign co-chair, urged Bernie to fight on, while Faiz Shakir and Jeff Weaver—who met with Robbie Mook in 2016 and created a Biden Super PAC in 2020—lobbied the Senator to drop out. If Bernie won 25 percent of the primary vote, he would have the leverage to appoint progressives to the Democratic Party's rules committee. In 2016 the Sanders Campaign was able to use their leverage to create the Unity Reform commission, which was able to eliminate 60 percent of the superdelegates, thus significantly rolling back their corrosive power and influence.

Briahna Joy Gray, the campaign's national press secretary, argued on Twitter that, "Four out of five of the largest Black populations in the country haven't voted. And some of you want to call off the primary. Your interest in the franchise is self-interest, and it shows."

RoseAnn DeMoro, when asked about senior staff members lobbying Sanders to quit, said, "They shouldn't be part of the campaign. If people want to go work on K Street right now—go. The base is attached to the movement and Bernie, not operatives."

Naomi Klein publicly encouraged Bernie to stay in the race even if only to pressure Joe Biden on the issues.

When Bernie finally made his concession speech on March 11th, the pain and grief set in—as if millions of people had been collectively gut punched and had lost a loved one at the same time. It was over. After five years of fighting, it ended not with a bang, but with a whimper. For many, the anger came quickly, compounded by anger over the shit show that was Trump's leadership in a pandemic.

Many of the grassroots organizers who'd previously held their tongues about the campaign leadership began speaking out. There were grievances, for example, about the campaign's failure to center Black leadership and policies to advance racial equality. Might this have been the difference in states like South Carolina?

After Bernie had suspended his campaign, Marcus Ferrell, the former African American outreach director for Bernie 2016, made the following statement on social media:

> *Let me lay it out there for you.*
>
> *Jeff Weaver blatantly told white senior staffers that he had no plans of doing serious work for the Black vote. After getting decimated on Super Tuesday he tried to shift all the blame on Black staffers. When I tried to quit he threatened me by saying 'it would be bad for my career.' Then he went on to blackball me anyway.*
>
> *This is just one incident. I have at least seven I could pull out proving issues of race on the grand ole Bernie campaign.*
>
> *I'm tired of being silent. That stuff messed up democracy.*
>
> *This is the real reason they lost both times. Not the DNC, not moderates. They just can't get along with non-famous Black people.*

We must all take account of the part we played, or lack thereof. We must always endeavor to do an autopsy to determine what worked and what didn't. John F. Kennedy once said, "Victory has a thousand fathers but defeat is an orphan." If I had it to do over again, I would have made stronger efforts to get the band back together and reassemble all of the original Avengers.

To its own demise, the campaign rejected relational organizing. And Bernie wasn't willing to play the game to win in South Carolina. Nor was he willing to dangle the possibility of cabinet positions in exchange for high-profile endorsements. There is no doubt that Kamala and Mayor Pete received offers of cabinet positions in return for their dropping out and falling in line behind Biden.

The Bernocalypse

As grassroots organizers, we must also reconcile our own short-comings. It is easy to simply blame the establishment, the media and the campaign staff. But I deeply regret not having done more and not having taken more drastic measures when it became clear that the campaign leadership was deeply, profoundly flawed, and that their electoral plans and theories of change were not sound.

In retrospect, I would have lobbied much harder for Rapi Castillo and others to reignite Coders for Bernie. In 2016, the decentralized affinity group created eighty-five game changing apps to support fundraising, volunteer efforts and many other areas of the campaign. In 2020 there was only a single Bern app made by the campaign. It was mediocre at best. I should have written more articles and spoken out earlier.

It was a mistake to keep my concerns to myself early in the campaign out of fear the establishment media would weapon-ize the information against him. In retrospect, we should have spoken up.

There are many within the political consultant class that would prefer not to have an honest debate about what really happened. The purpose of this autopsy is not merely to drag down a couple of seemingly self interested politicos. It's purpose is to offer a cautionary tale for future progressive campaigns, so that we may create safeguards against toxic political mercenaries who seek to control rather than uplift and empower the 99 Percent. But the end of the day campaigns are messy work and it is easy to speculate from the sidelines who is to blame.

While we offer this analysis let us keep some perspective and remember the words of Teddy Roosevelt who said:

"It is not the critic who counts: not the man who points out how the strong man stumbles or where the doer of deeds could have done better. The credit belongs to the man who is actually in the arena, whose face

is marred by dust and sweat and blood, who strives valiantly, who errs and comes up short again and again, because there is no effort without error or shortcoming, but who knows the great enthusiasms, the great devotions, who spends himself in a worthy cause; who, at the best, knows, in the end, the triumph of high achievement, and who, at the worst, if he fails, at least he fails while daring greatly, so that his place shall never be with those cold and timid souls who knew neither victory nor defeat."

The purpose of this work is to offer a modern theory of change, to wrest power from the oligarchy and shift it to the people. In this pursuit let us also not simply replace the old boss with a new so-called *progressive technocracy* and consultant class.

Lastly in our examination of the 2020 primary, there was never any advantage to allowing the opposition to brand Sanders a Democratic Socialist. In truth, Bernie and all who subscribed to his vision of a Scandinavian social safety net are actually followers of social democracy, not democratic socialism. Bernie never promised to end capitalism, only to make the billionaire class pay their fair share so working people could have health care and earn a living wage. If Bernie had simply focused on policies and not ideology, in my opinion his campaign might have been more palatable to older mainstream voters who still succumb to Cold War McCarthyist red-baiting propaganda.

In my opinion, ideologies are inherently limiting and divisive. Without the labels, most people would agree with socialist policies. What's more important? Getting everyone to believe in an ideology, or implementing common-sense policies that improve the lives of poor working people?

Language can be a tool or a weapon. Right-wingers are masters of co-opting the language of the American Revolution to reinforce the cultural hegemony of undemocratic structures in American society.

Consider how they have claimed and weaponized the word "freedom." They use it in a way that has no real meaning or practical application. It is rhetoric, used for the purpose of selling an illusion. We must reclaim this word. Conservatives and neo-fascists build power by creating simple messages that resonate, such as "Make America Great Again." This phrase would never stand up to any kind of serious scrutiny.

The Bernie Sanders movement had a robust policy platform that could transform society for the better, but we sometimes lacked the skill to communicate this simply and effectively to larger swathes of voters.

With this understanding, it is obvious that any worldview that gets to the root of our crises would be demonized by the political and media establishments who do the bidding of corporate donors and advertisers.

In reality the primary should have been postponed. There were ridiculously long lines of Democratic voters being endangered by voting in person during a deadly pandemic. People in Texas and California had to wait two to four hours to cast their ballots. Music venues, schools and universities, the NBA, and fucking Disney World all shut down, but citizens would literally have to risk their lives to perform their sacred franchise. Citizens were using 3D printers to make ventilator parts because the Trump administration had cut critical funding and had failed to respond. In New York City, the morgues were past capacity, so the dead were loaded onto ice in hockey rinks in black bags. Poor people of color were at greater risk, and yet the Democratic Party saw fit to have Michigan voters show up to the polls in person and form long crowded lines.

In Los Angeles, we delivered water to voters forced to wait in line until after midnight all over the city. Hospitals, meanwhile, were overflowing with patients.

But the Democratic establishment finally had their boots on the neck of the socialist menace once more and they would not take the pressure off even if it meant killing off a percentage of their base.

The political establishment clung to power with lead pipe mercenary cruelty—one befitting the character of Frank Underwood in *House of Cards*. The character of the lieutenants and generals Sanders picked would determine the course of the ship in the final days. Just when he needed people to push him hardest, to go to the lengths necessary to win, his kitchen cabinet told him to fold. How can you possibly fight on when your own campaign manager and closest confidants are urging you to drop out? Especially when some of them are already planning on launching Biden PACs to make money from the opposition?

It is best to view candidates as allies and vessels for ideas and tactics. Ideally, they become friends and allies. But it is more than likely they will disappoint you because they are human, and exist in a system that is designed to keep them out, absorb them, or limit their power. No, it is better not to get emotionally invested in candidates. They will just break your heart and damage your nervous system, even and especially when there is so much more work to be done.

In my opinion, leftist organizing does not focus enough on innovation. While Steve Bannon was reinventing political strategy in 2016 with Cambridge Analytica and psychographics, the left was still doing what it has always done—knocking on doors, sending fundraising emails, and cold-calling voters on the phone.

Decentralized applications made by Coders for Bernie in 2016 helped level the playing field, but we did not go far enough. Many of these new strategies and tactics were abandoned in 2020.

We did not leverage all of the resources that were at our disposal.

We must develop more sophisticated methods of identifying voters through the limitless digital tools and platforms available. We must take the data we gather knocking on doors and having conversations with people, and use that to create more sophisticated voter list segments. We must get better at polling these lists to learn about what these specific demographics care about, and then create media and messages that speak to those concerns through micro-targeted content. The left tends to shout with one megaphone, preaching to the converted, using language and jargon that appeals to the choir.

Unfortunately, for some organizers we did not have the luxury of quitting or secluding ourselves in the woods to sulk and lick our wounds. We could not sit idly by, to lament that humanity had lost the best chance it had to avoid the worst of the climate apocalypse under a Sanders presidency. We had to do our best to end the most imminent threat of full-throated neofascism our country had ever faced and salvage what was left of a workable battleground for the future.

Chapter 13

QAnon: Worst Storm Ever

The truth has no defense against a fool determined to believe a lie.
-fake Mark Twain quote found on the Internet

The Trump Q-ult

Mark Twain didn't really say the quote above, but he did once say that "It's easier to fool people than to convince them that they have been fooled." Following the election in 2016, Trump and his army of bad actors continued to foment populist rage on the right.

Some of our former comrades were seduced by neofascism, which they viewed as the only remaining outlet to fight "the elite."

No one had any illusions as to who Biden was, or any expectations that he would be an ally to the progressive platform. But it was clear that Trump would not only drag his feet, but would use McCarthyite red-baiting to mobilize his growing cult following of proto-fascist brownshirts. Conservatives cheered and defended counter protesters like Kyle Rittenhouse, a seventeen-year-old white boy who crossed state lines with an AR-15 and killed two unarmed demonstrators in Kenosha, Wisconsin. It's curious how heavily-armed white shooters are consistently taken alive, but black people selling cigarettes, or doing nothing at all, are killed by police for simply existing.

In 2017 we witnessed the first casualty of our movement when a thirty-two-year-old Bernie supporter named Heather Heyer was killed in Charlottesville by a white supremacist who drove his car full speed into a crowd of counter protesters against the Unite the Right rally. Heather had worked as a paralegal for a Black-owned law firm that fought for clients facing bankruptcy. She cared deeply for the struggles of working people.

When her murderer, James Alex Fields, stood trial, a taped phone call from jail between Fields and his mother was played in which he called Heyer a "communist … enemy." I spent a great deal of time infiltrating online conservative groups. It was very common for members to joke about running down protesters, and to say that Democrats were Communists who deserved death.

Cornel West was part of the Charlottesville counter protests. Speaking in a nearby church, he was held hostage by hundreds of white supremacists wielding torches and shouting the Neonazi chants of "Blood and soil," and "Jews will not replace us!" while defending the statue of the slave owner Thomas Jefferson. The police allowed the white supremacists to descend on the small group of clergy and moral witnesses, until an outnumbered group of antifascists came in to defend them with force.

Bernie made several statements about her killing. In one of them, he said, "Heather sacrificed her life in the fight for social and racial justice. She will not be forgotten. The best way for us to truly honor her memory is to make sure that, every day, we continue that struggle. Our condolences go out to the family of Heather Heyer who was killed by a terrorist as she protested Neonazism and white supremacy."

Trump refused to condemn the racist mob, saying there were "very fine people on both sides." He regularly scapegoated antifascists who mobilized against white supremacists and had an actual army of brown shirts called the Proud Boys who mobilized against the antifascists in turn.

There were no more questions as to what the next four years would look like. This is why radicals like Angela Davis, Cornel West, Frances Fox Piven, and Noam Chomsky declared there would be no possibility of a progressive agenda if Trump were reelected, and so threw their support behind Joe Biden. Chomsky warned, "Another four years of Trump may literally lead us to the stage where the survival of organized human society is deeply imperiled."

What do you call those who are against those that are against fascism?

You're not antifascist if you stand by and let fascists control one third of the government. Forty-Five was rolling out full-throated fascism. What started out as rhetoric had become a matter of policy by the time of Heather Heyer's cold-blooded murder.

To further complicate matters, in June of 2020 a white Minneapolis cop named Derek Chauvin kneeled on the neck of a black man named George Floyd for eight minutes and forty-six seconds, murdering him on livestream and sparking a global mobilization against racism.

There were uprisings in over two thousand cities and towns in over sixty countries in solidarity with Black Lives Matter. True to form, Trump's fascist Homeland Security goon squad started apprehending activists off the street in unmarked vans without reading them their Miranda Rights.

More than two hundred US cities responded by imposing curfews. More than thirty states activated over ninety-six thousand National Guard. By the end of June, there were more than forty-seven hundred demonstrations with 26 million participants. It was the largest mass civil disobedience uprising in United States history.

Trump's legacy of jack-booted authoritarianism continued.

Starting on July 14, 2021, federal police in downtown Portland wearing unidentifiable generic uniforms used unmarked vehicles to drive around and detain protesters. Mark Pettibone, one of the victims, called the experience terrifying. He compared it to a dark sci-fi novel by dystopian author Philip K. Dick, of *Do Androids Dream of Electric Sheep?* (which would later be remade as the movie Blade Runner) and *The Man in the High Castle* fame.

Unfortunately this was not fiction, but a scheme dreamt up by President Trump's Acting Homeland Security Secretary Chad Wolf.

In the beginning of June 2020, Trump invited military deployments to suppress Black Lives Matter demonstrations. Thousands of National Guard troops from ten states were patrolling the streets in Washington, DC or would soon deploy there alongside local and federal law enforcement. He threatened to send troops to every state in the union before retired generals publicly rejected the suggestion.

There was simply no ground to be gained under another Trump regime. There would have been further escalations in the mobilization of well-armed extremist militias against progressives and grassroots activists.

Then there was the more familiar violence of extreme inequality reinforced by nearly three hundred lobbyists invited to work for the Trump administration. The Trump hotel became the center of lobbying in Washington. There were countless instances of pay-to-play appointments and other forms of routine corruption. Corporate lackeys were appointed to oversee the agencies they'd hated in their prior roles. Under cover of the pandemic, $6 trillion was funneled to the top.

Life for undocumented Americans and their loved ones under the Trump regime was terrifying. The administration spearheaded a program to force migrant detainees in ICE facilities to have unwanted hysterectomies. This is not dystopian science fiction, it really happened.

As of election day 2020, the combined fortunes of the nation's 644 billionaires totaled a jaw-dropping $3.88 trillion—up 40.7 percent since 2017, the year before Trump's tax cuts went into effect.

Republicans had finally killed the estate tax, which they had rebranded the "death tax."

Some leftists and progressives still argued against voting for Biden. Of course, this had nothing to do with actual organizing. These feelings were understandable considering what was at stake and everything we had fought for. Nina Turner probably said it best: the prospect of voting or campaigning for Joe Biden was like "eating a bowl of shit."

But many progressives did it anyway. Because real leadership means being grown-ups, even when our elected officials fail us.

This was the general feeling in the fall of 2020. We should have been fighting for Bernie's presidency—fighting for a climate mobilization, to end systemic racism, and against income inequality. Instead, we had to be the fucking grown-ups and ensure the rickety proposition of Biden beating Trump in the general. The establishment had proved they would go to any lengths to preserve their power, and were willing to risk a second Trump presidency on a candidate that could barely make it through a public appearance without rambling or challenging a potential voter to a fight.

The Truth Has Changed

In 2017, Josh Fox wrote a book called *The Truth Has Changed*, where he shared his experiences fighting the fossil fuel industry, and the psychological warfare campaigns that the industry had waged to discredit his documentaries about fracking. This phrase—*the truth has changed*—perfectly described the deepening war on objective truth and science. Right-wing climate denial was not a random phenomenon. It did not happen out of nowhere, and the fallout of decades of intentionally propagated misinformation would set the stage for the neofascists to weaponize false narratives and conspiracy theories in a way never before seen, with a psychological operation called QAnon.

Since 1997, the Koch brothers have spent over $145 million financing more than ninety groups dedicated to casting doubt on climate science, and coordinating backlash efforts to slow the global policy response. The Kochs have been highly organized and highly strategic in their approach to killing the very impact of climate science.

To achieve this, they have used their almost limitless resources to wage war on an objective science-based reality.

This is a critically important phenomenon to understand in order to fully grasp how Trump came to power, and how so many millions of Americans could be led to adopt such a ridiculous set of propositions as those at the center of the QAnon cult.

In 1991, when the United Nations first began to meet to discuss mobilizing the world to address global warming, a Koch brothers-funded libertarian think tank called the Cato Institute organized a counter summit called "Global Environmental Crisis: Science or Politics?"

The summit literature attacked environmentalists, in defense of the billionaire class who might otherwise have to sacrifice a portion of their wealth and power. The Koch brothers even brought in the DonorsTrust, the same dark money group that pushed junk science for Big Tobacco.

The junk science project to discredit climate change marked the beginning of a decades-long assault on the truth, and on the movement to save humanity from itself.

It wasn't just Republicans who succumbed to the Kochs' will. The Koch brothers also employed a centrist Democrat think tank under the Clinton Administration, Third Way, and worked with them to undermine negotiations around NAFTA that would have affected their oil interests in Canada.

In 2010, the oil baron Koch brothers threw down the gauntlet for every Republican elected official: if they acknowledged global warming, they would face a well-funded primary challenge.

While we were occupying Wall Street in 2011 to protest money in politics and the corrupt bankers, they were using their obscene wealth to fund the Astroturf right-wing populist Tea Party movement that eventually took over the Republican Party.

At that time, Mike Pence became a valuable toady to the Kochs' network, and they were very pleased to make sure he was installed as Trump's vice president in 2016. He had, after all, helped convince Republican legislators to sign the "No Climate Tax" pledge put forth by Americans for Prosperity, another of the Kochs' propaganda outlets.

Although Trump got most of the heat, Pence represented an unholy alliance between the Christian right and Big Oil.

At least fourteen Koch-funded think tanks have been working together since 2010 to take over state houses and judicial offices. The goal is for them to pass voter suppression laws impacting Democrat-leaning Black and brown voters. If they control the government at the judicial, state legislative and federal levels, they can ensure continued corporate domination, not just in the fossil fuel sector but across the board.

How could two billionaire brothers so effectively tear apart the fabric of our democracy? Weren't there checks and balances to ensure that two oligarchs and their cronies couldn't undermine our political system for their own agenda?

The master stroke in their scheme to plunder the nation came in 2010 with the infamous Citizens United Supreme Court decision declaring that corporations and dark money groups were people, and thus entitled to free speech in the form of unlimited campaign spending.

In his book *The War on Science*, Shawn Otto breaks down the Koch Brothers' systematic war on climate science and truth itself, which I paraphrase below:

The Koch Brothers Playbook:

There is a formula to the Kochs' weapons of mass distraction:

— Hire outlier scientists that challenge the consensus of the scientific community by publishing fake reports casting doubt on peer-reviewed scientific studies.

— Send outlier scientists to do publicity and speaking events.

— Employ think tanks and fake nonprofits to release this information to compromised media outlets, often funded by phony foundations who are funded by the Koch brothers and other fossil fuel barons.

— Organize fake Astroturf grassroots organizations to give the illusion of public support.

— Enlist sympathetic conservative YouTubers, talk-radio and sock puppet social media accounts who reference these mainstream sources, react with outrage, and call for policy action.

— Shift mainstream opinion away from objective science to that of denial, thus creating political cover for elected officials in the pocket of Big Oil.

The goal is to create uncertainty in public opinion, and then to weaponize that skepticism. Again, the torpedo launched against the Kyoto Protocol was a demonstration test of their strategy. Kyoto was the first significant mobilization of sovereign nations to create an international treaty with specific timelines and objectives intended to roll back greenhouse gasses and stop the warming of the planet. The process took five years to ratify, and created a rough consensus around the need to reduce emissions.

This should have been the part in the movie where the whole world came together, like when the scary aliens attack or the meteor is going to destroy the earth. But as a result of the oil industry's coordinated organizing efforts, their elected lackeys in the US and

Canada signed the deal but did not stick with it, and fossil extraction projects continued to expand.

Basically, a death cult for Big Oil profits.

In 2015, 195 countries participated in talks to create the Paris Climate Accord after decades of failed attempts to comprehensively address the climate emergency. President Obama and Canadian Prime Minister Justin Trudeau may have played climate leaders on television, but their policy agenda continued to allow new pipeline projects. Obama and then-Secretary of State Hillary Clinton were largely responsible for selling fracking around the world on behalf of the natural gas industry.

The consensus was to collectively work to reduce greenhouse gas emissions with the goal of keeping global average temperature increases below 1.5 degrees Celsius, rising steadily to a projected 2 degrees. It doesn't seem like much, but the effects to the planet's climate are nothing short of catastrophic.

Intersectionality plays an important part here. Not only do fossil fuel projects most adversely affect poor communities of color due to all of the health impacts from extraction projects, but the climate emergency itself is an expression of white supremacy. The figure of 2 degrees Celsius is a global average—this would mean a 4 degree Celsius rise for predominantly Black and brown people living in countries in the Global South.

In other words, a death sentence.

The heart of the problem is this: capitalism compels the maximization of short-term profits over all else. The need to opportunistically extract as much money as possible in as short a period of time as possible regardless of the consequences is what crashed the housing market, and then the global economy, in 2008. The entire system that enabled predatory subprime loans and synthetic collateralized debt obligations was corrupt. It was an endemic failure from the regulators to the executives to the managers.

The difference here is that no one is coming to bail out the humans of planet Earth like the federal government bailed out the banks. Many Occupy Wall Street organizers understand that the fights for climate justice and economic justice are inexorably intertwined.

Donald Trump's following did not come out of nowhere. The conditions that gave rise to the alternate post-fact universe his supporters live in resulted from decades of right-wing attacks on objective science, and the branding of anyone that opposed the corporate state as evil, anti-American Communists. Predictably, this well-financed and well-planned project produced a monster that outgrew the old-line GOP's power to keep it under control.

Q Origins

In 2017, a new phenomenon arose from the swamp, called QAnon, which led a large swath of the conservative base right off the deep end. QAnon started as an obscure online live-action roleplay, or LARP, hosted on an anonymous message board in the dark corners of the web called 4Chan. Once this online game started to gain viral popularity and amass a huge following, it was hijacked to radicalize Trump's cult-following into an actual cult. A LARP is a game in which players pretend to be someone else, and others interact with them for fun. Think of a colonial village, Medieval Times, or a Civil War reenactment—except all the action happens online.

There were originally several message boards in the online chat rooms of 4Chan for these LARPs, including CIAAnon, HLIAnon (High-Level Insider), WH (White House) Insider Anon, and FBIanon, where members participated in an online fantasy world. It began with a live-action roleplay called Cicada 3301, which was an online game designed to bring together intelligent people to solve puzzles.

The premise was simple: there was an anonymous member of the military with "Q" level clearance, who started leaking information to the public about a secret war within the deep state and wealthy elite. Anons, or those that followed the imaginary whistleblower, believed with the utmost sincerity that Q was working with Donald Trump and his team to stop a cabal of Satan-worshiping Hollywood pedophile Democrats who were torturing children to harvest adrenochrome from their blood, which they would drink for longevity.

Take all the time you need to process that. More than 30 million Americans believe it.

The Satanic panic was an old standby right-wing tactic from the 80s, dusted off by "Q" to advance his vaguely-asked questions that invited readers down various rabbit holes. It all amounted to a conspiracy theory composed of many smaller conspiracy theories. When Q made wild predictions that never came true, they would create excuses and rationalizations.

During the 2016 election, there was a predecessor alt-right conspiracy called *#PizzaGate*. It claimed that Hillary Clinton and her top strategist John Podesta were part of a sex trafficking ring being run out of a Washington, DC pizza parlor called Comet Pizza.

On December 4, 2016, a twenty-eight-year-old man from Salisbury, North Carolina arrived at Comet Ping Pong, and fired three shots from an AR-15 into the restaurant while it was full of children and their families eating pizza.

He discovered that there was no dungeon, just a supply closet. He live streamed the entire shitshow. This is important, because it is the first of several instances where a right-wing conspiracy designed to uplift Donald Trump's candidacy resulted in a false shared reality and led to real-world violence.

As absurd as it all was, Q continued to take conspiracy theories to new levels. According to one Q-drop (post), John F. Kennedy, Jr. faked his death, was still alive, and was working with Trump the whole time. Anons believed that Trump was playing "4D chess."

I first became involved in tracking these efforts when I started getting calls about Lisa Clapier's connection to QAnon. Her involvement allegedly went all the way back to Cicada 3301. She was known as SnowWhite in these circles and it was alleged that her job was to onboard people from Cicada to QAnon. I had first met her through the comms tent at Occupy LA. We'd stayed in touch for the next several years, helping to launch the global meditation sync platform UNIFY and promoting fusion coalitions organizing for peace. We'd come together every year in September to celebrate the United Nations International Day of Peace. We both shared the opinion that the New Age and peace movements were out of touch with political reality.

We'd connected immediately at the Occupy LA camp, because it's not that often you meet people in leftist circles who are also into meditation and spirituality. Despite the fact that so many of the greatest political revolutionaries were members of the clergy or deeply spiritual, leftist and progressive culture tends to be biased toward atheism and agnosticism. The corporate state may have nearly infinite money, resources and manpower, but Mahatma Gandhi knew well that every one of us has access to the greatest power in the Universe within us—the Immortal Spirit.

This was the basis of his theory of *satyagraha*, or "truth force."

According to leaked emails and some of her own tweets, Lisa was apparently part of the organizing effort to co-opt the QAnon

LARP and weaponize it for political power. According to some of her social media posts, she thought that the ruse would lead to some kind of liberation for humanity.

She could not have been more wrong.

With time, it became apparent that QAnon was making inroads to indoctrinate—or "redpill"—other online communities like the New Age, yoga moms, alien disclosure, anti-vaxxers, and even Bernie supporters through a psyop called *#SaveTheChildren*. There was strong evidence to suggest that Lisa had played a major role in weaponizing QAnon to subvert the New Age community into supporting Donald Trump. It is unclear if this was her true intent, but it is clear she was a significant player at the heart of the intrigue.

Lisa's involvement was a terrifying revelation, because I had talked to her so many times about my theory of a vast untapped political power in the New Age and yoga communities. Organizing these communities and mobilizing them for political power was the mission of the non-profit I ran in 2011, Peacelink Live!

If Lisa was at the heart of these QAnon organizing efforts, had I unwittingly planted some of the seeds of this chaos? I was horror-stricken at the thought, and started connecting with others who were tracking the bad actors behind these efforts.

I learned that Lisa had been in prison for fraud from 2007 until 2010, and in 2016 had gone on the lam after an alleged hit-and-run vehicular manslaughter charge. I felt sick at the thought of her killing someone and going on the run. She was last seen in the Philippines in 2016.

Back in 2011 I'd stood on my soapbox with very little discrimination, evangelizing this strategy to anyone who would listen. Lisa's story gave me pause, and I now try to exercise more discernment when it comes to whom to trust and share certain strategic ideas with. In retrospect, most of the problems I've had in organizing spaces stemmed from not being more careful about the integrity of those I allow into my inner circle.

This led me to another soul-crushing discovery: my old dear friend from Bernie's Avengers, Mikki Willis, was a part of these efforts as well. I had seen Mikki at Standing Rock, but had not known that he and Lisa had traveled there together. Mikki became infamous for a short documentary film he'd made called *Plandemic*, which suggested that Covid-19 was intentionally created as a bioweapon for mass control. One discredited researcher that Mikki interviewed in the doc claims that "wearing the mask literally activates your own virus. You're getting sick from your own reactivated coronavirus expressions."

Yup. That was a thing she said.

Mikki claimed that after YouTube and Facebook banned the video, it gained almost a billion views due to sharing on peer-to-peer platforms like WhatsApp. The corporate media often tried to paint Bernie supporters and Trump supporters as the same. It is important to understand that only a small percentage of Bernie supporters fell for QAnon, not because they were the same, but because Sanders appealed to a diverse range of voters, some of whom were already into conspiracy theories. Bernie got people engaged in the political process who did not traditionally vote or participate. They had seen the liberal establishment collude to crush the political revolution. It makes sense that a small percentage of those voters would be attracted to a highly coordinated psyop that promised to bring Hillary Clinton and her cronies to justice. QAnon preyed on the disillusioned.

Luckily there was also a coordinated network of activists working to track and expose the bad actors behind QAnon.

Some of the "Anti-Q" organizers were fascinated with the fact that I knew two people of interest said to be operating behind the curtain.

Engagement in QAnon was exploding. Alt-right ideas had infected millions of Americans like a virus. Relationships were torn apart as friends and family members succumbed and joined one of the most ridiculous cults of all time.

The theory that the Deep State was behind the pandemic originated with QAnon. Before long, all of these conspiracies merged in one supergroup of misinformation. It was a conspiracy theory composed of conspiracy theories—like one of those transformers that makes a super robot out of smaller robots—except instead of robots they were red herrings.

I joined a number of existing efforts to track the organizers behind this movement. Throughout 2020 it spread like a cancer, consuming people who felt disempowered and disconnected. With the mandated Covid lockdowns, so many people were scared, angry and had nothing to do but spend hours searching the Internet. QAnon gave them the feeling that they were part of something important. Just like all of Trump's rhetoric, the narratives were false, but had a kernel of truth. People had a vague sense that a monolithic cabal of powerful and wealthy people were pulling the strings of society and were largely to blame for the suffering in the world. They felt that the corporate media was lying to and manipulating them.

The greatest irony was that there was a real conspiracy, to co-opt conspiracy theories and weaponize them for Trump. In other words, Anons thought they were fighting those who were behind the curtain, when in fact they were really just useful idiots being manipulated by a real cabal that included theocratic con-servative ex-intelligence community members and usual-suspect political operatives.

This was pure projection, right out of the Joseph Goebbels playbook—in other words "accuse the other side of that which you are guilty of."

Derek Beres, Matthew Remski, and Julian Walker had a great podcast called *Conspirituality* that deconstructed QAnon and the unholy convergence of the New Age and Alt-Right communities. Desiree Kane from Bernie's Avengers and Standing Rock introduced us to Jim Stewartson, who had a background in live action roleplay and augmented reality. They did a TEDx talk together dismantling the QAnon network. Jim was an incredibly dedicated activist who uncovered and mapped many of the identities of the players behind the curtain.

Aubrey Cottle, one of the founders of hacktivist group Anonymous, came out of retirement to help take down the far-right conspiracy network.

Alex Ebert from the Avengers, and Ben Lee the Australian singer-songwriter, were also committed to tracking and disrupting the real cabal. I had known Ben Lee since he performed at our Peacelink 11.11.11 show.

This is important because the stakes were so high. Hundreds of thousands of people were dying unnecessarily because of Covid conspiracies driven by QAnon. Trump and his corporate junta of the worst bigots and vulture capitalists were ushering in actual neofascism. What few checks and balances were left in our already broken system were crumbling. If our friends and comrades continued to join them, there would be no chance of staving off the climate apocalypse.

How QAnon was Organized (Or, The Allegory of the Cave)

Imagine a person who is a prisoner in a cave. They've spent their entire lives with other prisoners, chained to the confines of the cave. Their necks and legs are chained so that their heads are fixed in a position that only allows them to stare at one of the walls. They see nothing else. There's a fire behind the prisoners that throws shadows on the walls of the cave as their captors pass in front of the fire. The objects they carry form various shapes that move with the firelight.

They hear the captors talking and, as the sound reverberates, they assume that the voices come from the shadows.

They know nothing of the world outside of the cave. It doesn't occur to them to try to escape. Then one day, a prisoner is freed. They look around to discover that it was the fire that was the true source of the shadows on the walls. They leave the cave and see the sun for the first time. They couldn't have conceived of the sun while living in the cave, or the smell of the fresh air, or the great expanse of a clear blue sky.

The freed prisoner goes back to the cave and attempts to tell the prisoners the truth of what they have seen. To their surprise, the prisoners don't want to hear about the sun or life outside the cave. They become angry, and even want to kill the liberated one who has seen the light.

The Allegory of the Cave was taught by Plato to demonstrate the innate nature of humans to protect their illusions, even when presented with the truth. It illustrates the lengths humans will go to to remain imprisoned, even when freedom is within their grasp. It's just as relevant today, only instead of shadows on the cave wall we experience more of our reality through small digital screens than through real life. The shadow puppeteers in front of the fire are think tanks, consultants, political party hacks, advertising media, the entertainment industrial complex, and corporate news pundits.

How do political revolutionaries free themselves, and then free others? How can we be sure that we're not like the prisoners subscribing to a reality that is nothing more than shadows on the wall?

To understand QAnon, one must first understand the digital primordial ooze from whence it emerged.

Q first appeared on the anonymous message board 4chan, before migrating to 8chan and eventually 8kun, by posting as "Q Clearance Patriot." These anonymous boards were the home of meme lords, trolls, and shitposters who derived a sense of shared meaning. These anonymous message boards were basically the seething subconscious of humanity online. Anonymity allowed people to express their true feelings and biases—unedited. Unfiltered.

There were hundreds of message boards for communities of video gamers, neonazis, child pornography enthusiasts, occultists, and fundamentalist Christians. This was a place for edgelords to shitpost, or to deliberately make provocative or off-topic comments on social media, typically in order to upset others or distract from the main conversation. Shitposts are intentionally designed to derail discussions or cause the biggest reaction with the least effort possible.

This is a place where the worst aspects of humanity come together like a horrible gumbo. Several white supremacist mass shooters have posted their manifestos to 8Chan before their murder sprees and have been celebrated there after their crimes. People took this whole thing seriously, despite the fact that it was put forward in the place people go to play pretend and troll anonymously in search of a reaction.

All of the members were anonymous users, hence their self-designation as "Anons."

This psyop was similar to other fringe extremists, like jihadists and neonazi efforts to recruit and indoctrinate followers, with the exception that these campaigns usually target the young and vulnerable, whereas QAnon largely appealed to gullible Baby Boomers.

From the beginning, the conspiracy played on a narrative of right and wrong, and depended on extreme dehumanization of the opposition. This is how civil wars and genocide begin. As it happened, the QAnon trope of the "gathering storm" was an old favorite of Nazi propaganda. The Hutu in Rwanda were referring to Tutsis as "cockroaches" before their genocide began, even in parliament.

Not surprisingly, anti-Semitism and white supremacy were common QAnon threads. Jewish billionaire George Soros was a go-to arch villain, along with Antifa super soldiers and Black Lives Matter.

Whoever was posting as Q was essentially crowdsourcing their theories. By the end, there were over five thousand posts or Q-drops. Each drop was numbered and contained vague predictions called "bread crumbs." Q would tell people to "do their own research," which essentially invited them to participate in the creation of the conspiracy theory with no formal system to vet their veracity. The genius of it, if that's the word, was that people would fill in their own meaning and create their own evidence, usually out of thin air. Everyone could play a part.

Most QAnon followers were not on 4Chan or 8Chan at all. Instead, they received their theories from "bakers," who took the bread crumbs and tried to make obscure, far-fetched connections.

Apophenia is the tendency to perceive meaningful connections between unrelated things. The term was coined by psychiatrist Klaus Conrad in his 1958 study on the beginning stages of schizophrenia.

People need ways to explain a dangerous and chaotic world. QAnon promised to reveal a hidden reality. It invited people to follow Neo from the Matrix and "take the red pill," except this pill led only to delusion and blind obedience to Trump.

Those indoctrinated into QAnon would reflexively answer any question about the inconsistencies in logic or fact with the automatic rebuttal, "You're just brainwashed by CNN," or they would say, "dO tHe rEseARch." It was often amazing to learn that I had been brainwashed by CNN when I don't watch corporate news and haven't owned a television since 2001.

Anyone who disagreed was called a "tool of the Deep State."

According to their beliefs, elite military personnel working under Donald Trump were going to arrest the corrupt members of the Cabal, as well as their leader, Hillary Clinton. This was known as "The Storm."

According to one theory, Donald Trump was a time traveler—something made possible by his uncle's access to Nikola Tesla's research. Believe it or not, the part about his uncle is true. The most effective psyops are based on a kernel of truth.

Donald Trump legitimized Q by retweeting some of the phrases and narratives or making vague references to them when talking to the press, which would cause Anons to go wild. It also caused some non-anonymous followers to celebrate: Roseanne Barr, Curt Schilling, and MyPillow CEO Michael Lindell all went full potato for QAnon.

Did it never occur to them that Trump had people on the inside of the operation or at the very least had his staff tracking the Q posts that 30 million other citizens had access to, and was responding to them because they were his most feverish followers?

Trump once made a cryptic comment from the West Wing to the press following a meeting with military leaders where he referred to the "calm before the storm." Online pandemonium ensued.

At one point, Anons believed that Hillary Clinton and John Podesta were already detained and in custody. When these predictions never came to pass, QAnons would simply say, "Trust the plan." Tom Hanks, Ellen DeGeneres, Lady Gaga, and Oprah were all allegedly baby-killing members of the Cabal.

At the center of this was the perpetual hope that Hillary Clinton, Joe Biden and their cronies would be brought out in handcuffs. The punchline was to brand Biden and the Democrats as demonic baby rapers in an attempt to drive voters to Trump. It was framed as an end-times battle between the forces of good and evil, but really it was a child's game played in the service of a mundane political outcome to reinforce the status quo.

Sure enough, it wasn't long before Q started encouraging people to focus on the 2018 midterm elections.

The Origins of the Alt-Right

In 2014 a group of gamers organized a hate campaign against a female programmer named Zoë Quinn for developing a game that didn't focus on violence but attempted to lead players through the experience of depression in a non-traditional format. She received rape and death threats from these pathetic misguided souls.

Gamergate Anons pushed back against feminist critique of video game culture. They used the anonymous chat forum 4Chan to doxx and harass their critics. They were supported by conservative pundits like Mike Cernovich and Milo Yiannopoulos, who channeled their rage into white nationalism and an all-out war against "social justice warriors" or SJWs.

Out of this milieu the alt-right was born.

As a movement, the early alt-right began by repeating old canards about the liberal media. Beginning in 2016 as part of his digital operations for Trump, Steve Bannon ran psyops to harness the online 4chan and 8chan communities into a battalion of trolls.

"You can activate that army. They come in through Gamergate or whatever and then get turned onto politics and Trump," he explained. Bannon used the right-wing platform Breitbart.com to promote sympathetic *#Gamergate* narratives and gain followers.

Bannon targeted *incels*, or men who hate women because they are virgins and don't believe they will have sex—involuntary celibates. Several have been connected to mass shootings. This is one of the unintended consequences of the extreme atomization of society in end-stage capitalism, when poor working class men feel isolated, alone and powerless in a world that is seeing the absolute power of white men diminish. They become easy targets for demagogues and batshit crazy ideologies.

Neonazis in the 1980s saw the hardcore punk rock music scene as a target-rich environment to recruit disillusioned youth. With all the debate about Antifa in modern times, I can't help but remember that it used to be understood that if someone showed up to a punk show to flex some nazi shit, they would probably get knocked the fuck out.

In any event, Bannon would go on to tour the world, spreading his doctrine of populist nationalism. He was an advisor on Jair Bolsonaro's campaign to win the Brazilian presidency, a man who has been under investigation before the International Criminal Court in The Hague for crimes against humanity, genocide, and ecocide.

Andrew Breitbart once described Bannon as "the Leni Riefenstahl of the Tea Party movement." Riefenstahl was one of the more effective propagandists for the Nazis, having produced and directed

Triumph of the Will. Bannon did not dodge such comparisons. He once told an interviewer, "Darkness is good. Dick Cheney. Darth Vader. Satan. That's power."

Imagine the supreme irony of right-wing Christians believing that Trump was sent by God to vanquish Satan-worshiping Democrats, at the same time being manipulated by one of Donald's operatives who quite literally was a fan of Satan. If that wasn't crazy enough, Trump's online army created an entire mythology around Trump that included an Egyptian deity name Kek, who took the modern form of Pepe the cartoon frog, who was a master of a form of black magic called "meme magic," and who turned Donald into a demiurge called "God Emperor Trump."

Q is Co-opted

QAnon may have started as an online game, but once its popularity skyrocketed, it was taken over by Trump operatives who manipulated the insanity to Trump's advantage.

As QAnon's following exploded, operatives close to Trump himself began to enter its inner circle. Just as the Koch brothers had co-opted the Tea Party and channeled populist rage to serve their own interests, the Trump clique used QAnon to advance its broader war on truth and its political enemies.

Once the QAnon LARP had been co-opted, it became a psyop to onboard conspiracy subcultures and radicalize them. It wasn't enough to pander to the gun nuts and Christian fundamentalists—they needed to expand the conservative voter base without promising anything that would compromise the wealth and power of their corporate masters.

Jim Watkins and his son Ron were co-founders of 4chan and 8chan. Jim Watkins was a businessman who ran his operations out of the Philippines.

They emerged as two of the most central players in the QAnon intrigue. According to some accounts, they were the ones who took control of the original Q account.

Incidentally, our old pal from Occupy LA, Lisa Clapier, also went to the Philippines to evade arrest after committing vehicular manslaughter in Ojai.

Trump campaign advisor Roger Stone allegedly funded Jim Watkins's political website The Goldwater. Roger Stone was arrested for lying to the FBI about his interactions with Wikileaks and Russian operatives. He and Republican strategist Jerome Corsi were both indicted in the investigation.

In 2004, Corsi was the co-author of *Unfit for Command: Swift Boat Veterans Speak Out Against John Kerry*, who helped ratfuck George W. Bush into a second term.

Corsi was also the author of the white nativist Obama birther conspiracy theory that proposed Barack was born in Kenya, not the United States and was therefore ineligible to be president (even though his mother was a full citizen). This was the first fringe conspiracy community where Trump had built his core political following. Corsi made thousands of dollars per livestream promoting QAnon conspiracies. It was also a big breakthrough for right wing operatives like Corsi who saw a new strategy at their disposal to indoctrinate new followers.

He later became the bureau chief of Alex Jones's InfoWars, which in its own way helped to create the swamp QAnon climbed out of, with insane right-wing conspiracy theory rhetoric that accused the Sandy Hook massacre of being a hoax and Hillary Clinton of being an interdimensional demon.

As QAnon's following exploded, operatives close to Trump himself began to enter its inner circle. This is a consistent tactic of the Republican Party. The Republican Party has never stood for policies that benefit working people. They have pandered to niche constituencies like the NRA and the Christian right that use wedge issues, dog whistles and fear-based rhetoric to move votes. The problem is that demographics across the nation have been shifting to become more Black, brown and progressive. It should come as no surprise that Jerome Corsi was one of the first Republican operatives to jump on the Q-train.

The Koch brothers used their billions to co-opt the Tea Party and channel the populist rage into building up their own political power. One of the factors that made the ground fertile for QAnon and Covid misinformation was the war on objective science waged by the Koch network of think tanks combating climate research.

Imagine the worst Venn diagram ever, of alien disclosure people, Illuminati conspiracy theorists, white supremacists, New Agers, Flat Earthers, anti-vaxx yoga moms, anti-Zionist anti-Semitics, Christian fundamentalists, and Alex Jones fans who believe in globalist Reptile people from the Vatican. Once this LARP was co-opted, it became a psyop to onboard each of those communities and radicalize them.

Each of the conspiracy communities brought their own spices to the worst gumbo ever made. It was like a schizophrenic online hivemind. By falling for a conspiracy theory that was at bottom a psyop organized by an actual criminal conspiracy, Trump fans managed to murder irony itself, then sit dull-eyed and triumphant on its rotting corpse.

In 2020, twenty QAnon believers ran for Congress. Two of them—Georgia's Marjorie Taylor Greene and Colorado's Lauren Boebert—serve in the House of Representatives as I write these words.

Retired three-star General Michael Flynn was Trump's national security advisor and a major person of interest who was fired for lying about his back-channel communications with Russia. Trump of course pardoned him. Flynn had written a book on fighting against militant Islam so he was well versed in their recruiting tactics. He also elevated conspiracies that Hillary Clinton was part of a child sex-trafficking ring.

Michael Flynn and his family went on social media asking Trump supporters to "take the oath" to be digital soldiers. It was important to the narrative that this Q person supposedly had high level access to the secret world of government and the aristocracy, so Flynn's involvement legitimized the story in the minds of Anons.

Lead technical director of the NSA Bill Binney, and one of Roger Stone's operatives named Jason Sullivan, made contact with Ron Watkins. Retired military operatives were working directly with "QTubers" to drive narratives. Sean Stone, son of director Oliver, was also part of the operation along with an ex-CIA spook named Robert David Steele.

Steele could give Alex Jones a run for his money when it came to Reptile people conjecture about the British royal family and the Vatican, which often veered into the wildly anti-Semitic. Steele and Corsi were connected to a LARPer that had gotten QAnons to elevate a fake news story about a dirty bomb that closed down the Port of Charleston. I asked an acquaintance named John Kiriakou, a former company man who was jailed by Obama for being a CIA whistleblower, about Steele. He told me that the CIA and larger intelligence community is enormous, and there are bound to be a few crazies.

QAnon spread to Germany, the UK, Australia, Canada, New Zealand, France, South Africa and the Netherlands. Let's keep in mind that the US military and the CIA have been running psyops all over the world to influence foreign elections for over a hundred years. Also as economist Mark Blyth has elucidated, Trumpism is a global phenomenon that is the result of decades of neoliberalism.

QAnon's premise was that the common people were working with Trump to take on the evil Cabal. The supreme irony is that all of those who drank the Kool-Aid became useful idiots in a sophisticated psyop to deliver Trump a second term—in other words, they were the victims of an actual conspiracy organized by an evil cabal that weaponized conspiracy theories for indoctrination.

Under Trump we saw the House and Senate go to a climate-denying GOP. Within days of Trump winning the presidency he appointed Rex Tillerson, the former CEO of ExxonMobil, as Secretary of State. The Secretary of the Interior Ryan Zinke opened up federal lands to lease to oil and gas companies. We saw coal lobbyists appointed to head up the EPA. He signed the executive order for the Dakota Access Pipeline as one of his first acts in office.

He waged war on immigrants and Muslims.

The Covid death toll and the number of cases in America dwarfed that of every other country. Four years under a Donald Trump presidency felt like being in the passenger seat with a drunk NASCAR driver going a hundred and fifty miles an hour into oncoming traffic.

In a sane world, Trump's campaign would never have survived his campaign announcement speech where he called Mexicans rapists, and if that were the case, a quarter of a million people would not have died unnecessarily from gross Covid mismanagement. According to a study conducted by *The Lancet*, a British medical journal, 40 percent of Coronavirus deaths were avoidable. There is no doubt that by the time this book is published, this tragic figure of people who didn't have to die has increased.

There were no more questions about who Trump and his cronies were and what their agenda was. It was clear that the establishment was fine with another four years of Trump. The wealthy Democratic Party donors were doing great under his tax scam for the billionaire class. BiPoC organized, and voters and progressives showed up in force.

Bernie and many grassroots leaders set aside their pride and campaigned hard for Biden. It was a bitter pill. We were aware of the establishment Democrats' gambit to play Trump roulette. No one had any illusions about who Biden was or whether he represented the same establishment we had fought against for the last five years. The truth, though, was that the field of battle would be more conducive to making gains under a Biden administration, and that another Trump presidency was too dangerous to permit.

Trump and conservative hacks leading up to the election pushed a narrative that the only way he could lose was if the Democrats stole the election. This trope was first started by Roger Stone when he pushed the *#StopTheSteal* hashtag in 2016. After Biden won, Trump's base went completely off the rails. They alleged that the election was stolen.

In Bob Woodward's book, *Peril*, he records that General Mark Milley, the Chairman of the Joint Chiefs of Staff, was "certain that Trump had gone into a serious mental decline in the aftermath of the election," and so took countermeasures fearing Trump would launch a nuclear attack on China. He had already escalated nuclear tensions with other nations like North Korea to levels not seen since the Cold War.

In the end, Trump lost.

This was largely due to the efforts of Black and brown progressive organizers in Georgia and Arizona who campaigned hard to defeat Trump. Despite all that had happened, Bernie, the Squad and a good percentage of his army showed up in full force to defeat the regime.

Perhaps the most glorious end to Trump's presidency was the press conference after his defeat. The election year of 2020 was a never ending barrage of dumpster fires. There was one shining moment however, as though it were a gift of manna bestowed from on high by the celestial gods of irony. Trump's brand was always that of the pomp and circumstance of obscene wealth. He even flaunted a gaudy 18-karat golden toilet.

The recently deposed president's team had meant to book the lavish Four Seasons hotel in Philadelphia with the hopes of whipping up a media circus to promote false narratives of a stolen election. Instead Team Trump accidentally held the press conference outside Four Seasons Total Landscaping, a small mom and pop store in front of a white garage door next to a sex shop. Giuliani sweated profusely while spouting rhetoric and trying to play the incident off, as well as the fact that Trump had lost badly. It was a glorious moment.

It wouldn't last long, however, as Trump's cult would not concede without incident.

The January 6 Insurrection

Leading up to the election, Trump whipped his base into a frenzy by making statements like, "The only way we will lose the election is if it is rigged." After the election the daily chatter in the QAnon threads we tracked reached levels of crazy we could not have imagined. One theory was that Joe Biden and Trump had had surgeries to remove their faces so that they could trade places like in the 1997 Nicolas Cage and John Travolta movie *Face/Off.* They thought that Joe Biden was really Donald Trump. Others suggested that Biden was the president for show, but that Trump was really secretly in charge of the White House.

No, I'm not joking. The Trump Q-ult really believed this at one point.

On January 6, the day Congress convened to certify the results of the election and codify Trump's defeat, a *#StopTheSteal* Trump rally was held at the Capitol. It had been all over the QAnon message boards. Trump himself addressed a frenzied crowd of thirty thousand of his most rabid and cult-like followers with wild rhetoric about a stolen election.

Just a few weeks prior, Mikki had invited me to join him in Austin, Texas where he and his new right-wing extremist pals allegedly lived in a compound of sorts. It was heartbreaking. Mikki and I had a history going back over a decade. A few weeks later, his cryptic message made more sense in the light of the Capitol Riots of January 6.

Mikki even spoke at the rally. He claimed that the demonstration was going to be peaceful.

He spoke about the connection to life and the creator. He said there was a psychological war. It was the alt-right agenda packaged in a love and light New Age message.

When Trump spoke at the Stop The Steal rally, he inflamed the crowd of supporters by saying, "all of us here today do not want to see our election victory stolen by emboldened radical-left Democrats, which is what they're doing," he said. "And stolen by the fake news media. That's what they've done and what they're doing. We will never give up, we will never concede. It doesn't happen. You don't concede when there's theft involved. Now it is up to Congress to confront this egregious assault on our democracy. And after this, we're going to walk down, and I'll be there with you, we're going to walk down, we're going to walk down."

When they got there, tens of thousands of people rushed the barricades outside the Capitol Building. These barricades were a joke compared to what we faced outside the Democratic National Convention in Philadelphia in 2016, or the resistance that the BLM organizers had faced during the George Floyd protests.

Trump's all-male brown shirt paramilitary group, the Proud Boys, were there in force shouting "1776" and "Fuck Antifa." All of a sudden, the law-and-order crowd picked up barricades and started smashing the cops over the head. The horde overwhelmed the police, who were outnumbered a hundred to one. There was a sea of white, bearded men with red hats, American flags, Trump and Confederate flags, baseball bats, and pitchforks. It looked like an invading mob of angry villagers.

They smashed windows and climbed up the walls. It looked like something out of a zombie movie, when the undead hordes finally swarm the main complex. The cops largely let them in without resistance. This was in stark juxtaposition to demonstrations for Black Lives, which were met by standing armies of law enforcement. Eventually it was clear that this was a full-scale riot with potential designs on targeting members of Congress with violence.

The demonstrators even built a gallows outside reserved for Mike Pence, whom Trump had accused of disloyalty for agreeing to do his constitutional duty to certify the 2020 election. When there were altercations between the Trumpers and police, many were astonished that the cops met them with pepper spray, because normally they were the biggest supporters of police—even when they brutalized unarmed demonstrators and murdered people of color. The white privilege on display was mind boggling.

More than a hundred officers were injured in the riot, and five people died. By contrast, when we shut down thirty-five state capitals every weekend for six weekends in a row during the 2017 Poor People's Campaign, more than two thousand people were arrested, but zero people were hurt or killed, and no property was destroyed.

Yet according to conservatives, radical leftists were the lawless ones. QAnon promoted the idea that the Covid-19 epidemic was a dark plot for control orchestrated by Bill Gates, China and the Democratic Party. It accused the George Floyd uprising of being a "deep state psyop." It claimed that the Democrats were in league with Antifa super soldiers.

Over two hundred people were arrested for their role in the Capitol siege, a number of them associated with militant groups such as the Oath Keepers, the Three Percenters, and the Proud Boys. These were far-right neofascist groups committed to political violence, and which had sworn fealty to Donald Trump. It turns out that both the Proud Boy and Oath Keeper leaders were coordinating with the FBI as informants to track antifascist groups. In other words, federal law enforcement officers were working with extreme right-wing paramilitary groups to target Antifa organizing efforts against white supremacists.

Take all the time you need to let this sink in.

Military generals. Ex-CIA officers. Right Wing militias. All of them had coordinated with a white nationalist strongman president with fascist inclinations, and were part of a conspiracy to instill fear and obedience as a cult overran the Capitol Building under false pretenses to maintain unlawful control of the government.

It eventually came out that even Supreme Court Justice Clarence Thomas's wife had pressured Trump's Chief of Staff to not let Donald concede, driven by conspiracy theories. They exchanged twenty-nine text messages. She even attended the Jan. 6th Stop the Steal rally.

We must pause here to fully grasp just how close this country may have been to entering into the next phase of a burgeoning *Hunger Games* or Gilead-esque dystopian fascist ethno-religious state. Trump and his cabal had followed the autocrat's playbook to achieve absolute power.

Hitler rose to power in a time of economic crisis by driving conspiracy theories that international bankers, Communists and Jews were all in league to oppress ordinary working people. He preyed on their existing biases to assume power. Trump and QAnon also used the fear of Communism and dehumanizing rhetoric against ethnic groups. There was an occult aspect to his rise, including the branding of the opposition as a supernatural evil. His supporters attributed magical qualities to him. The red MAGA hat was like a uniform. He encouraged his supporters to commit acts of violence against counter-protesters at his rallies. Fear and hatred are important to controlling the minds of the masses. Fear and hatred cause mental activity to be centered in the reptilian brain, causing people to lose prefrontal cortex cognition and the ability to reason. People look to a strong authoritarian leader when they feel threatened.

Ultimately QAnon, Trump's victory, and the coda of the Capitol riots revealed how vulnerable the country's democratic institutions really are, as well as how easily a populist uprising can be co-opted.

In the end, the feedback loop between QAnon and Trump may have contributed to his undoing. The Covid conspiracies that arose from QAnon would influence Trump's narrative and policies (or lack thereof), which likely contributed to him losing the election. Over half a million Americans died in 2020, representing 25 percent of total Covid deaths globally. Some data suggests that beyond the first hundred thousand deaths, much of the decimation was preventable. Had Trump taken appropriate measures to contain the virus and to provide adequate aid to suffering working class Americans, he might, according to some projections, have defeated Biden handily.

A New Age bare-chested man with runic tattoos and a giant viking helmet carried a sign that said, "Q sent me," and wielded a spear with an American flag. QAnon Congresswoman Lauren Boebert tweeted up a storm suggesting that the insurrection was "1776." Like many of her Anon cohorts, she believed that the mob would be successful in taking over the government to reinstall their führer.

Video captured Mikki Willis at the heart of the mob, camera in hand, trying to get into the Capitol Building. He later claimed to just be there as a journalist.

The Capitol rioters attempted to breach the doors of the Speaker's Lobby, a long corridor with portraits of every Speaker of the House who has ever served. The doors were barricaded with a stack of chairs to keep Trump's mob at bay while congress-people and staffers were being evacuated. With cries of hatred, they began smashing the window and ramming the double doors. They were about to break through when a shot rang out, killing Trump supporter Ashli Babbitt—an Air Force veteran who died on the spot.

At one point tens of thousands of protesters were bottlenecked at a tunnel entering the Capitol Building in a 45-minute standoff with a handful of riot cops, like a giant, horrible rugby scrum.

There was an all out mêlée where Trump supporters used a variety of blunt weapons to bludgeon the cops. It looked like the scene from the Battle of Helm's Deep in the second book of the *Lord of the Rings* trilogy, when an ocean of orcs attempt to take the stronghold of the Hornburg. In the aftermath, four of the cops who responded to the insurrection died by suicide.

We must confront the possibility that Trump could have attempted to declare martial law, avoid the certification of the results of the election and retain power. This has happened in other countries, sometimes as the result of our own CIA having orchestrated it—having been successful at least seven times in Iran, Guatemala, Congo, Brazil, the Dominican Republic, South Vietnam, and Chile, and having attempted it on at least seventy-two other occasions. We should not forget that Hitler failed at his first coup attempt.

These people intended to take the Capitol Building and reinstall Trump as president. Many had believed for months that a civil war was coming and that this was the moment.

Regardless of what might have happened, this was a populist uprising. Very often the agents of the corporate state will attempt to discredit leftist uprisings by conflating them with radical right-wing populism. They tried to paint Occupy Wall Street and the Tea Party with the same brush. They tried to say that the Bernie Sanders movement and Trump's cult were cut from the same cloth. This could not be farther from the truth, as our leftist and progressive movements have stood for economic, racial, health, and climate justice, whereas conservative populism still worships capitalism and the billionaire class as its religion, and stands in solidarity with the police state to not only uphold the status quo, but to regress our society back to a time when straight white Christian men ruled the world with complete impunity.

What radical right-wing and leftist movements do have in common is that they are fueled by decades of neoliberal policies that have decimated the working class. The rage that fueled these insurrections has stemmed from the powerlessness and desperation that the majority of Americans feel as they have watched the leaders they've elected to serve them avoid all responsibility for selling out to "the elite" and destroy all hope they have for a good life.

How could this happen?

Decades of global neoliberalism. Jobs shipped overseas. The death of unions. Stagnating wages. Trillions being funneled to the billionaire class out from the poor and middle class. Decades of stupid, immoral, expensive wars. Corporate media-driven political football to keep the political ad money rolling in. Social media algorithms corralling us into echo chambers so that we could be easier to market to. A systemic failure of our journalistic institutions. A strategic takeover of all structures of power by corporations.

QAnon and the January 6th Insurrection are the logical result of the Democratic Party establishment working to suppress healthy populist movements for justice and equity.

Poor conservatives felt that they had no voice or representation in the government. They felt shut out of the political process. So they violently occupied the Capitol Building, the enduring symbol of the government.

QAnon's second American revolution did not only happen because the aim was to win a second term for Trump. It was also fundamentally rooted in the paradigm of white supremacy, which was very much the status quo. It never truly sought to fundamentally transform the system to uplift poor people or people of color. It never sought to challenge the hegemony of corporations.

This is a cautionary tale.

Not only must we contend with the climate crisis, but we must be prepared to meet the continuing rise of neofascism, which has become a global phenomenon. The QAnon Trump cult is not going away.

According to *Grid News*, at least seventy-eight QAnon candidates decided to run for office in 26 states as of 2022. Ron Watkins—whom Cullen Hoback, director of the HBO documentary *Q: Into the Storm*, suggests is "Q" himself—was one of them. Just to give you an idea of Ron's brand of leadership, in January Watkins appeared at a school board meeting in Scottsdale, Arizona, where he accused "communist creeps" in school boards of indoctrinating children with "transexual propaganda" and critical race theory.

I believe this is only the beginning. Marjorie Taylor Greene and Lauren Boebert are the canaries in the coalmine.

We can only speculate at this point what world we would have been living in if the Obama administration had heard the cries of Occupy demonstrators around the country, brought the corrupt bankers to justice and passed policies for poor working Americans. We can only wonder what might have happened if the Democratic establishment had let democracy have its day and had not put its thumb on the scale in the 2016 and 2020 primary elections against the strongest candidate, or if they had actually fought for a people's agenda.

If Occupy Wall Street and the Bernie Sanders Movement has done anything, it's upended the idea of what was normal. Both movements have revealed that there was an unholy alliance between the ruling class, the political establishment and corporate media. Both smashed the simulacra of the American dream and put a chink in the armor of the perception that the corporate state was too powerful to challenge. Both brought mass protest back into the

DNA of the nation. Both were driven by decentralized technology and ordinary people using social media platforms to make their voices heard.

For good or ill, QAnon and the Capitol riots would most likely not have happened without the grassroots populist uprisings of OWS and the Bernie Movement transforming the landscape of America. History has shown time and time again how fascists and right-wing authoritarians will come to power on the back of leftist movements. This in my opinion is one of the most compelling reasons that we must succeed in the end and not fall short of occupying the structures of power.

As John F. Kennedy once said, "Those who make peaceful revolution impossible will make violent revolution inevitable."

Epilogue

Bernie's Mittens

We didn't lose the game; we just ran out of time.
-Vince Lombardi

When Inauguration Day finally arrived, no one expected that Bernie would figure into the festivities. He appeared on television sitting in the audience on a folding chair with his arms crossed, wearing a gray jacket that most likely came from Burlington Coat Factory, and a pair of mittens knitted by a friend and supporter in Vermont.

It seemed like attending the ceremony might have been on his to-do list, but wasn't the most important thing he had going on that day. Before the ceremony had ended, the Internet had erupted in renewed love for Bernie, sparked by the image of the old man and his mittens. For at least four days, thousands of "Bernie's Mittens" memes dominated online spaces and media narratives. The image was inserted into classic paintings, album covers, movie scenes, and historic photos.

It broke the internet, and totally eclipsed coverage of Joe Biden's big day.

Marianne Williamson described the phenomenon by writing, "All the Bernie memes today are a spontaneous eruption of America's collective unconscious. We know who we love and we just weren't gonna let the day go by without saying so."

Right on cue, the corporate media hacks tried to blame Bernie for taking over the day, while the liberal intelligentsia sulked for not having their vapid opinions on Lady Gaga heard. I think Sanders's give-no-fucks posture was the perfect expression of our collective reaction to the Biden-Harris ascent to power.

The barrage of memes was a nice moment, but small consolation for the fact that we had come so close to taking over control of the White House and the military and executive powers that come with it. We should have been mobilizing to begin the fight for Medicare for All and a Green New Deal, and instead we had just helped the corporate Democrats win the office we had fought so hard to occupy.

The establishment candidates and policymakers who had fallen in line for Biden were well rewarded. Kamala was given the vice presidency, making her the first Black woman to hold the second-highest office in the land. While progressives and leftists hold grudges, neoliberals understand that it's all about power. No one batted an eye over the times Kamala had told Biden in the debates, "That little girl was me,"—riding to school, in response to Biden's opposition to desegregating school buses. Neera Tanden, one of Bernie's greatest detractors, was nominated to be the Director of the Office of Management and Budget, but was defeated when progressives rose up to oppose her nomination.

For all of his efforts to swing the election for Biden, Sanders was appointed as the Chairman of the Budget Committee. This was a powerful position—and he wielded it as such. According to Alex Woodward of the *Independent*, "The Vermont senator held congressional hearings on wealth inequality and corporate bailouts, forced a vote on the Senate floor to raise the federal hourly minimum wage to $15, introduced several pieces of legislation aimed at raising taxes on the nation's ultra-rich, and critically, ushered into Congress a definitive piece of legislation that encompassed Joe Biden's American Rescue Plan, one of the largest-ever measures in US history to combat poverty. Meanwhile, he has rallied organizers and Amazon workers in Alabama."

This list paled in comparison to what he could have done had he won, but it was impressive nonetheless.

As for the Fellowship of the Bern, we did not hold together after the election. There was no unifying vision or candidate to rally around and, in many cases, we turned on each other instead. In the wake of Bernie's concession, a swath of armchair leftists became active opposition, even going so far as to accuse Sanders of sheep-dogging, or acting as a sort of controlled opposition.

The extreme antipathy toward the Democratic Party drove some factions of the left to sympathize with right wingers. One of the problems is that conservatives look for converts and the left looks for traitors. The right understands the need to build power and will go to any lengths to do so, whereas leftist movements have been infiltrated by agents of the corporate state since the early days of the labor movement and therefore we are more conditioned to accuse one another of treason. Some were influenced by the old adage of, "the enemy of my enemy is my friend."

Some members of Bernie's Avengers and other accomplices seemed to be more attracted to the right-wing Legion of Doom.

Jimmy Dore doubled down on right-wing anti-vaxx tropes. Tulsi picked the weirdest hill to die on by throwing herself in with transphobes. Jimmy and Tulsi both defended Kyle Rittenhouse, the poster boy for conservatives that fantasize about killing leftists and falsely accuse BLM of being a terrorist organization.

Bobby Kennedy Jr. compared the suffering of the unvaccinated to Anne Frank, a Jewish victim of the Nazis. Sameera Khan got fired from RT for going full tankie (someone who claims to be a leftist but defends authoritarian regimes like North Korea) and publicly standing for Joseph Stalin.

Josh Fox was publicly accused of toxic behavior by his ex-girlfriend Lee Ziesche, who was joined by other activists and organizers in calling for accountability for bad behavior. Wes Clarke Jr. began displaying signs of serious mental health issues and our beloved brother David Braun ended up on the streets battling drug addiction. The physical, psychological and emotional toll that frontline activism may exact can be too much to bear if we aren't intentional about getting the support to process the trauma.

Tim Tagaris, who helped run Bernie's digital fundraising in 2016 and 2020, and his Aisle 518 consulting firm took on right wing billionaire real estate oligarch Rick Caruso's vanity campaign for Los Angeles Mayor, which was just too gross for words. It wasn't enough that his firm made $16 million off of the political revolution.

On top of it all, while Bernie was out in full force campaigning for Karen Bass to beat the rapacious developer, Cenk Uygur also chose to personally endorse Caruso.

Fuck me.

And the schisms didn't stop there.

Jimmy Dore also launched an all-out offensive against AOC and the Squad for not adopting his strategy to force a vote on Medicare for All by threatening to challenge Pelosi's position as

Speaker of the House. There was nothing wrong in principle with the *idea* of the Force-The-Vote strategy, but there was no real advance organizing behind it, and when all the attacks started, it drove a giant wedge in the movement that destroyed much of the solidarity and good will that had been built in our ten years of movement building towards a broad leftist-progressive alliance. I tried unsuccessfully to de-escalate with back channel communications with Jimmy and Cenk—after all, we all had a lot of history together, but passions were running too high and the efforts were unsuccessful.

This "bucket-of-crabs" infighting is a long-standing paradigm on the left, which is a big part of why we can't have nice things. This is also why we must cultivate a culture that also emphasizes doing the uncomfortable inner work of healing our trauma and transforming our consciousness. We need processes for transformative justice so that when problems arise, we can work things out together in a healthy way, as opposed to public call-outs that create no healing and just give the opposition ammunition to attack us with.

No one could manage to try to see the other's point of view. Personally I think everyone was wrong for fighting in the first place, while the establishment sat back and laughed as progressives attacked one another.

r/WallStreetBets

On another front, the spirit of Occupy continued on January 22, when a Reddit subthread called WallStreetBets initiated a short squeeze on GameStop stock. Big hedge funds like Citadel had shorted the stock (meaning that they sold the stock before they bought it). The idea was to punish short-sellers, and for the little guys to pummel Wall Street by uniting the decentralized network of users with the common goal of buying and holding the stock, thus driving up its price and forcing the big investors to have to buy back the stock at massively inflated prices—causing the "hedgies" to lose billions. The idea of Occupy Wall Street took on a new meaning for the almost 10 million followers of the subreddit, who also experienced Wall Street fight-back, when it exerted its leverage on online trading platforms, who suspended trading for individual investors.

On July 30, 2021, Squad members Cori Bush, AOC, Ayanna Pressley, and Jamaal Bowman occupied the Capitol steps to protest the end of the eviction moratorium. Members of Congress were going on vacation during their recess while 40 million Americans were in danger of losing their housing. Representative Bush had experienced eviction and being unhoused before she was elected to Congress, and called for the House to pass legislation to extend the deadline to keep the eviction moratorium in place. When she couldn't get traction, she went back to her activism roots and used direct action and her platform to elevate the issue. They slept out on the Capitol steps while calling on the White House, the Congressional Progressive Caucus and Speaker Pelosi to take action.

This was a hearty action, but my great fear is that the Congressional Progressive Caucus does not do nearly enough to work with the grassroots to create a working inside-outside strategy. Not only do they fail to capitalize on the enormous people power available to pressure the establishment, but when the base is disconnected from the inside baseball of Beltway politics, people begin to feel disempowered and disillusioned.

★ ★ ★ ★ ★

Ultimately, the pandemic forced us to see just how fragile our way of life and the systems we take for granted truly are. There were bread lines miles long and grocery stores with entire rows of shelves that were empty. These were things that were only supposed to happen in socialist countries like Venezuela. We learned in real time that all of the assumptions that kept us from demanding that our own tax dollars be used to benefit poor and working people were false.

We learned that our government could house the homeless.

We learned student loans could be forgiven.

We learned that frontline minimum wage workers were the glue that held our society, economy and way of life together—the technocracy, it turned out, not so much.

We learned that minimum wage workers, not the technocrats, were actually the most essential workers in our society and yet they were still deemed to not be worthy of a living wage, free healthcare or hazard pay.

We learned the power of mutual aid to empower citizens to support one another, especially to care for the most vulnerable.

We learned that people did not have to be evicted from their homes.

We could keep poor people from getting their utilities shut off.

We learned that Bernie was right about his platform.

The entire healthcare system is broken.

In 2008 the banks got bailed out but the people were left to suffer.

When we asked for a living wage they always said, "How are you gonna pay for it?"

When we asked for free state universities they said, "How are you gonna pay for it?"

When we asked for access to free healthcare like every other industrial nation they said, "How are you gonna pay for it?"

In 2020, corporate America got bailed out again to the tune of six trillion dollars without so much as a discussion.

In the midst of a pandemic, the billionaire class extracted over three trillion dollars from the poor.

Hedge funds made $320 billion during the pandemic, while 300 million more members of our human family went into extreme poverty.

The US is the richest country in the history of the world. When it comes to corporate subsidies for fossil fuel companies, the Walmart Waltons or big stupid wars, no one ever asks, "How are you going to pay for it?" When it came to denying relief to working people, the establishment shills dug in like they were fighting at the Battle of the Bulge.

Of course the corporate media narratives continued to ignore or dismiss Sanders's achievements but, after the election, Uncle Noam Chomsky once again brought clarity to the national conversation:

> *"It's common to say now that the Sanders campaign failed. I think that's a mistake. I think it was an extraordinary success, completely shifted the arena of debate and discussion. Issues that were unthinkable a couple years ago are now right in the middle of attention.*
>
> *The worst crime he committed, in the eyes of the establishment, is not the policy he's proposing; it's the fact that he was able to inspire*

popular movements, which had already been developing—Occupy, Black Lives Matter, many others—and turn them into an activist movement, which doesn't just show up every couple years to push a lever and then go home, but applies constant pressure, constant activism and so on. That could affect a Biden administration."

And indeed it did, even if it was met with predictable opposition from the corporate centrists in the party.

Bernie, the Squad and progressive grassroots leaders exerted their power to push for Build Back Better, Joe Biden's infrastructure spending bill. It started out as a $3.5 trillion FDR-style new New Deal, to expand Medicare and Medicaid, provide free higher education for working-class students, fight child poverty, and address the climate crisis.

It was opposed by every Republican in Congress as well as the drug companies, the insurance companies, the fossil fuel industry and the billionaire class, and the bill was gutted. The Democrats had the votes to push it through, but ultimately it was allowed to be torpedoed by two Democratic Senators: Joe Manchin and Kyrsten Sinema, who are virtually indistinguishable from Republicans themselves. Manchin represented poor working people and yet owned a yacht and Maserati, and worked tirelessly against their interests for the corporate donor class. Kyrsten Sinema, known for her brightly colored Forever 21 fashion sense, voted down a $15 minimum wage amendment to Biden's Build Back Better bill with a flippant curtsy. Service workers suffered horrible indignities in life-threatening conditions during the pandemic—overworked and underpaid. This was a clear fuck-you to the 99 Percent.

Previously, in June 2021, Greenpeace UK did an op where they impersonated a headhunter interviewing a former Exxon lobbyist named Keith McCoy, who unwittingly gave them closely held secrets about Manchin, Sinema and nine other members of the Senate. McCoy described Manchin as the Senate's "kingmaker," and went on to say that they are in dialogue at least once a week. He indicated that the Democrats would never pass any meaningful climate legislation because the oil giant essentially owns the Exxon Eleven.

Like our DSA comrades in Nevada, West Virginia Berniecrats would not simply lie down and let Dinosaur Joe and the establishment hacks rule with impunity. In June 2022, progressives took control of the West Virginia Democratic Party. They were able to use the party's own rules against them, won a majority of seats on the executive committee, and thus ended Manchin's unimpeded rule of the state party.

Just Look Up!

The violent riots of January 6th left much of the nation in a dark and apprehensive mood. This included veterans of the Bernie campaign. But, with few exceptions, we did not fade away or sink into despair. As in 2016, the movement continued to push, lighting a pathway forward with unexpected victories in struggle after struggle, from sea to shining sea.

Everywhere one looked, activists affiliated with the Bernie movement were rejecting complacency and doing what they do best: successfully reframing debates around vital issues. They remained at the forefront of a growing renters' strike movement. They organized unions in new industries. They fought pipelines and the Big Banks that finance Big Oil. In the case of the Public Bank LA movement (formerly Divest LA), they successfully steered the passage of two laws that allowed Los Angeles to create the country's first-ever Municipal Public Bank on October 5, 2021.

There were also wins inside the electoral system, including those holding implications for 2024. In March of 2021, a slate of progressive Democratic Socialists of America candidates swept all five party leadership positions in Nevada—effectively taking over the leadership of the state's Democratic Party. The effort was aided by solidarity fundraising emails signed by Bernie Sanders, AOC and Cori Bush. (Faced with imminent defeat, the old-guard Nevada Democratic Party leadership shifted their funds to the DSCC, rather than hand it over to the DSA-Bernie wing of the party.) Beyond Nevada, Bernie-aligned groups like Justice Democrats and Brand New Congress continued to fight for progressive candidates in states both red and blue.

Bernie veterans also generated strong waves on the culture front. The Oscar-winning writer and director Adam McKay, who endorsed Bernie through the Bernie Wizards team, partnered with political journalist and senior Bernie 2020 advisor David Sirota to write a satire about climate inaction in the mold of *Dr. Strangelove*. Released on Netflix in December of 2021, *Don't Look Up!* told the story of two scientists, played by Leonardo DiCaprio and Jennifer Lawrence, who discover a comet that is going to destroy all life on earth. The metaphorical punchline was all too familiar: no one will take the imminent threat seriously. It quickly became one of the most streamed movies in the history of Netflix and won an Oscar nomination. (The campaign's DNA extended to the film's cast, which featured Bernie surrogate Ariana Grande and endorser Bon Iver, who contributed to the soundtrack.)

Nor did campaign allies and veterans let up the pressure on the environmental front. In March of 2022, I got a call from my old friends Mark Ruffalo and Alex Ebert who asked me to organize a *#BankExit* campaign targeting City National Bank and their parent company, Royal Bank of Canada, over their funding of the Coastal GasLink pipeline in British Columbia. We had seen this exact movie play out following the 2016 election at Standing Rock, the most famous of several pipelines being pushed through sovereign indigenous land. This time, the brutality was being inflicted on the Wet'suwet'en tribe.

To fight the Coastal GasLink project, I contacted my old Occupy comrades Harry Waisbren, Kelli Daley, and Brad Gans at Act.tv. Only a few months previously, we'd collaborated on the tenth anniversary celebrations of Occupy Wall Street in New York, Boston, and Los Angeles. Soon we had formed a *#BankExit* team connected to Bill McKibben and another team of activists who were organizing around the energy created by the success of *Don't Look Up!* The crossover efforts soon extended to active roles for Adam McKay and Meryl Streep, who played the US president in the film. Life was imitating art in the best way.

Like me, Adam had read the IPCC report in 2018 that gave humanity until 2030 to cut carbon emissions by 45 percent (and until 2050 to transition off carbon-based energy altogether) if we were to salvage any sort of sustainable future. This new alliance between our pipeline and McKibben's climate group was aided by former Occupy LA activist Steven Starr, who had tapped his new Extinction Rebellion friends to organize direct actions at City National Plaza in Downtown Los Angeles. It was the old gang infused with some young blood: Youth Climate Strike, Sunrise Movement LA, XRLA, and Jack Eidt from SoCal 350. Shannon Rivers and Dawna Shuman, meanwhile, wrangled the press.

Shannon, George Funmaker (the Lakota activist who'd helped inspire *#BankExit* had been with us for the Jane Fonda protest), and I led an unannounced action inside the bank just before the main rally on City National Plaza on March 18th, 2022. Before the bank's security and staff had any idea what was happening, George and Shannon began banging a big ceremonial drum and singing the Mni Wiconi song from Standing Rock while I read our list of divestment demands. The staff and security just stood there nonplussed. Normally when we do an action against one of the big banks like Wells Fargo, they know we are coming and have prepared significant counter measures, but on this occasion we caught them unawares.

Feeling good about the morning's work, we headed back to the rally to fire up the troops and muster reinforcements.

After the press conference, we returned to the bank with a hundred people marching behind banners. To illustrate the urgency of the climate crisis, we held up a giant clock with a timer counting down eight years, synchronized according to the IPCC climate report projections. We held hands and did a circle dance in the plaza as the news cameras bore witness. The next day, Mark, Adam, Meryl Streep, and Bill McKibben took part in a powerful broadcast I produced with Avaaz and Act.tv, together with Canadian Indigenous leaders. It was called, "Just Look UP! Stop Big Oil!"

★ ★ ★ ★ ★

As the dust settled after the event, I reflected on our collective journey. Specifically, what it said about the vitality of the movement that once again lacked the organizing vessel of a national campaign. By elevating an important struggle that had received almost no media attention, the *#BankExit* campaign demonstrated the resilience, effectiveness, and—yes—fundamental importance of the sacred community formed in Occupy and nurtured in

Bernie's two campaigns. We were not only battle-scarred, but uniquely capable of uplifting and onboarding a new generation of young people into the movement.

Nowhere was this clearer than in the momentum around a generational nationwide surge of labor activism.

Strike!: The Rebirth of American Labor

Bernie Sanders has always been known for his long and principled solidarity with American labor, which dates well before he ever ran for president. But if the years after Occupy sparked a resurgence of interest in labor, Bernie's two presidential campaigns allowed him to continue elevating union organizing to a new place of prominence in the national consciousness.

During the run-up to his 2020 campaign, Bernie seemed to be everywhere that workers were fighting for better wages, rights, and benefits. He came to the aid of Disney and Amazon workers to help them win nationwide wage increases; he walked a picket line with thousands of striking research and technical employees at UCLA; and he pledged his support to 1,700 striking General Electric/Wabtec workers, whom he inspired by saying, "Americans are sick and tired of corporate America and their wealthy CEOs ripping off working families."

Bosses clapped back with fake sock puppet accounts posing as employees, and silenced dissent on Twitter. Elon Musk, the world's richest man in 2020 (otherwise known as *"Space Karen,"*) railed against unionization and safe conditions.

Labor organizing, however, was not exclusive to the United States. In November, ten trade unions and left-wing parties across India organized the largest general strike in the history of the world, with over 250 million participants. It wasn't surprising that these historic events garnered almost no attention from the American corporate media.

But even with all the activity on the labor front in the post-Occupy decade, few predicted the surge of strikes and organizing activity that followed on the heels of the 2020 election. From the campuses of elite universities, to for-profit hospitals, to big-box corporate icons of minimum-wage precarity, workers were standing up and walking out, demanding the economic justice that was at the center of Bernie's recently concluded campaign.

It was clear these stirrings were deep when, on May Day 2020, thousands of essential workers at Instacart, Target, Walmart, Amazon, and Whole Foods announced a general strike. Career labor watchers and organizers were shocked again later that summer when McDonald's and Walmart employees led a Strike for Black Lives that mobilized a mass walkout in 160 cities in protest of the murder of George Floyd.

As the pandemic continued to push supply chains to the breaking point, employees in many industries were forced to work twelve- to sixteen-hour shifts without fair pay. Bernie was often present at rallies held in support of these actions, such as strikes by workers at food processing and packaging plants who stopped work in protest of mandatory overtime policies. Dedicated 2020 Sanders surrogate Danny DeVito temporarily lost his Twitter verification in August of 2021 for tweeting, "Support Nabisco workers striking for humane working hours, fair pay, outsourcing jobs. NO CONTRACTS NO SNACKS!"

One development that drew heavy media attention was the December 2021 union vote by Starbucks employees in Buffalo, New York. Prior to the vote, Bernie had joined a webinar with the employees leading the union drive. One of them, Gianna Reeve, detailed the company's union busting tactics, including the use of a hundred spies. Was this the 2020s, or the 1920s?

The Buffalo Starbucks union vote triggered a wave of agitation at thousands of Starbucks across the country. Maggie Carter, one of the first baristas to pass out union cards in Tennessee, reported that Bernie Sanders was her greatest inspiration for the campaign. "Bernie Sanders is my everything," she said. "I love him more than anything."

By summer 2022, over a hundred Starbucks locations had voted to unionize. As the trend spread through the country, Starbucks CEO Howard Schultz—who six years earlier had been rumored to be Hillary Clinton's pick for Labor Secretary—announced that the company would refuse to comply with the National Labor Relations Act's legal requirements to engage in good faith dialogues with unions about workers' rights.

Within just one year, 267 Starbucks stores were unionized, covering around 6950 employees.

As dramatic as the union conflict at Starbucks was, it did not catch the nation's imagination as much as another unexpected locus of organizing—one targeting the world's biggest online retailer, led by one of the world's richest and most unabashedly exploitative CEOs.

Taking on the Yellow Giant

It all began on March 30, 2020, when a worker named Chris Smalls led a walkout at the Amazon fulfillment center in Staten Island, New York center. Following his protest over what he described as a lack of safety protocols, Smalls was immediately fired. Refusing to lie down after his wrongful termination, he immediately began to organize the Congress of Essential Workers.

His successful career in labor organizing was helped by the job he held before taking a job at Amazon to support his family. For years, Chris had pursued a career as a rapper and even toured briefly with Meek Mill. He was a powerful speaker with charisma to spare—combining the unionizing instincts and leadership of Eugene Debs with the style and flair of RZA from the Wu-Tang Clan (also Staten Island heroes).

Smalls had no previous training in union organizing; nor did he have funding or institutional support from existing labor organizations. What he did have besides his own talents was three dedicated and talented co-conspirators in Derrick Palmer, Gerald Bryson, and Jordan Flowers. The three held meetings at the Queens bus stop where Amazon workers commuted to work. But not just any meetings. They made bonfires and had cookouts for employees after their shifts. Empowering workers through barbecues and S'mores proved to be an incredible and effective tactic. The company tried to and failed to blunt the union drive with everything at its disposal, including the use of fake employee accounts to badmouth unionization on Twitter.

This New American Labor Movement continued to gather steam during the pandemic. Indeed, in March of 2021, one of the pandemic economy's iconic images was born: the piss bottle that one worker described having to keep in his Amazon delivery truck because the company did not allow him bathroom breaks. Discontent within the company continued to spread, and on April 1, 2022, factory workers in Staten Island voted to join the Amazon Labor Union. A *New Yorker* story published that month on the labor activism rattling Amazon noted that "many of the organizers are young, like the ALU founders, and appear to have absorbed the horizontalism of Occupy Wall Street, Black Lives Matter, and pandemic mutual aid."

She got it right, with the exception of forgetting the contribution of Bernie Sanders and the movement behind him as a continuation of these uprisings.

★ ★ ★ ★ ★

I first became aware of the activity at Amazon in August 2021, when I saw a fellow activist and Occupy veteran named Justine Medina post about infiltrating Amazon to help start a union there. Like many of us, Justine's politics continued to evolve during her involvement with the Sanders campaigns. In 2017 she helped to found the Queens branch of the DSA, and went on to work as a political consultant on AOC's congressional campaign.

When I reached out to her about her interest in the Amazon drive, she informed me that she was pursuing a strategy, called "salting," in which someone gets a job at a company to agitate for the union. Justine told me, "Don't get a 'salt job' if you aren't committed. To be in true solidarity with the workers, expect to be there at least a year."

I have known some truly dedicated revolutionaries over the years, but Justine's plan to work for a year or more in Amazon's substandard sweatshop conditions—in the middle of a deadly pandemic, no less, just to help incite a worker's rebellion—was one of the hardest and most inspiring things I had ever heard of.

A familiar voice was no doubt helping inspire her and others who got involved in the union drive. In response to Jeff Bezos's union busting thuggery, Bernie challenged the CEO in a blistering address on May 5, 2022. "Given all your wealth, how much do you need?" the senator demanded to know. "Why are you doing every-thing in your power, including breaking the law, to deny Amazon workers the right to join a union so that they can negotiate for better wages, better working conditions and better benefits? *How much do you need?*"

After Smalls won the vote to unionize, he traveled to Washington, D.C., to advocate for the Protecting the Right to Organize (PRO) Act, a bill that would prohibit bosses from bullying employees into voting against unions. As part of his trip, he met with President Biden while wearing his signature red-and-black jacket that declared, in big yellow cartoon letters, "Eat the Rich."

Chris Smalls would go on to become the founder and president of the ALU, or Amazon Labor Union, and together with his comrade Derrick Palmer was named one of *Time* magazine's 100 Most Influential People of 2022.

Writing the article about the two men for *Time* was—who else?—Bernie Sanders.

To Sum It All Up

One thing Bernie's Mittens proved is that we are ubiquitous. Our numbers have grown to millions of people who will no longer sit idly by and allow the oligarchs to conduct business as usual. We will not be ignored.

Occupy and Bernie's Political Revolution forever shifted the political discourse in America. It radicalized millions of citizens who were part of a mass awakening around income inequality, neoliberalism, climate justice, racial justice, health justice and a host of other issues impacting our society. Over the course of a decade, a national network of activists has emerged and continues to grow.

Occupy and the Bernie Movement brought back the spirit of a by-gone era of Frank Capra populist films like *It's A Wonderful Life*, and *Mr. Smith Goes to Washington*, representing the time before McCarthyism waged war on leftism in Hollywood. In popular culture, movies and television shows reflected the shift in zeitgeist.

Films and series like *The Dark Knight Rises, Elysium, The Big Short, Mr. Robot, Ozark,* and *Billions* continued to bring the issue of inequality and class warfare to the forefront of our popular consciousness. *Dopesick* chronicles the tragic saga of how the Sackler family knowingly created an opioid epidemic and defrauded the public, killing over five hundred thousand Americans and destroying millions of lives to make billions in profits on their drug OxyContin.

No one went to jail, proving once again that oligarchs are not beholden to the same laws that poor working people are, and they will continue to get rich off of our sweat and blood.

Boots Riley, a former Occupy Oakland activist and radical leftist hip hop artist and Bernie supporter, wrote and directed *Sorry to Bother You*, a film starring LaKeith Stanfield and Sanders surrogate Danny Glover. Riley's film used elements of magical realism to bring to life the issues of race, militarism and vulture capitalism.

In 2020, Bong Joon-ho's *Parasite* became the first foreign language film to win the Academy Award for Best Picture. Joon-ho had previously directed a 2013 dystopian film called *Snowpiercer* which imagines how a class war might play out in the aftermath of the climate apocalypse. Chris Kantrowitz's wife Mickey Sumner got a featured role when the film was adapted into a television series in 2020. The South Korean series *Squid Game* also became an overnight sensation with its overt commentary on life in late-stage capitalism. The trend continued through 2022 with Ruben Östlund's *Triangle of Sadness* earning an Academy Award nomination for it biting satirical commentary on the lifestyles of the rich and famous, and Mark Mylod's *The Menu* garnered critical acclaim for going full *eat the rich—literally.*

If *Adbusters* had never put out that call to action in 2011 or had the folks in Zuccotti Park not responded, the world we live in would be a very different place. Before 2004, the term "progressive" wasn't even a thing and as of 2021 there are millions of people who identify as such. It is important to understand that for many Occupy activists, the occupation never ended and the Bernie Campaigns were just extensions of the class war we've fought for a solid decade. It was all part of a long road to build movements that would bring people in to transform our society.

If activists had never pushed Bernie and generated grassroots enthusiasm, he would most likely not have run. If Bernie had never run in 2016 and 2020, the world would be a very different place.

In 2011, there was a great chasm between liberals and radicals. By 2016, liberals who were mostly focused on electoral politics had been radicalized and were taking to the streets and engaging in direct actions against Trump. By 2021 leftists and progressives who had never thought of becoming politically engaged were joining campaigns at all levels of government, inspired by Bernie's Political Revolution.

There is a Frederick Douglass quote that encapsulates Bernie's lifelong struggle for justice when he said that "No man fails, or can fail, who so grandly gives himself and all he has to a righteous cause."

Bernie Sanders showed that it was possible to fight for working people in a corrupt system and never sell out to corporate special interests. He proved that you could run at the highest level and still be wildly committed to being your most authentic self—not just a hollow suit and a mouthpiece for the oligarchy.

He broke all campaign fundraising records with small individual donations, which shattered the illusion that politicians could only build power by aligning with wealthy donors and machine party bosses. Bernie demonstrated that you could run an issue-based campaign that shifts the Overton window at a national level for people-centered policies that were once considered too radical.

He inspired generations to become politically active, run for office and create organizations committed to electing progressives to elected positions of power.

Occupy and the Bernie campaigns brought millions of people together and changed the national dialogue around the issues. We helped break the illusion of the American Dream to reveal what had always been true—that a small group of wealthy and powerful people controlled the government and economy and when challenged, would go to any lengths to protect their own wealth and power.

We proved that people could stand up to the corporate police state. We have advocated for system-changing legislation like public banking and the $15 minimum wage. We collectively made Medicare for All and the Green New Deal a litmus test for candidates on the left.

Campaigns like *#BankExit* not only shifted billions of dollars in capital from toxic banks, but they helped link the idea in people's minds that they were funding fossil fuels and the climate crisis, as well as private prisons, wars and Indigenous genocide. Since then, shutting down banks with direct action has become a go-to tactic for climate activists.

Occupy paved the way for every mass mobilization that followed, from Black Lives Matter to the March for Our Lives, and the Youth Climate Strike. In the case of the Women's March, Occupy and Sanders activists were behind the scenes organizing. In a way, the Occupy movement was like the outside strategy and the Bernie Movement evolved to become the inside strategy. Brand New Congress and the Justice Democrats helped bring us the Squad, and they arose out of these movements. Occupiers like Nelini Stamp went on to be a force in electoral politics with the Working Families Party.

As a hybrid organization with decentralized chapters engaged in direct action and electoral organizing, Sunrise represented both the inside and outside strategies, and could trace its lineage back to these movements directly.

It is clear that the Biden Administration was not the leadership that progressives wanted or had fought for, but without the continuous struggle of Occupy political revolutionaries, not only would Trump likely have won a second term but Joe's cabinet would surely have unabashedly embraced a doctrine of militarism and business as usual for the corporate state. The progressives who fought for the 99 Percent throughout the last decade created a political awakening that has taken the fight for the soul and survival of humanity to the highest levels of government, where leftists have previously remained but a small fringe element of society with no political power.

My hope is that our greatest moments are yet to come, that all of our efforts have merely been a prelude to the next awakening. It is going to take everyone giving their very best and bringing their unique gifts to address the climate apocalypse, species extinction, the rise of neofascism, the total takeover by the oligarchy and the corporate state, the health crisis, the next economic collapse, the continued genocide against BiPoC and every other problem before us.

The Occupy and the Bernie movements brought organizers together and created a context for new leaders to emerge. Over the course of a decade, many of us have found each other. There is a vast, growing network of progressive activists who have gotten to know each other over the last ten years with many different skill sets.

Naomi Klein, in an interview with Amy Goodman, perfectly summed this up:

"More than anything else, I think what the campaign did is help us find each other. And by "us," I mean that huge "us" of the "Not me. Us." campaign. And he did this not just in this campaign, but in 2016, where he really broke the spell of the Reagan era, that spell that has lasted for four decades, that told people, who believed, that this system that was funneling so much wealth upwards and spreading insecurity, precariousness, poverty and pollution for everybody else— everybody who saw that system and thought there was something deeply wrong with it, what the neoliberal era told us was that we were the ones who were crazy, we were a tiny minority of fringe people, and that we should just accept it.

And what the Sanders campaign did in 2016 is tell us that we had been lied to, that, in fact, there were so many millions of us who saw that this world was fundamentally upside down. And all of the incredible organizing, including digital organizing but also in-person organizing, wove this amazing web, and we were able to find each other and find that we were many and they were few. And so, I don't think we can ever thank Bernie Sanders and the campaign enough for that. And being part of the campaign as a volunteer—but I did go to four states for the campaign—[were] some of the greatest moments of my political life. I mean, I was in Nevada when we won, and got to be part of that incredibly joyful moment and just got to meet so many other like-minded people."

As Naomi stated, we have found each other, inspired one another and worked together. Countless progressive campaigns have come out of these movements. Not all of us get along, but many of us quite like and respect one another. We share a bond, having fought side by side in countless fights, in a war as old as the labor movements that arose out of the Industrial Revolution.

You won't hear about this on corporate media, but take heart: our numbers are growing, especially with the next generation of young activists emerging. We invite you to join us on the playing field, where the experience is much more exciting, empowering and fulfilling than on the sidelines or the bleachers. You will surely meet us along the way if you do.

It will take every one of us standing up to meet the great challenges we face. Your voice matters. Your contribution matters.

Who knows, maybe it will be your story that will be told one day in shaping the course of history. I certainly would never have dreamed of the places this path would take me.

The greatest journeys always begin with a single step.

Prologue: This is Not the End

This is not the end, but the beginning.

Bernie Sanders is not the protagonist of this story. I am not the protagonist of this story. This story is not about any one of us. It never was.

This is about you.

Whether you are a veteran activist or have never organized before, this moment must be a new beginning. We must reevaluate the way our society functions and our entire way of life. We must look once again to organizing on a local level. We must look for new ideas to solve old problems. (Here's one: as of 2019, there were over 550,000 unhoused Americans, and more than 17 million vacant homes across the United States.)

Organizing is a wonderful thing to feel a part of. Getting involved with others who share a similar vision to make life better for our fellow humans is deeply fulfilling.

Start from wherever you are. Find a few like-minded confidantes. Form an affinity group. But choose wisely who you let into your circle of trust. Remember that the most meaningful change usually happens on the local level. Your experience level doesn't matter. Experience comes to those who act.

Abandon your identity as a consumer.

Martin Luther King, Jr. wrote in his 1963 *Letter from a Birmingham Jail* that "Freedom is never given voluntarily by the oppressor; it must be demanded by the oppressed."

Bring local leaders together to organize coalition-based progressive primaries, and work together to discuss the issues facing your communities. Create meaningful experiences together, ones that foster solidarity. Focus on transformational relationships—don't be transactional.

Align with the candidates and policy makers that will be your allies, but remember in this realm there are no permanent friends or enemies.

Build fusion coalitions with inside-outside strategies. Occupy the structures of power. Study prefiguratism as a concept, and think your plans through. Always know your outcome and how it will play.

Let us bring all movements to stand together as one.

Create voting guides to educate and inform your community. Share your resources.

Heal your trauma. Your triggers are your treasures. They illuminate the path to wholeness when we are brave enough to face our shadows.

Performative wokeness is not antiracism. White supremacy, patriarchy and colonialism live inside of us. Do the inner work.

Meditate every day. It will change your life in ways you can't imagine. You are more powerful than you know. Challenge your biases and assumptions. Embrace self-care. Don't just do it to put yourself back together, but make it a regimen and a way of life. This will give you longevity and make you a better comrade.

You cannot liberate others if you cannot liberate yourself. Transformative justice means tolerance, patience, and compassion.

Call folks in before you call them out. Create processes for mediation and transformative justice.

Never underestimate the power of cultural hegemony. Hack into culture and transform it. Seek out artists and creatives who understand the language of the heart and what stirs it. Don't just react to the opposition's plans, think ahead and control the narrative.

If you don't like or agree with this book, write your own. Make spicy memes. Make documentaries—short ones, long ones. Tell better stories. When you do, don't just talk in the language of your particular group, but speak so that others outside your clique can receive what you have to say. Try to connect with what is important to those you hope to draw into your movements. Use language that they can hear.

Be bold. Be brave. Be powerful. But above all, be kind to your comrades.

Be true to your word. Your word is everything.

Don't gossip, and try not to take yourself too seriously. Even if the work is heavy, there's no reason you can't also have fun. As Alan Moore once said, "A revolution without dancing is a revolution not worth having."

Enthusiasm is infectious. Be relentlessly passionate, especially when the vibes are heavy. Some people have fun, and some people are fun.

If you feel like you're struggling, it's because you don't have enough support. No one succeeds by themselves.

Don't be afraid to be vulnerable.

It is impossible to have been raised in America and not to have experienced trauma. Do the inner work to heal. There is no pathway to societal liberation without personal liberation, and vice versa.

Accept that the life of fighting for justice will break your heart. It will break it over and over again. It will leave you wanting to crawl into a little whimpering ball in the shower at times.

Let it.

Your heart will heal stronger in the broken places, if you do the work. There is no birth without pain. There is no magic without a sacrifice.

This will give you a medicine that you will carry, to heal others. It will help you build resilience.

Learn everything you can. Seek out mentors who are older, wiser, and more successful, but don't be afraid to learn what young people can teach you about the changing world and the fresh perspectives they may offer. Be patient with them when their views lack perspective, and the wisdom that comes with age and experience.

Organize leadership trainings to build capacity.

The work will often be thankless. In victory, you'll give your team all the credit. In defeat, you'll take the blame. People will even blame you for things you never did. You will get past it. A pure heart is the best defense and eventually if you are consistently a person of character and integrity those minor character assassinations won't matter in the long run.

Don't be an asshole—honor people's time, especially when they give it freely. Honor them for their contribution. Do this publicly. Make sure you tell them directly and make sure it lands with sincerity. Strive for excellence but don't let the idea of perfection be the enemy of the good. Perfectionism is self-hatred.

Understand the complexities of the problems, but don't let your focus be held captive by them. Don't give in to anger and despair. Above all, let all of your actions be guided by an incomparable love for all humanity. In my ignorance, it is possible I have done the reader a great disservice by writing words that inspired feelings of anger or resentment. For this, I beg your forgiveness. Every member of the human race is part of the same family, even those who, in their unconscious pursuit of wealth and power, create harm and suffering on this planet. Remember that any time you give way to anger, you are giving away your power.

Take it back.

Forgive everyone, especially yourself. It is said that holding onto bitterness and resentment is like drinking poison and expecting someone else to die. This doesn't mean to accept or condone evil. The greatest alchemy is to transform this anger into loving, courageous, conscious, strategic action. Anger is a fire that burns out quickly.

Stay committed to the footwork, but surrender the results. At the end of the day, it is about the hearts we touch and the lives we positively impact. As Bell Hooks once said, The transformative power of love is the foundation of all meaningful social change …

When all else has fallen away, love sustains.

Envision the world as you wish it to be. Make big calls to action for sweeping change. Paint a picture people can see in their minds. Passionately enroll emissaries that can carry your message.

One thing we definitely got wrong during Occupy was when we said, "There are no leaders of this movement." We should have said, "*Everyone* is a leader of this movement." Remember that no one is coming to save you. If you are looking for a savior, look in the mirror.

Who knows, you could be the next Bernie Sanders.

Find like-minded people who align with your values. Start an outlandish and foolhardy quest to make a difference. Fail. Learn from your failures. Take away the victories no matter how small.

Build victory gardens. Play to win, but hold fast to the moments you share with those who stand with you and for something greater than themselves.

Cherish those who honor you, stand by you and are willing to tell you the truth even when it is something you don't want to hear. Choose your allies wisely. Admit your mistakes and shortcomings. There is no problem that cannot be solved through committed souls working together with love, wisdom and vision.

As the old adage says, "We do not inherit this earth from our ancestors, we borrow it from our children." Despite the ugliness, the divisiveness, the fascism, the war, the racism and inequality, there is still so much beauty in this world and the generations that follow us deserve a chance to inhabit a livable planet.

The climate apocalypse is now.

It is as Tennessee Williams once said, "We all live in a house on fire, no fire department to call; no way out, just the upstairs window to look out of while the fire burns the house down with us trapped, locked in it."

Only the people's movement, to overcome the regressive systems placing greed and power over life, will save us. You are that movement. So if you are still looking for someone to save you, look within.

In her novel *The Dispossessed*, Ursula K. Le Guin said, "We have nothing but our freedom. We have nothing to give you but your own freedom. We have no states, no nations, no presidents, no premiers, no chiefs, no generals, no bosses, no bankers, no landlords, no wages, no charity, no police, no soldiers, no wars. Nor do we have much else. You cannot take what you have not given, and you must give yourself. You cannot buy the Revolution. You cannot make the Revolution. You can only be the Revolution. It is in your spirit, or it is nowhere."

The time to do all of this, to make a stand, is now.

And always remember—all things are possible!

To support the *Be The Revolution* mission:

1. Take a picture of the cover of this book.
2. Post on your social media accounts and send it to your friends directly with links to where they can purchase it.
3. Leave a positive review on whatever digital platform it is available for purchase.
4. Call your local bookstore and request they carry it.
5. Contact political science professors and recommend they add this book to their curriculum.
6. Buy copies for local activists, schools and libraries.
7. Start a book group to read and discuss the content, or suggest anyone you know that is part of a book group to select it.
8. Sign up for our mailing list to learn more about *Be The Revolution* organizing activities.
9. Make a selfie video testimonial about this book and post it to your social media platforms
10. Become a Patreon supporter: www.patreon.com/BeTheRevolution

venmo   PATREON

To support the author:

venmo   Paypal

About the Author

Jay Ponti is a grassroots political organizer, trainer, and consultant who has participated in some of the most important social movements of the last decade, including Occupy Wall Street, Standing Rock, and Bernie Sanders's two presidential campaigns. He is the co-creator of the #BankExit fossil fuel divestment campaign and has organized campaigns and direct actions across the country. This is his first book.

More info on the author and mission:

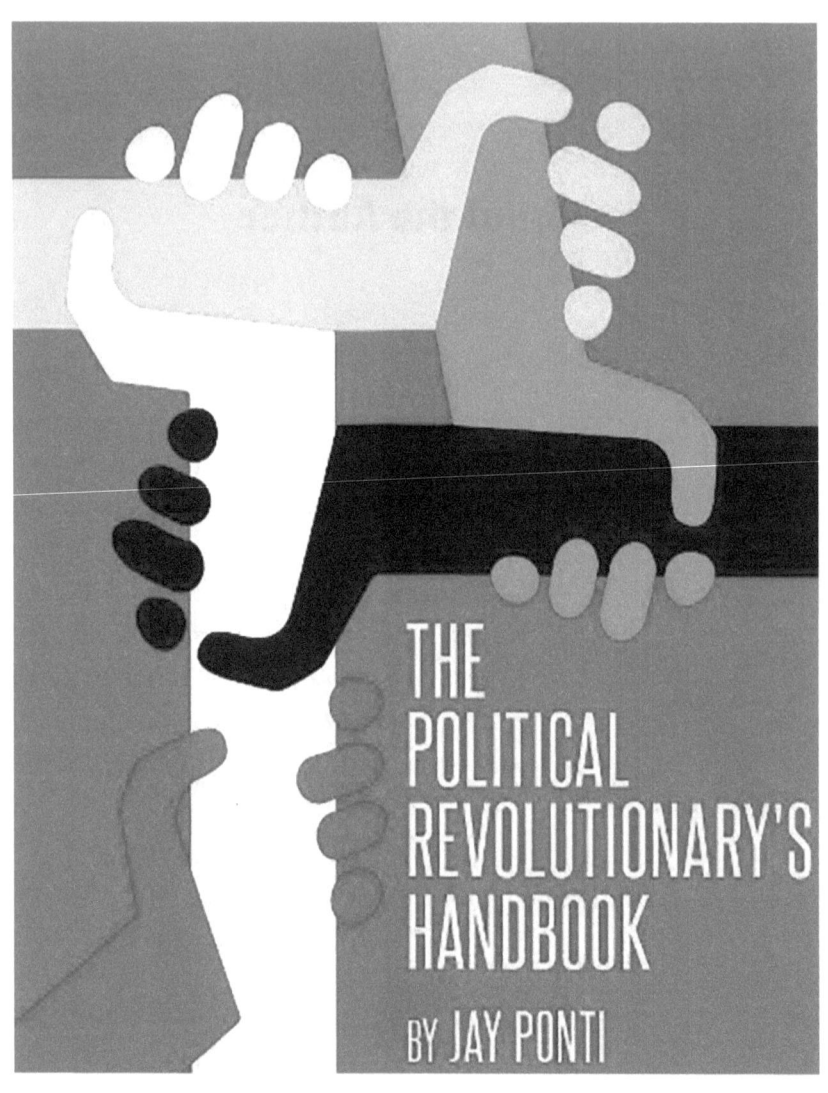

Stay tuned for the *Political Revolutionary's Handbook.*